Praise for Alan
Reverence, Obedience and ι.   .... ~........

Alan Chadwick's contemporary, E.F. Schumacher, referred to him as "the greatest horticulturist of the 20th Century." Why was this so? No doubt, he was referring to AC's metaphysical labours in the tangible world, quite literally, replanting the "vital root" of existence. To us, his apprentices, he had succeeded. The world became charged with beauty and productivity that was unrestrained and infectious.

It was the 70's and we were young and high on hard work. We were breaking through the hardpan of established thought and custom, building fertility of the soil until it was effusive up into the very atmosphere; soil that became so fertile and open, it was possible for one person to double-dig a 200 foot by 4 foot bed in a single day!

One could stand up from one's labours and look around at a world made new: fruit, flowers, selected weeds, vegetables and herbs, bird song, monarchs, hummingbirds, scent—all in the unity and quantum coherence of a handmade paradise; each species highlighted en mass for full effect and expression; always there was a claire-voyez towards the infinite...in our case towards Medicine Mountain.

AC's profound frisson was between "origin and culture", the root of his horticulture, the mother of all the arts.

He was cut from both original and ancient cloth.

The greatest of his "magics" was to be up with the morning star and actually live in the circadian rhythms of the day, the lunar month, and the full inclination of the masterful sun.

When one opens the garden gate of his metaphor it is like being on a mountain top.

AC is still the grandest human being we have ever known.

Two years "classic technique" apprenticeship with AC was riches enough for a whole lifetime.

— Chris and Stephie Tebbutt, Filigreen Farm, Boonville, California

This collection of talks by Alan Chadwick is comprehensive and covers much of Alan's philosophical, practical ideas and approach to horticulture.

I followed Steve Kaffka as student president of Alan's Garden Project at the University of California, Santa Cruz, in 1970-71. During that time, Alan gave his initial lecture cycles to university students and faculty. His audience soon grew to encompass large numbers of the general public throughout California.

Alan used to say that we were not in fact interested in gardening or horticulture, but that the whole reason for our work was similar to that of a musician. His approach to horticulture was for each individual to work together as in an orchestra, for each individual to become attuned to the spiritual world. Only then could we become creative in the proper way, not for the sake of merely creating an abundance of produce, which would come as a matter of course from our work if our approach was correct.

The whole purpose of the Garden was to uplift, to sanctify and to consecrate the earth, the plants, and the elemental beings that dwell there. In fact, it was apparent to anyone with sensitivity who visited Alan's garden at that time, that there was an intense atmosphere filled with spiritual forces.

It was a very sacred place.

We can be inspired even now, upon reading these lectures, by the work of this great man. And in some small way, we may bring his inspiration into our own lives, so that we live not merely for our temporal selves. We can become in tune with the infinite, and bring the blessings of Eternity into earth existence. In so doing we bless and uplift the Earth planet, and ensure its future.

— Dan McGuire, Retired Horticulturalist and Beekeeper

Steve has written a most beautiful book in transcribing Alan's lectures into a language wherein the reader can receive the spirits as they come through Alan Chadwick's field of perennial wisdom of Reverence, Obedience and the Invisible in the Garden. This book is a national treasure to all gardeners and lovers of the Earth.

— Barbara M.V. Scott, M.Sc., author of *The Joy of Biodynamic Agriculture: Living with the Unseen Forces Behind Nature* and *Transmissions from the Canid Nation*

I feel about Alan's garden like I do about Frank Lloyd Wright's buildings...they are incomparable and should be protected at all cost so we can always be reminded of the courage, tenacity, and level of commitment required to have the working relationship with nature that both Alan and Frank had...to me, it is not so much their human design genius (which is obvious) as it is the ability each had to tune into the message and design collaboration with nature to produce such amazing manifestations.

I grew up with Alan Chadwick as a family friend and the Biodynamic French Intensive method was the assumed norm of interaction with nature in a garden or small farm setting for our family—then as it still is today. In 2007 I founded the Institute for Man and Nature International for the purposes of bringing the philosophy and principals of Alan Chadwick's teaching, among others, into the agricultural work we do in the Rainforests and tropical areas around the world.

— Emily Mattison, Director, Institute for Man and Nature (International)

I feel sad when I think how I could have met this beautiful wizard of plants, but didn't know Alan Chadwick was there to meet. But at least these years later, it's as if he's sitting right here addressing this crazy lost time, his implacable hopeful blast of the do-ability of peace as a thing of living through plants sprouting inside us as a great medicine.

If you are already a plant person you probably know Alan Chadwick and will love this book.

If you aren't you'd better read *Reverence, Obedience and the Invisible in the Garden.*

— Martin Prechtel, author of *The Unlikely Peace at Cuchumaquic:*
The Parallel Lives of People as Plants: Keeping the Seeds Alive

It is not often that a horticulture teacher has such a profound, positive effect on so many young people that their lives are forever altered by his influence. Alan Chadwick was just such a master gardener. I was headed for an academic career in literary studies as a student at the University of California, but after meeting Chadwick, my life changed its course; I became devoted to raising flowers! My wedding business, the Flower Ladies, has afforded me the opportunity to grow hundreds of varieties of old-fashioned flowers and introduce them to happy customers and their wedding guests for more than forty years.

Alan's inspiring words are set forth in this book, but to hear him utter them in person was an unforgettable experience. His garden at UCSC, and those gardens that followed were phenomenal.

We former apprentices cannot claim to use all of Alan's methods, but we take our planting very seriously. Many of us seem to hear his words, as we participate year after year in the creation of our gardens. I, who never grew anything in my first nineteen years, cannot imagine a year in which I would not tend the flowers, vegetables and fruit trees. Chadwick was younger than I am now, when I first met him, yet his image and his words remain clear and strong many decades later. As you read this book, perhaps his words will inspire you to create your best garden yet!

— Nancy Lingemann, co-owner of the Flower Ladies in Santa Cruz

In my early twenties I had the fortune of working for two years with Alan Chadwick helping him build his first California garden. Thus I was steeped in practical and specific garden techniques—digging beds, mixing soils, sowing seeds. Around the lunch table at the garden chalet we had the joy of eating the beautiful vegetables we grew—limestone bibb lettuce, fresh snow peas, french carrots and beans. In the early morning light we cut flowers to give away, old-fashioned roses, zinnias, dahlias, anemones and annual phlox.

When I read his lectures I hear the cadence and passion of his voice and remember his guests, including Norman O. Brown, Page Smith, Donald Nichol and Paul Lee. Alan's eyes sparkled, his smile was deep and mischievous. He was intensely alive, alert and full of love for all the beautiful things that fill this planet and make it warm and soft and tasteful and fragrant. He loved plants and reminded us of their gifts—clean air, food and medicine, fiber and flower. He loved birds for their singing and flowers for their enchantment and beauty.

Alan was an inspired, disciplined, and energetic gardener who, with the help of many young people, transformed a hillside into a productive garden. He was there working from dawn to dark each day. Beautiful, fresh and high quality organic vegetables and vibrant flowers flowed in great abundance to the community from this garden while its soil grew more friable and fertile each year.

May Alan continue to light a fire inside the hearts of those who read his words and visit his archive.

— Jim Nelson, Camp Joy Gardens

A magnificent work from one of the plant geniuses of our time. Essential reading for all who want to deepen their relationship with plants and the Earth.

— Stephen Harrod Buhner, author of *The Secret Teachings of Plants and Ensouling Language*

Alan Chadwick demands rigorous thinking while, at the same time, offering to his readers and students an invitation to enter a world that we might call fanciful but which is real enough to result in the most inspiring gardens imaginable. Reverence, Obedience and the Invisible in the Garden is an essential book for the gardener and plant person of any stripe, to be read, savored, and read again.

— Deborah Madison, author of *Kitchen Literacy and Vegetarian Cooking for Everyone*

Little did I know upon leaving the kitchens of Cowell College that fateful morning in June, 1969, that my life would change forever. My first notion that something had altered was the sight of a group of students breakfasting at a table nestled on a rose bowered patio overlooking Monterey Bay. Quickly hiding the small box of dry cereal I had brought with me, I stepped into a new world.

After a cordially greeting, I was led to a finished lettuce bed which needed a preparatory digging for a new planting of beans (or so I was told...). I had entered a new classroom, seemingly small on that first day but one which has grow to encompass all of life. But who was the teacher...that I was soon to learn and have been grateful from that day forward.

You will learn much from and about Mr. Chadwick in this book. His style of delivering knowledge to students was never dull nor pedantic. He had the ability to give wings to the imagination and fire the will. Yet, he always said he was never a teacher; and finally, I have come to understand what he meant. To Mr. Chadwick, Nature was the teacher, and perhaps he was just reminding us how to open up all of our senses to the real Teacher.

And though, he didn't believe himself a teacher, I believe he gave to me the greatest gifts a teacher can bestow: a sense of wonder and reverence for Life and the World, the tools to work with Nature, and the drive to carry projects through to the end. And all gardeners know (as did Mr,Chadwick) a (The) Garden demands nothing less.

— Gregory H. Hudson, Waldorf Teacher, Eurthymist, Musician, and Gardener

It was late September, 1967, when I first encountered the kingdom of Alan Chadwick. What was that place, all that color? A brilliant blooming hedge of four foot zinnias, stretching hundreds of feet along the top of the bank, was backed by another row of what I learned were tithonia, Mexican sunflowers—crayola orange, velvety grey-green hollow stems, favorite of the monarch butterfly. I wondered about that place on the hill. As spring came, I began to attend a meditation class that was held in the garden, on the porch of the garden chalet. I'd open my eyes to the light and see the young roses and the shimmer of the ocean far away but visible from where we sat. This was what I wanted—to be part of this garden on the hill.

The man who directed the garden turned out to be a charismatic and charming Englishman in his late 50's named Alan Chadwick. Tanned like ruddy leather, dressed in crisp nautical blue and white, often only shorts and boots, with a shock of gray hair that he'd toss back abruptly, he'd always be working somewhere. I'd come down the path to find him and say "I'd like a job."

Leaning on the spade, tilting his head to the side like the blue jay that would perch on the handle when he left it to go pull a hose, his blue eyes would sparkle. "Heavy or light?" he'd ask me.

Time spent in the garden became the only reality for me. By spring break, I was spending almost all of my time there with the small and dedicated cadre of workers who'd fallen in love with the man and the site and placed themselves at his service. Reaction to Alan was mixed. There were those in authority who worried about allowing the students to be influenced by this mad magic man. "Of course there are Undines and Fairies and Elves!" he once began a lecture.

He talked of "sensitivity, observation, and obedience to the laws of nature"—what a concept for California kids in the late 60's! We knew this was about something larger than vegetables. The Vietnam War was still raging, and for all of us it was a defining issue of our time. It was such a relief to be shown a role for humankind of nurturing the earth as stewards of this growing garden on this particular piece of land. His unbending insistence on proper techniques and the acquisition of a discipline based on authority beyond human rules and regulations was novel.

This awareness of having a place in the life of the natural world was Alan's gift to those of us who worked with him. He made it real to us that plants are alive, they give us everything, and that the soil is the skin of the earth to be treated with tenderness.

Life was timeless in Alan's orbit for those of us who were his merry band and constant companions in the very early days of the garden. Alan is quoted saying, "It's not the gardener who makes the garden, it is the garden that makes the gardener." The garden that he made inspired those of us who were lucky enough to work with him and those who continue to experience that garden long after he has gone; we will continue to make other beautiful gardens (and eat beautiful food, and smell beautiful flowers, and write beautiful poems) in his memory and in his honor.

— Beth Benjamin, from the Introduction to *The Chadwick Garden Anthology of Poets*

Reverence, Obedience and the Invisible in the Garden

Talks on the Biodynamic French Intensive System

by
Alan Chadwick

Edited by
Stephen J. Crimi

Introduction by
Dr. Rodney Blackhirst

REVERENCE, OBEDIENCE AND THE INVISIBLE IN THE GARDEN
TALKS ON THE BIODYNAMIC FRENCH INTENSIVE SYSTEM
by ALAN CHADWICK

Edited by Stephen Crimi
Introduction by Dr. Rodney Blackhirst

LOGOSOPHIA

Logosophia Books
Copyright 2013 Reverence, Obedience and the Invisible in the Garden, Logosophia, LLC

Logosophia, LLC
90 Oteen Church Road
Asheville, NC 28805
www.logosophiabooks.com

Library of Congress Cataloging-in-Publication Data

Chadwick, Alan, 1909-1980
Reverence, Obedience and the Invisible in the Garden: Talks on the Biodynamic French Intensive System
Crimi, Stephen J., Editor

ISBN 978-0-9815757-3-5
1.Gardening and Horticulture 2. Organic Gardening 3. Biodynamics

Cover art "In the Garden," by William Henry Price. Back cover photograph by David Field.
Cover design and layout by Susan Yost.

For fledgling heartseeds emerging aquiver...

Epigraphs

We want to use astro-alchemical means of healing, as well as conventional bio-remediation, not only to cure this land but also to restore its authentic significance. To re-enchant it. Hence, not just bioremediation is required but georemediation of a specific topos or geome. If it were prairie, we'd attempt prairie restoration; if forest, we'd attempt re-wilding. But since it's a field, we'll use "celestial agriculture" as our goal. It will be done alchemically, meaning that the redeeming of matter on all three levels (body, soul, spirit) will constitute our method. We want to do this for the common wealth and we want to do it in communitas. But we also want to do it as a spiritual exercise, as alchemy in which the lab/oratory is found outdoors as well as within ourselves; as an action in what Novalis called the necessary poeticization of science: alchemy as an art form with ramifications on both individual and social levels.

– Peter Lamborn Wilson, *Green Hermeticism: Alchemy and Ecology*

The thought recurs that education—cultivated thought—can best be combined with agricultural labor, or any labor, on the principle of thorough work—that careless, half-performed, slovenly work, makes no place for such combination. And thorough work, again renders sufficient, the smallest quantity of ground to each man. And this again, conforms to what must occur in a world less inclined to wars, and more devoted to the arts of peace than heretofore. Population must increase rapidly—more rapidly than in former times—and ere long the most valuable of all arts, will be the art of deriving a comfortable subsistence from the smallest area of soil. No community whose every member possesses this art, can ever be the victim of oppression of any of its forms. Such community will be alike independent of crowned-kings, money-kings, and land-kings.

– Abraham Lincoln, An Address Before the Wisconsin State
Agricultural Society in Milwaukee, Wisconsin, September 30, 1859

now the goldmine is abandoned
leavin' treasures unattended
rusty coal cars standin' frozen
and scattered cages sprung wide open

– Malcolm Holcombe, "Hannah's Trading Post"

Table of Contents

Foreword

All birth comes out of darkness.
                                            – Alan Chadwick

This book is a follow-up and deepening of the first book of Alan Chadwick's lectures Logosophia Books published in 2008, *Performance in the Garden*. In *Performance* we were establishing the parameters and preparing the ground of the garden of the future, a garden always planted and harvested now; and with this second book, in the French intensive tradition we are double digging it, as it were, loosening the fertile subsoils, delving deeper to where the plenteous nutrients are.

To root out the gist of this further: it seems that by 1979, toward the end of his life, Alan had established a particular series of introductory lectures, which is what comprises much of *Performance*. He gave those at his last garden project in Carmel, Virginia. We laid the talks out in the order Alan did, letting him speak for himself. Those talks are all basic to the approach of biodynamic horticulture—cosmic cycles, cultivation, propagation, fertilization, fertility. The field of approach is unfurrowed there.

But the biodynamic French intensive bed cannot be planted until fully prepared, double dug, composted, watered and visioned. Ten of the lectures collected in *Reverence, Obedience and the Invisible in the Garden* are from the Garden Project at Covelo, when the garden there was well-established. These particular talks are all on utilitarian-sounding garden topics—composting, irrigation, raised beds, seed—but they all talk about the same thing, or more accurately, speak *from* the same place, and reflect upon each other beautifully. According to his students, Alan spent many hours preparing for these talks, often taking pages of notes with him, frequently abandoning them to say whatever needed to be heard in the moment.

Each of these talks attempt to undo the mechanical cultural presuppositions we bring in our approach to the garden. What are we carrying to the gate? Which lodestar sways us? Thoughts of utility and profit, or visions of beauty and fertility? One does not fully preclude the other, but the former feeds humanity's hungry-ghost ego, and the latter creaks open doors to the invisible.

You might be getting to the end of a lecture, and suddenly ask yourself, "Well, when is Chadwick going to talk about composting?" At which point you may put the book down and watch one of a thousand YouTube videos on technique. Or maybe, just maybe, you'll go back to reread the beginning, and realize that Alan has been talking about composting the whole time, only in a special way that requires a different ear. Composting, irrigation, bloom, fertilization, grafting—are all happening in the garden, and *within us simultaneously*, if we have the longing for the inner silence necessary to open up to it. Once the beds are prepared within and without, then we can go on to the care of individual plants, with their individual requirements. As we care for them, plants can care for us.

The concurrent project with the publication of these books is The Alan Chadwick Archive. The goal of the Archive is to collect, digitize, remaster and transcribe all of the available talks by Alan Chadwick, and do the same with the available video. All this, along with photos, student notes, forcing house logs and letters are to be made available to the public. We envision an interactive website where one can listen to talks while reading the transcripts, view videos, and search for notes on any specific plant. Anyone looking for information or wishing to help us in this goal can reach us through thealanchadwickarchive@gmail.com.

This book has been lightly edited from transcript tapes that were less than optimally recorded, and are sometimes extremely difficult to discern. Some of what we couldn't hear after a multitude of passes is edited out, but hopefully, soon the complete Alan Chadwick Archive will be available where the original remastered talks can be heard along with the best transcriptions possible. The words are Alan's, and all of the edits reflect our attempt to translate into a readable form that which is an intense verbal transmission from Alan's august *presence* direct to his students. Many consider it impossible to do this, but that has been thankfully confuted by the wonderful feedback we received from people encountering Alan for the first time through reading *Performance in the Garden*. Something does indeed come through from reading, and even more from rereading. We hope this book brings ambuscades of beauty into your life.

S.C. *Asheville, All Hallows Eve, 2012*

Introduction

Alan Chadwick's Alchemical Horticulture

At the centre of the alchemical tradition is a profound paradox: the basest of elements are the keys to the highest realities, and the person with the greatest insight into the transformations and innate wisdom of creation is the humblest of workers, the blacksmith at his forge. This same paradox extends to other traditional crafts, sciences and industries, too, including the alchemy of horticulture and farming. It is not the scientist or the professor who understands the most intimate secrets of Nature. It is the humble gardener, the person with a strong back and dirt under his or her nails tending to the transformations of the compost heap, the turning of the seasons and the mysterious metamorphosis of plants. This is certainly true of Alan Chadwick. He arrived in America at a juncture of social and cultural ferment. Students at the University of California, Santa Cruz—disillusioned by the Establishment institutions and their entrenched 'experts'—skipped their academic classes and headed down to the campus garden to hear an eccentric Englishman discourse on methods from the ancient 'Era of Alchemy' and traditions long shunned or completely forgotten by technocratic officialdom. The students sensed that here—in the garden, not the classroom—was what they needed to learn and what the world needed to hear.

They were attracted by another feature of alchemy characteristic of Chadwick too, namely the total inseparability of theory and practice. Alchemy, it has been said, is *metaphysics made tangible*. Tangibility is not something for which Ivory Tower academics are known. The gardener—Chadwick—on the other hand, was not offering either empty theories or a soulless utilitarianism, but rather a beautiful fusion of *theoria* and *praxis*, an engagement with practical realities so deep as to be spiritual. Chadwick once said to Dr. Paul Lee, his ally in the Faculty in Santa Cruz, that he had achieved "a huge marriage between vision and practicality." It is not an idle boast. This 'marriage' (noting the alchemical nuptial symbolism) was the work of a lifetime. Students found in Chadwick a

1

seamless unity, a synthesis in which the highest philosophy illuminates the lowest reality, the earthworm and the manure pit.

The alchemical background to Chadwick's horticulture is not always obvious. His talks were intended for apprentices and had as their purpose practical instruction rather than historical curiosity. On a careful reading, however, his roots in alchemy become clear. Indeed, there are hints here and there that suggest that he was deeply familiar with what are today extremely arcane and neglected traditions. When he talks of the 'Sun's Sun', for instance, modern readers are likely to be puzzled, unaware that this is a doctrine going back to the Pythagoreans and beyond. He makes certain connections in one of his talks and other connections in another talk; it is only from both references that we realize that he knows, and means, much more than it seems. He says in one talk, for instance, that "the Moon is born out of the mind of the Sun." What is a modern reader to make of such a statement? What did his apprentices make of it? In another much later talk, however, he expands on this when he says:

The Moon, like Pallas Athena, when Pallas Athena says: "I am truly another. But in origin I am one, because I am out of the mind of Zeus." And here you must look upon the Moon. The Moon is out of the Sun.

We then realize, putting the two talks together, that Chadwick is drawing upon arcane understandings embedded in Greek mythology (where Athena is born from the head of Zeus). Chadwick, like the Neoplatonists, interprets this myth cosmologically. Where did he learn such things? It is hard to say, but he drew freely from the Greek 'Era of Alchemy' that, in his account, continued down through Socrates and Plato until its demise in the time of Alexander the Great.

The corner-piece of his gardening method—double-dug or 'trenched' permanent raised beds—he also attributes to the ancient Greeks and describes it as a method taken by mimesis from the natural processes of earth-tremor and landslide. This makes it a method belonging to the earth-shaking Vulcan, the blacksmith of the gods, whose arts are exactly alchemical. The origins of Western alchemy are in these layers of Greek mythology, mediated from Egypt. We must remember that the word 'al-chemy' comes from etymologies meaning 'the black soil' [of the Nile].

2

If anything, the alchemy of farming came before that of the blacksmith.

Chadwick does not present extended discourses on any of this, but he drops hints, makes references in passing, or statements that are otherwise cryptic, that demonstrate that he knows these connections very well. It is not a bookish learning, though. It is a tangible knowing. There is a distinct and identifiable tradition upon which he draws. It is Athenian—he is an Athenian man—but it is not the stale classicism of the British schoolmasters. For example, instead of the Socrates of the polis that we meet in Plato's *Republic*, Chadwick knows the agrarian Socrates of Xenophon's *Oeconomicus*. His Platonism—he counts Plato as one of his ancient alchemists—is through that lens.

This Athenian aspect of Chadwick is little appreciated but crucial to making sense of some of his accounts of the processes of Nature. Notice, for example, the key role of the element Air in his cosmology. He knows, but rarely mentions, that Athena is the Air (cloud and atmosphere) goddess. His beloved Ruskin wrote a little book about it called *Queen of the Air*. Chadwick says in one of his talks: "Let's be led by the great depths of myths and then interplay them with our realities." Air is the subtle element in horticulture. Gardening is not so much about soil and water— and even less about nitrogen, phosphorous and potassium—as it is about Air. This has been lost in the brutality of industrialism. Chadwick defines horticulture as "how to prepare the soil with the atmosphere." Elsewhere he says, "The air of an area, the atmosphere, produces the soil." Those who want to understand such statements and their full background should read Ruskin's account of the mythology of Athena. Clearly, Chadwick is in the same universe of ideas, looking at Nature through the same ancient traditions, myths "interplayed with our realities." But, as he says in the talk 'Nature's Medicine Chest' in the present volume:

Much of this was understood in the days when talking was very little and doing was quite a lot. There was the practice of alchemy...

Nearer to our own times, some of Chadwick's alchemical legacy is easier to trace. He stands in the tradition of Paracelsus. Most prolific is his use of Goethe, mediated through his personal tutor, the great Goethe scholar and visionary, Rudolf Steiner. From Goethe Chadwick takes the categories of *idée* and *metamorphosis*. From Steiner he takes the development of Goethean sciences and in particular the application of a Goethean view of Nature to farming in Steiner's *biodynamics*.

True to his teacher, though, Chadwick was a student of life more than he was a student of Steiner's books. If he rarely used Steiner's alchemy—namely, the so-called 'preparations' that these days seem to define Biodynamics—it is because Steiner inspired him to find his own. He meets Steiner in alchemy. For example, Chadwick has appropriated Steiner's terminology in his use of the polarity Ahrimanic/Luciferic. It is familiar anthroposophical jargon, but as Chadwick uses it, it is an adaptation of the alchemical polarity Sulfur/Sal. There is a universal principle of contraction and solidification (Ahriman/Sal) counterpoised to a universal principle of expansion and dissolution (Lucifer/Sulfur). Life, the third term, is a dynamic between these two extremes. This is a cornerstone of Chadwick's cosmology. It is important to understand it. There is not a single talk by Chadwick that does not make use, implicit or explicit, of this threefold schema.

In other respects, his use of Steiner is selective and distinct, like his construction of a rural Socrates. It is not the anthroposophical Steiner that we find in Chadwick; it is an alchemical Steiner seen largely through one work, *The Four Seasons & the Archangels*. He takes from Steiner what he needs. He needs the structure of the year and the calendar of the invisible. Otherwise, as Chadwick once said, Steiner planted seeds within his young pupil that would mature of their own accord. It is remarkable that some people quibble over how 'true' Chadwick was to Steiner. Rudolf Steiner—who taught individuality, integrity, autonomy as virtues of our Age—had no more authentic or accomplished protegé.

In the threefold scheme just mentioned it is not the polar extremes (Sulfur/Sal) that are important but the middle term. The middle term is the key. The Sun, Chadwick says, is Luciferic and the Earth Ahrimanic. Between them is the plant. In a different cross-section, between the extremes of Fire and Earth is Air, the middle element. The air-filled double-dug permanent raised beds so central to Chadwick's method are designed to create a *middle realm*—a type of filter or sponge—between the atmosphere and the earth. Chadwick is always concerned with the 'inter-realms' of Nature. His whole technique is to open them and nurture them.

The alchemical triad reappears throughout his thinking. An important formulation is, as he puts it: "The invisible-the intermediaries-the visible." The alchemical cosmology consists of a single reality divided into two realms—the visible world and the invisible world. Between these two realms is an intermediate zone. It is a borderland between the two worlds. Chadwick's horticulture gives attention to this intermediate zone. The threefold pattern is repeated at many levels. Most fundamentally, between earth and atmosphere is soil. Living soil is an intermediate zone where things can flow between the two realms. In an interview he was once asked what he thought had gone wrong with the world. He thought long and hard and then answered with a single word, "Compaction." The inter-realms of the world have all been crushed out of existence. He talks about the disappearance of 'bloom'. What he calls 'bloom' is the intermediate and subtle layer, the middle term. It is the "bloom" that allows the passage of the invisible into manifestation.

Unique to Chadwick, he extends this to the metaphor of the theatre. Again from 'Nature's Medicine Chest':

Aura of discontinuity. Aura. Emanation. Skin. That through which everything pulsates. Can breathe out and can breathe in. And is that area that separates an entity into a self. Every picture on the wall literally has to have a frame. Otherwise, it only belongs to the world. And a theatre has to have a proscenium arch. The audience has to be dark and that—the stage—has to be light. Areas of discontinuity and bloom.

For Chadwick, an old thespian, everything is seen through the magic of theatre. A garden is a performance. A flower is a performance. The world is a stage. The underpinning metaphor in all of Chadwick's metaphysics is: *there is the lit stage and the dark theatre, and between them the proscenium. It is through the filter of the proscenium that the magical transformations happen.* Theatre as alchemy. In many ways, this, above all, is the key to understanding Alan Chadwick. The intermediate realm is of utmost importance because it is the medium for transformations. It is through it that the invisible manifests—miraculously—in the visible world. This is the role of soil between earth and air.

It is also the realm of elemental beings, gnomes, sylphs, fairies, angels, creatures of the inter-realm, the same inter-realm that the great scholar of esoteric religion Henry Corbin called the *mundus imaginalis*. The imaginal (as opposed to the merely imaginary) is between the real and the ideal, between *idée* and *metamorphosis*. Chadwick was not a spiritualist, but the denizens of this realm were a natural part of his scheme. In one of his talks he said of this:

Of course there are elves and fairies and undines! They are names. Names for what? For the magic that the four elements—earth, fire, air, water—bring about in the perpetual marriage of the invisible into the visible.

Chadwick's main contention, alchemically speaking, is that, by nurturing the inter-realms, life can be drawn endlessly from the 'invisible' in defiance of the laws of physics (but not the laws of Nature). He had discovered a cornucopia. This is the main claim of biodynamic farming in general. A biodynamic farm is a closed system, a self-contained unit, and yet it runs perpetually without outside input. It exports produce every year without ever exhausting the soil and without ever bringing in fertilizers from outside. This goes entirely counter to conventional, quantitative agriscience. (It is achieved, amongst other things, through the proper use of the ley.) Chadwick speaks of "an unending cornucopia that will never cease." The alchemist has found the key to the endless bounty of Nature. "How much is a tomato?" Chadwick asks the audience rhetorically in one talk. "The same as it has always been. Nothing!"

Contemporary readers should note that Chadwick did not subscribe to the myth of scarcity. He believed in the overflowing abundance of life and in *enthusiasmos*. He was bemused by John Jeavon's brilliant streamlining and adaptation of his techniques to apply them to the food security problems of the Third World. It was not Chadwick's agenda at all. He complains at one point:

The major question that one sees printed and asked everywhere is: "I say, how are we going to grow the food for the millions?" It has got nothing to do with it. It has never had anything to do with it!

It had, instead, to do with Beauty. In this respect we see him at his most Platonic. He was not setting out to "feed the millions" but rather to bring beauty to the world, a Platonic enterprise arising out of an adoration of Beauty from which abundance is merely an overflow and an excess. Contemporary ecologists, thoroughgoing utilitarians, rarely speak about Beauty. For Chadwick, it is the central concern.

We find the roots of his world-view stated in Plato's dialogue, *Timaeus* 30A sq., a key text in the transmission of the philosophy of occidental alchemy. It would be wrong to cast Chadwick as a Platonist in any formal sense, but his interest in Beauty (with an upper-case B) surely puts him in that camp. He is Platonic in at least three main ways. First, the adoration of Beauty is central to his world-view. Second, he believes that creation is intrinsically good and overflows (emanates) from God's goodness, and third he shares Plato's concern for the real against that which merely seems real; he thinks of the modern advent of synthetic chemicals and artificial flavorings as a 'deception' and the modern era as a whole as an Age of Deception.

There were, perhaps, times in his life when his pursuit of beauty was self-indulgent, but Fate conspired to take him to America to find his true mission. Paul Lee quotes him as saying that he had spent most of his life in the "selfish pursuit of beauty," but, unwittingly, and not without resistance, he found himself called upon to teach others and to show the beauty to them. His ultimate objective in this was to transform the Earth into a Garden of Eden. His vision is Arcadian. It is a pact he made with Countess Freya Von Molkte in South Africa in the smoldering aftermath of World War II—a world and a mankind transformed by gardens. Towards this Chadwick, almost single-handedly, made an heroic start.

As in classical metallurgic alchemy, though, it is not the transmutation of metals but rather the transmutation of the alchemist that is important. Chadwick said:

The garden is all secrets. The whole miracle of the garden is made up of secrets, and I've been granted the chance to expose a few others to this incredible thing which, itself, is the teacher. It is, you see—though many people find the idea amusing—the garden that makes the gardener.

Gardening, for Chadwick, is first and foremost an arena for transformations. Transformation is the dream and the duty of the alchemist. The alchemist is servant of the coming dawn who labors to hasten the day when man ends his sojourn of folly and returns to Paradise renewed. It is a noble *theoria* that Chadwick has and it is perfectly wed to his extraordinary command of horticultural technique. The horticulture of Alan Chadwick speaks for itself. It is an eminently rational, logical, clean system of high yielding optimum organic gardening of unsurpassed simplicity and productivity. It is also an expression of a sublime vision coming out of a deep and ancient tradition of which this man of the soil was an unlikely representative.

> – Dr. Rod Blackhirst is the author of *Primordial Alchemy and Modern Religion*, and a teacher at La Trobe University, Australia, for over 20 years.

The Proscenium Arch:
An Approach to this Book

Stephen Crimi

There is a wonderful line in the *Corpus Hermeticum* perfectly reflective of an approach to encountering Alan Chadwick. In the midst of an intensely spiritual discourse, Hermes' son Tat has just asked a question indicating he didn't quite get what his father was saying. Hermes replies:

The listener, O son, should be of one mind and soul with the speaker, and his hearing should be quicker than the voice of the speaker[1].

In order for a spiritual transmission to happen, there has to be a oneness of speaker and listener on the soul level. Both have to be resting in the same place, so that soul is expressing itself to itself. How the listening can be quicker than the expressive voice is certainly a mystery to be pondered.

What is translated here as 'mind' is *nous*, a complicated Greek philosophical term, equivalent to the Latin word *intellectus*, and the Sanskrit word *buddhi*, but basically it is the human faculty that apprehends, on each of our human levels: the Real, the True, the Divine. It requires a stillness of listening through one's whole being, impossible for anyone with a discursive mind ravenous for data. In this classic sense, it is *nous* that receives what Alan calls *idée*, a term derived from Plato for the spiritual ideas or archetypes in-forming this world. Alan often 'quotes' Plato as having said, "I do not know. But I do *perceive*." *Idée* and the perception of *idée* are one. The ephemeral and evanescent *idée* is creative of all that is good and true in the garden, which includes insect pests. *Idée* is vision, a spark. Alan says, "*Idée* is the inert information of Truth. It is so brief that with the average contact a person is unaware of the flash. It is so instant. And instantly, reason and intellect are preying upon it and it is vanished."

Luckily for us Alan is not average in any imaginable way. He is permeated with a spiritual vision that sometimes trips over itself in expression, sometimes pierces like a saving-bell through a fog. His linguistic expression via odd and archaic noun and verb formations is far from pedestrian. Yet these neologisms somehow manage to express the Real in an elliptical way, preventing our reason from fooling itself into nodding sagely that it has understood.

So this is no ordinary gardening book you hold. Yes, there are some potato planting procedures, specific qualities of dozens of herbs, tips about composting, watering and fertilizing. But this book imparts a vision of what we need to *see* before toting our spade to a compost pile; a vision of what fertility *is* before we dump a bag of additives on the soil; the whole constellation of con-*sider*-ations (with the stars) before we start dousing plants with water; and most importantly, how to approach the garden in terms of what we don't—but will—see: the Archangels in their obedient performance, bringing the invisible into the visible, through our spiritual vision, our *idée*, in reverence to Nature. She has been abused and exploited long enough.

Sorry to say, this is not a book to *get* on the first pass. Maybe not even the third. Not because it is not clear, but because is it expressive of the ineffable. That is why there are myths invoked amidst the garden. They all *point to*. It will reward the reader, the *listener*, who is of one soul with Alan. There is a way to read with one's whole being, awash in stillness, without worrying about remembering facts. To read that deeply a certain invisibility is required. Once we get out of our own way, we will know what we need to know when we need to know it.

Of course, Steiner's seminal book of lectures on biodynamics, *Spiritual Foundations for a Renewal of Agriculture*, is notoriously obtuse, and for many the worst place to begin an understanding of the topic for the untutored novice. On the other hand, it truly rewards the persistent reader. Is this book a better avenue of entry? Maybe for those who understand the need to return to the origin vision, just as you must return fruit back to root stock for fertility and renewal, before it warps into a disease-ridden aberration of ego. The true approach to biodynamics pauses at the garden gate, and enters in reverence, obedience, love, joy and awe of the invisible becoming manifest for you, with you, as you.

As a help, here's a sort of Chadwickipedia of terms Alan uses that may initially confuse, but will eventually deepen this approach to the vision of the garden. These are by no means official, or static definitions. They are the outcome of a long-term grappling after hundreds of hours of listening to Alan's talks. There are many other interpretations, just as valid, but maybe these can hopefully lubricate a rusted gate for someone green to Alan's vision.

Ahrimanic and Luciferic: These terms come out of Rudolf Steiner's work, by way of Zoroastrianism. Alan uses them in a number of different ways. They are different directions of spiritual movement manifest in the world. Ahrimanic is downward, toward the material, toward darkness, and luciferic is upward, toward the immaterial, and toward the light. Root growth, for example, is ahrimanic, while shoot growth is luciferic and upwards. Both are obviously necessary, and like the yin/yang have elements of one contained within the other. Balance is always the key. We live in an excessively materialistic ahrimanic age, and anyone sensible suffers acutely from that imbalance. Much of what is called 'New Age thought' reacts to this by displaying overreaching luciferic tendency: 'everything is light'; 'we are all ascending to the nth dimension', etc. In Chadwick's biodynamic garden, everything has a place, a duty, and plays within a dynamic equilibrium. The difference is between bringing the stars into the garden, and abandoning the garden for the stars.

Archangels: Archangels are immensely powerful spiritual beings, absolutely obedient to the Divine. They are the spiritual force and presence behind everything that happens in the garden and elsewhere. Each of the four major Archangels is in ascendency for a season, and the changing from one to another is called the passing of the Grail Cup. Uriel is the intense effulgence and light of summer; moving to the decay of fall with Michael and his sword of iron; to the quiet-essence of Gabriel's winter; waking again to the uprising current of Raphael in the spring. For Alan, they are the spiritual forces behind all manifestation in the garden. The elementals—the gnomes (earth), undines (water), salamanders (fire) and sylphs (air)—all work under the direction of the Archangels. All of these are given different names in various cultures and times, but the reality of how this world of experience continuously emerges from the invisible is ineluctable. Sometimes Alan mentions a fifth Archangel, the Dove, too exquisite to even speak of for him, the single reality giving rise to the four faces of the Archangels. There is a spiritual reality behind each physical reality, as when he speaks of the Sun's Sun, "too vast, too black" to be seen. These are mysteries within mysteries and can only be pointed toward.

Clairvoyer: In classical art, and with some classical estate gardens, the border extending a line of sight out of view and up through the skyline above the gardens is referred to as a *clairvoyer*. Crafted correctly, it has the ability to move one's experience of the garden from the visible right through to the invisible realms.

Conservatoire: A conservatory within the garden. In the French intensive system, one plants often in a hexagonal array, allowing the mature plant leaves to fully cover the ground themselves, after the fertility-enhancing weeds are plucked, creating a stable atmosphere of gasses and moistures, protecting and magnifying growth and fertility.

Divertissement: the movement from origin energy into plurality and more dissipated energy. In the case of an individual plant, the further it is from origin, either due to hybridization or propagation, the more prone it will be to the forces of disease and exhibit lack of vigor.

Equinoxes: Basic to understanding Alan is his correlation of certain divisions of time and space. Therefore, noon is equated with summer, sunrise and sunset are respectively the spring and fall equinoxes, while midnight is winter; then the equator is again noon, while the equinoxes are the Tropics of Cancer and Capricorn, moving to the midnight of the Arctic Circles. The equinoxes are the luscious maritime climate between excessive dry and hot, and excessive cold and wet.

Idée: Spiritual insight before it is rendered into words. The term originates in Plato, and is taken up by Goethe. Alan follows Goethe in contrasting the spiritual reality of *idée* as seed, with metamorphosis, the physical and particular fulfillment of *idée*. *Idée* is not only behind the vision of the garden, but informs all classic art. That is, art that is derived from the spiritual, as opposed to most of modern and contemporary art, which is derived from the individual.

Image: *Idée* and *image* are nearly interchangeable. The imaginal realm is where the human and divine intertwine: from whence the crabapple becomes a GoldRush apple; whence prairie grass becomes wheat and corn. In all traditional cultures, it is direct communication with the plants that shows humans what can be done. There is an element of human desire in this, but also the desire of Nature to work with us, as long as we are obedient to her laws. This conversation takes place through the faculty of human *image*, in the imaginal world[2].

Participle: Alan usually means participant or participating here. It begs the question as to why an articulate Shakespearian-trained English speaker uses terms obviously not of the lexicon. One guess is that instead of using words the mind thinks it knows—and doesn't—he uses terms that *point to*.

Présentement: Alan often refers to a crown *présentement*, by which he seems to refer to the area of discontinuity between the root and the stem, between the soil and the air. He apparently is taking poetic liberties with the French word, which translates simply as 'present', or 'now'. He has said that this is where the cosmic, the *revolutionibus* actually enters the plant, which underlies its importance, especially when planting. It must be exposed—presented—to allow for maximal interplay with the cosmic. Possibly the gravest gardening blunder a student of Alan's could make is to transplant by pinching a seedling at that place, rather than gently grasping by the new leaves.

Revolutionibus, Prima Mobile, Secundus Mobile: These Latin terms come out of medieval astronomy and astrology, mostly by way of Copernicus' *On the Revolution of the Celestial Spheres* (*De revolutionibus orbium coelestium*). *Revolutionibus* is frequently used by Alan, and is essential for his gardening. It consists of the continuous, never repeated, movements of the seven classical visible planets (the *secundus mobile*: the Moon, Mercury, Venus, Sun, Mars, Jupiter and Saturn), the 'fixed' stars of the constellations (the *prima mobile*), and the ætherial realm, invisible and beyond the stars. The whole of biodynamics is to open the garden to this cosmic influence, bringing the spiritual literally into the plants.

Totem, Totemism: Alan seems to make *totem* synonymous with 'totality', 'the all', 'everything', the Latin phrase *in toto*. But it makes little sense, until you find his favorite passage from Maurice Maeterlinck's *The Life of the Ant*. Somehow the ant's complete happiness and inseparability from the joy of Nature is in *totemism* as Alan uses it. Worth quoting at length:

Unlike ourselves, the ant has the good fortune to be far more sensible to pleasure than to pain. Amputated or truncated, she does not deviate from her path, as though nothing has happened. But if a sister solicits her she stops and shares with her the delights of regurgitation.

With us happiness is mostly negative and passive, and is hardly perceived except as the absence of unhappiness; in the ant it is before all things positive and active, and seems to pertain to a privileged planet. Physically, organically, the ant cannot be happy unless she is giving happiness to those around her. She has no other joys than the joys of duty accomplished, which for us are the only joys that leave no regrets, but which most of us know only by hearsay. The transports of love, in which we think to surpass ourselves and escape from ourselves, are merely and essentially egoism concentrated or exasperated to such a point that it brushes elbows with death or annihilation—the very things that it seeks to annihilate. The ant knows other joys, which instead of contracting happiness enlarge it, multiply it, and lavish it upon her innumerable sisters. She lives in happiness, because she lives in all that lives around her, because all live in her and for her, and she lives in all and for all.

She lives, above all, in immortality, for she is part of a whole which nothing can destroy. Strange as this assertion may at first appear, the ant is a profoundly mystical being; she exists only for her God, and does not imagine that there could be any other happiness, any other reason for living, than to serve Him, to forget herself, to lose herself in Him. She is wholly steeped in the great primitive religion of totemism: the most ancient of all religions, the most widely distributed of all the religions practiced by man. At the root of all other religions, underlying all the gods, totemism is the earliest pursuit, the first conquest, by that which dies, of that which does not die. The totem was the collective soul of the tribe.

Wordism: Thinking that you know what something is by its definition; knowing a word by other words, rather than the essence of that word. Related to **verbosity**, which seems to be pretty much the same, referring to wordism clanging about the head. Either word describes the trap of believing you can understand anything through thought.

Capitalization: we have tried not to over-burden the reader with it, but the simple fact is that when Alan is talking about the Sun and planets, or Nature, he is referring to experienceable spiritual realities, and not solid orbs somewhere out in unreachable physical space. Nature is a Goddess, and if you show her due reverence and obedience, she will show you unimaginable treasures. Likely, if you are holding this book, this is not so much of a reach for you.

As mentioned in Dr. Blackhirst's introduction, there is a can of worms that really needs to be making compost: Alan and the biodynamic preparations (or lack thereof). For many, the nine preparations outlined by Rudolf Steiner in his *Agriculture* lectures are the unalterable core of what biodynamics is. Briefly explained, there are two basic sprays, one from silica for the atmosphere, and one from cow manure for the earth, each buried for six months in a cow horn. They are then dis-interred, and mixed in rainwater for an hour, alternating one minute clockwise and one minute counter-clockwise, with special attention paid to the chaos between vortices.

These are sprayed at certain times of the year. To understand why they work involves a lifetime study of etheric forces, plant alchemy, and sacred geometry, among other things. But, as Alan likes to point out, understanding and perceiving are two different creatures.

There are seven more preparations made from specific plants and herbs, in various ways, that are used to generate biodynamic compost. They are very esoteric in preparation, easy to administer, and have proven to be very effective in restoring vitality and fertility. In our own farm experience, we were able to grow crops with fair success in the face of successive years of record drought, rain, and heat, after using these preps for years. Any more of a detailed explanation will take us too far afield.

Back in the early 1920's Steiner worked with farmers to create these as an emergency procedure to deal with the increasingly debilitating effects of the chemicalization and mechanization of horticulture. This also would have been around the time that Alan, a teenager, was tutored by Steiner. Mechanized food lacks spiritual qualities. When eaten as a regular diet, there results a lack of any spiritual structure within us; there is no place for the Holy to hang itself on. What was true then is frightfully so now, and how this leads to lock-step compliance with fascism is another intertwined story.

But what seems to be missing in the conversation is one, the preps are an emergency procedure, designed at a specific time, using flora and fauna native to Western Europe; and two, these were developed at the end of Steiner's life, and his exhortation was for horticulturalists to grab hold of what was being done and continue to move it forward, because this was just a start. We are some ninety years down the road, and the scenery is little changed. There were a few poineers, like Hugo Erbe, who took the impulse and ran with it, creating 'new' preps out of his vision, but the great majority of biodynamics today is a clenched holding to and replication of Steiner's prescriptions. Where are the indigenous North American or Australian or Indian preps? Part of the lulling is that they seem to be effective everywhere. But we can do better, and some people are trying.

Now comes Alan's great contribution. There are more than a few people who claim that Alan didn't do biodynamics because he didn't use the preps, in spite of the fact that no one turned more people on to biodynamics in this country than he did. There is a hint of why he didn't use the preps at the end of the Composting lecture included here. He worked with the preps when younger, and subsequently found ways of fertilization, ways of composting, ways of planting that were "much, much, much more." Anyone who has experienced the ebullience and fecundity of an Alan Chadwick garden would be hard put to argue against all the universe inhabiting each and every flower, vegetable and spadeful of soil.

But more, over and over in these lectures Alan reminds us that nothing is static, everything is ever-different, and it's only seeming the same to the mind that makes it so. Unless you are tuned to this continual shifting, and shifting your approach in accordance with it, you will endlessly repeat, until the vital root is diminished and anemic. So there is a danger in calcifying and endlessly repeating Steiner's indications, until he is up on an unassailable pedestal, static and in a cage he never wanted. As one of Alan's student put it: "My take on Alan and the preps is that he worked on you in another realm, in freedom but with a strict discipline. To this day I have never met anyone who can get you into the space of sensing or perceiving, as he would say, the rhythms that were happening. Alan worked with horticulture but he gave me impulses that make me perceive what Steiner was saying."

None of Alan's disciples are doing what he did to the letter. They have taken his indications and made them work for their own gardens, their own locales, their own lives. Some use the preps and some don't. In the end it doesn't matter; what matters is whether you go through the gate to the center of the garden, which is the true center of yourself and everything surrounding. From there you can go anywhere.

Before we part the curtain, a brief story of Alan Chadwick's life. There is a much more detailed account in *Performance in the Garden*, Robert Howard's *What Makes the Crops Rejoice*, and in Paul Lee's new account of the founding of the garden in Santa Cruz, *There is a Garden in the Mind*. On 27 July, 1909, he was born to a mother steeped in anthroposophy, and a father from an ancient aristocratic line and lived at Pudleston Court in Herefordshire, England, an expansive estate with large gardens. He grew up with two main loves: Nature and the theater. He was personally tutored by Rudolf Steiner as a young teenager, and spent time in Dornach, apparently learning the essence and techniques of biodynamics there. By his own admission, he studied classic horticulture and also French intensive techniques, from various centers in England, France and Germany.

At twenty-one Alan gave up his inheritance to join the theater, learning his craft at the school of Elsie Fogerty. He performed Shakespearian and contemporary plays throughout Great Britain. He was a conscientious objector during WWII until the bombs drove him to enlist. He severely injured his back on a minesweeper twice. Sadly, this was nothing compared to the deep internal damage from living through war. The destruction he witnessed left him disconsolate and bitter towards humanity. He eventually vacated England and did itinerant repertory theater throughout South Africa. Here he met his great friend, another expatriate, Countess Freya von Moltke, a dedicated anti-Nazi, whose husband was executed by the Gestapo.

He began large scale gardening at estates in South Africa, followed by the Bahamas and Long Island. By 1967 Alan was ready to move into obscurity to New Zealand or Australia, when Countess Freya von Moltke recommended him to Paul Lee after an idea was floated to put a garden on the new UC Santa Cruz campus. She charged him with giving back all that he had envisioned and learned, and as difficult as it was for him to make that leap, connect with the hippie culture, and keep his vision of the garden alive during the crest of mechanization, he kept true to that charge to the day he died. The last talk in this book is given in his final week here with us.

Alan spent five years at Santa Cruz constructing the garden that still bears his name, followed by garden projects at the Zen Center in Green Gulch, a community garden in Saratoga, California, five years in Covelo at the invitation of Richard Wilson, where most of the talks in this book are from, and the better part of two years in New Market, Virginia, where he orchestrated his final masterpiece. He spent his last six months in hospice at Green Gulch, where cancer finally overcame his lionhearted spirit on 25 May, 1980.

But the lights are dimming. We've skimmed the program, and now it is time to slide the playbill under our seat, leave our rational minds at the door, and as the curtains part, pass through the proscenium arch and enter the soul of the performance...

---

1   10.17; *The Way of Hermes: New Translations of* The Corpus Hermeticum *and* The Definitions of Hermes Trismegistus to Asclepius, *Translated by Clement Salaman, Dorne van Oyen, William D. Wharton, and Jean-Pierre Mahé.*

2   See any of the wonderful works of esoteric philosopher Henri Corbin on the *mundus imaginalis.*

Nature's Medicine Chest

L.A. Biodynamic Conference
27 July 1975

Greetings, and among some of us, re-greetings! It is so wonderful to be asked to come and join you. I know so little, and know that in a hundred years I will say that I know less. And therefore, I repeat Plato and say, "I do not know, but I do *perceive*." Herbs are the weeds of the world. They are classic origin. They must not be cultured. They must be our masters. And we must live with them, study them, adore them, and revere them. And out of them have always come, and do come, and will come, every blessed thing that we have in this world.

Is it an important subject? There is nothing in the whole world, but the comings from this area: the whole law of Nature. We make and create nothing, but we do manipulate. The herbs, in origin, the weeds: when horticulture began, the whole talk was growing herbs, and out of it came the word 'herbaceous'. And herbs were, as you know, through Ptolemy[1] to the ancient Orient, and then to the Persians, and then to the Phoenicians, and to the ancient Greeks, they were the matter of food for the body, food for the mind, and the vision of the spirit. What a deep and incredible matter to consider in the world of plants!

How ludicrous that today, the major question that one sees printed and asked everywhere is: "I say, how are we going to grow the food for the millions?" It has got nothing to do with it. It has never had anything to do with it. Within the whole secret of the law that governs the growth of herbs is an unending cornucopia that will never cease, and the quantitive is endless, and the qualitative is more endless.

Therefore, out of the origin herbs has the great *image* of man—the seed of his mind that germinates magic—out of this *image* has come all the exquisite things that we know to eat. And that is only the basic beginning, for the eating is nothing. How incredibly little do we understand what magic meals we have upon sight, upon scent, upon textural touch. What huge meals we have out of the scent of a flower, out of the greeting and observation of the dawn, and the rising of the Dog Star, and of its very opposition, the eventide, the equinox of spring of day, and the equinox of sleep, of night, which are complete opposites.

Are we aware of these things? Do we perceive them, or are we hypnotized with gadgets and machines and incredible thinkings in gurglings of words? Are we hypnotized? Are we aware of the infinite magic that is happening every second of every day? And it is always new, and never repeated. Everything, even classicism, is not static, nor education, nor knowledge: for knowledge is a journey. And behind the whole of this journey is a pathway, and that pathway is crystal clear. It is the pathway of the herbs beneath the government of the stars, and the aperture is the law of God.

Are the herbs important in our lives? Out of the whole of herb origin—and one talks, of course, of trees and shrubs, and flowers and roots and leaves, and many other things that we are going to touch upon that are almost indelible—but out of all of that has come, via the great horticultural University of Padua, commenced in the 1400's, the great horticultural gardens that are schools, such as Kew (Royal Botanic Gardens), the sister of Wisley (Royal Horticultural Garden). Out of those gardens, out of those mastery of horticultures, from those herbs have come every single fruit, every flower, every vegetable, and everything that we look at, enjoy, smell, and eat.

What a gateway, what an enormous gateway this is! Where is one? Where is one here in the United States? Where is such a school in California? Then what are we talking about? Are we not talking about an enormity that is the revelation of the whole law of the universe? And are we not hypnotized into oblivion and not perceiving it?

In those very herbs, and the outcome of those herbs that are all the fruits and vegetables and flowers, there is as you realize, no difference at all. You can't really talk about flowers, for the cauliflower that you boil is perfectly good in the herbaceous border. And you get married holding the *Asparagus plumosus nanus* (asparagus fern) whilst you eat *Asparagus officianalis*. And of course the whole background of asparagus is really very interesting because the name began in the Greek period, which is *asparagos*, which of course was used as it should be in America, in the Senate. When anybody got up and spoke too long, they simply said:

(*thump*) "Asparagos!" And it was the duty of one man to pick up a wand of asparagus which always weighed about two pounds, which they grow in the Aegean wild in such a way, and strike him on the head, which of course did him no harm, but decidedly quieted the whole issue.

Now out of the whole matter of this is the vision which that remarkable person, Rudolf Steiner, so largely brought about, and which has not greatly been focused upon: relationship and dis-relationship. You are aware that every one of the herbs is governed by a planet or planets, and that every area of the body is likewise governed by planetary system and planetary invocation, and that therefore the interpolation between those two is so perfectly obvious.

If you question this matter you have only to put a bowl of water beneath a cucumber. The cucumber, as you know, is governed by the moon, and the cucumber will immediately grow downwards. If you place the water above the cucumber in a bowl, the cucumber will immediately go up to the bowl, or placed to the side, and it will go to the side. And as you know, if you place a bowl of oil beneath the cucumber, and the cucumber will go in the opposite direction. If you place the bowl of oil above the cucumber, it will go down. If you place it to the right, it will go to the left. It is governed, as they all are, sometimes by two planets, sometimes by three, usually by one, sometimes by many.

And the areas of the body, also. Therefore there can be no question about this interplay of the essences of the herbs and the appropriations to humanity. Likewise, you understand that we are very much inclined to think of plants *ad toto*. And, of course, just as there are night birds and day birds, there are night plants and day plants, and the in-betweens of the equinoxes, all interweaving in relationships and dis-relationships.

Now, not only is that interplay between man and his limbs and the plants, but likewise between all the birds, the animals, and the insects, and everything else that lives. For every grain of sand that comes from the rocks has spirit matter within it. It is a living entity somewhere. And all water is not just water. It is endless sisters of drops. A whole family, as mountains are families of mothers and fathers and children. And indeed when you look at a tree and you talk about a tree, what unutterable nonsense! For every bud which grows on every bough of every tree is a single entity, and you can indeed take it, and it will root and grow, and it has a root in the tree just like the roots of a tooth. Do you grow your eyelashes each day? Do you attend to the top of your ear and the bottom of your ear? And yet it all falls off and renews all the time as the skin of the trees and the plants does. Nothing is static—it's always changing all the time.

Likewise such things as temperatures. If we talk again about the cucumber and you take a day like today and you would say, "Well, the temperature today at noon was seventy-nine." Very well, you put your thermometer in the cucumber. And what is that crazy saying about 'cool as a cucumber'? Why? Because of the moon. Is it as hot at noon at night as it is at noon in the day? Why not? Aha! Why not? And when you put the thermometer in the cucumber at noon today you will read about forty-nine. And when you place that thermometer amongst the roots of, shall we say, heirloom lilies—just to take a differentiation, you could put it among anything if you like and it will be all variations—but when you place it amongst the roots of heirloom lilies it will read one hundred twelve.

Relationships and dis-relationships: here you have science, *scio*, 'to know': the knowledge of the law of God. The total knowledge, and here it sits in the very seat of herbs, to be observed and discovered and lived with. Out of this magic of the attitudes of biodynamics is the focus upon fertility.

Fertility is of course a vast marriage. It's the marriage of it all. It is the marriage of soil with moisture, with breathings, with decays: with life-into-death-into-life. And with plants and with birds and with insects, and with atmospheres, and with clouds. This is the knowledge of fertility. When man enters the world of herbs and creates the world of gardens, the world of horticulture, and from there steps into the world of agriculture—for there is no other path—to build a garden of an acre, it begins to teach you that you can build a field of twenty acres, and so on.

And so, this relationship and dis-relationship of the whole of the plants is being governed by the *revolutionibus* of the whole ordinance of the government of the Sun, with the *prima mobile* and the *secundus mobile*—the stars that we can see and the ætherial world that we cannot see. All of which is revolving and changing—in hundreds of thousands of years—but changing all the time. Even classicism is changing, and that is the seat of the import of the herbs.

For the herbs are origin. They began when we began. And they have not changed, and they have not been lost, and they have not been destroyed by man's unbalances. Only the plants that we grow in the garden are the exhibition of that. They become unbalanced—or less unbalanced or more unbalanced—according to our environment that we create. No garden lettuce has the lactucarium that the wild *Sativa* has. From the wild lettuce you will take probably sixty-eight grams of lactucarium. From the garden lettuce, in most cases, you would be lucky to get eleven or sixteen grams.

If you want the ointment of camomile, do not go to *Anthemis* 'Moonlight', go to *Anthemis nobilis* (Roman chamomile), or *Anthemis cotula* (stinking chamomile) and you will get your camomile in its full ratio. The totality of Nature, the absolute totality. And everything that we, out of our *image*, construct out of that totality must be to some small infinitesimal degree a lessening. Because we are self; we have selfishness. Now perceive: *self* must go if you wish to be a gardener.

This matter concerning the herbs in origin and the plants that we grow that bring about varietal disintegration is so much faster than any change that takes place in Nature's origins. Those changes are taking place when the forests have seed, and the trees are slowly changing. As the mountains grow in their families and the children spring up, those mountains are changing shape. The oceans change their areas. But it is all within the whole ordinance of the government of the Sun and the *prima mobile* and the universal law of God.

The moment that you enter agriculture and horticulture you have a new, a lessened, government. You have the government of: "Excuse me. We want something to eat! I like it like this! I'd like a pink apple. I want the pears with the seeds outside." "Very well, my child, you shall have it. If it is in your *image* and it is a desire, it will take place." Have we not got expressways with millions of flying boxes?

And it is always possible to have the Garden of Eden.

Therefore, one points out the enormity that the whole of this matter of herbs in origin, what they have to tell us, what they have to direct us with, and what they have within them to take either as seed, or juices, or relationships to our bodies, with the planetary system that will at all times put right and rebalance our imbalances, and reguide us, and show us a path that we cannot talk about, but is only perceivable.

How is it that we have such great libraries? There have never been so many books. Indeed, it takes the poor student today one hundred years to read one hundredth of them. And we know less than we knew. We make noises about everything. We write down the expression of those noises, and we pass people out sheepskin on graduations for regurgitating them. We know nothing about the origin that they have come from. We know nothing about the whole spirit character of the world from which they come. And as a result of this we have become hypnotized by our selves, by our self, and by our requirements. That's why we are all screaming our heads off, "What are we going to eat!" And the whole cornucopia is there.

What is the price of a tomato? It is what it has always been. Nothing. And it will give you a hundred thousand tomatoes again next year. One tomato. And it costs nothing. In fact it can't cost anything. It's our obscenity that costs a terrible lot. And so obscene has it become in its commercial and ludicrous unbalance that you can hardly afford one, and when you can, you wish you hadn't got it.

Out of the whole study of herbs, the way they grow, the way they're governed, to understand them and to sense them, out of this comes this magical matter that I now wish to place before you. You must never, never forget it again. Or lose it or leave it. It is the birth of fertility in the *image* of man. When you create fertility in the soil, and in the plants that you grow and the trees, and the birds and the insects and the fish that you introduce with it, something happens that is outside your verbal understanding. You are connected with the cornucopia of the birth of the spirit world, of the invisible through the four elements into the perpetual visible and temporal. And out of that creation of that fertility brought about by the *image* of man through the life force of biodynamics into the living world, comes a birth and a consummation that you cannot calculate, that you cannot count, and that is without profit. It is so endless. And more than the utter fulfillment of all requirement.

And suddenly in the new cycle of the *revolutionibus* enters the entire magic of the matter. You discover within this little nonsense that you've created, of a few yards, you find new weeds that you have never thought of, and with those weeds come insects, and with those insects come birds, and animals and breathings and moistures, and new trees and new plants, and new *image* forever in ascendency towards the stars. A magnification of all that there is. And never, never, never, to usurp, never to turn self against the whole origin of the herbs.

So much was this understood in the days when talking was very little and doing was quite a lot, there was the practice of alchemy. And here you discover in the whole of what people call today 'magic': truth. For you must perceive that even with the joking today about fairies, elves, nymphs, undines and dwarves: it is ludicrous to turn around and giggle, because it is so unutterably true. You have only to look at what happens at the dawn, and you are stymied in stupidity. Of course there are elves and fairies and undines, and they are names. They are names for what? For the magic that the four elements—earth, fire, air and water—bring about in the perpetual marriage of the invisible into the visible. And this is a stupendous matter today that almost nobody, almost nobody who has ruling and authority, and leadership, ever thinks of spending: living tempo in the whole world of eternity, which is invisible. The only thing we talk about is 'food for millions'. Eating.

Food has almost got almost nothing to do with eating. The greatest delight of food is smell. When you enter the house you say, "Oh! What have you been cooking?" And you'll go much more to heaven than you will when you eat it, generally.

Likewise, I refer to this period of food and medicine and magic and healing. Now you understand that the ancient Greeks, from the other ancients upwards, realized that what they ate was an emphatic interplay of their physical body, the uplift of their mind into vision, and the living in spirit. And this enormity lived through that whole era of alchemy. And you perceive it because, they knew so well, as much of the medical world is beginning to discover, and openly admit: you can't get rid of anything. You can't get rid of disease. It's part of huge balance. If you do something, *you've done it*, and there is a balance. Day and night. Hot and cold. Summer and winter. Spring equinox and fall equinox. And good and bad.

They realized, so clearly, that you can't get *rid of*. What you must do is to have a joyful inducer. Therefore they used herbs, or relators that would attract this thing known as dis-ease, and urged it either into water, or into an animal, or a cat or a dog or a horse; or into a formation, or a ring, or magical drawings. And then to use a driver-out. That driver-out was very seldom a pill or an injection. It was odor; it was focus, focus of dynamic approaches. The scent of certain apples were used. Invariably were herbs burned in the area, often beneath the bed. And in this way, first of all the herb-inducer was used, away; and then the herb-driver was used. And therefore you merely pass one from another.

Do you understand in the whole world of biodynamics you can't even think about garbage? It's ridiculous. There is no such thing as garbage. Everything in Nature is life into death into life. It is *revolutionibus*. You can't have cellophane bags that you can't get rid of. It's impossible.

I want to run through a few lists of plants and extractions and things that do relate to this and relate to that.

In one further remark about herbs and their origins, I want to talk about this very important matter: area of discontinuity, aura, emanation. Skin, that through which everything pulsates, can breathe out and can breathe in, and is that area which separates an entity into a self. Every picture on the wall literally has to have a frame. Otherwise, it only belongs to the world. And a theatre has to have a proscenium arch. And the audience has to be dark and the stage has to be light. Areas of discontinuity and bloom. Bloom—I am referring not to blossom—I am referring to that delicate matter which is infinitely more precise and articulate than the flower. It is that which rests on the stalks, the foliages, the roots, the whole emanation of the plant. It is emanation, it is a give-off, and it is all around all plants, all fruits—even molecules, even buds, even a hair has an area of discontinuity that contains bloom.

The earth, the soil, is the skin of the world, the delicate flesh of this revolving world. It needs a guard, and the guard is herbs. The herbs were created to cover the skin with a mantle. And man in participation, was partially then created with a whole ordinance to magnify this enchanting and exquisite magic. This is one of his great delights and works. And the whole of Nature adores and requests mankind to enter the scene and build and magnify that which can go on forever and ever into a magnification, until we find ourselves in this eternal garden of perfections.

Snails have lived for several of millions of years, which historians and other people will tell you a lot of rubbish about. It's known as Tyrian purple, and a beautiful dye comes from it. There are none actually living today, this is part of the change of origin. There are eight hundred million tons of *murex* in the Dead Sea, from snails, from dragonflies, from birds, from wings, from beaks, from teeth, from beetles, from spiders, from gnats. What magic! What endless magic are all these creations that are participle in the whole world of these origin herbs.

You can't have a garden without them. You can't have a garden for 'me', because that is the beginning of the end. Your garden is one that you must enter forwards and go out of backwards, in utter reverence and obedience to the great law that governs it. You can not and must not say, "I will do this. I will have this here. I will have that. I will have ten thousand dollars!" Because you'll get it, and it's horrid.

The whole world is full of *murex*, of chalk, of sand, and all of these silly words that we give names to.

Now enters the whole thinking of Steiner, and those enormous visionaries, at the time when he was beginning to point, saying, "There's a precipice. Look where we're going." And they all discovered a huge import of this matter: that if you take the contents of an herb, or if you take the contents of water, or an insect, and separate it and give it names, you haven't got the total of the plant or the insect at all. It doesn't add up.

I will give you an instance, of Dr. Bunge[2] in 1921, of Bath, who kept white mice, and fed them all upon milk, and they were terribly happy and terribly well, and proliferated. And so, since this was the huge calumnious time of the industrial age into agriculture, he wanted to prove certain things. So he said, "Now, we will go into the laboratory, we will take milk to pieces, and then we will put it together and feed the mice." So they took the milk into the laboratory, they took it into its five areas, and they fed the mice upon the partitions put together. And all the mice died. So they went back into the laboratory, and they dissected it properly, and took it to pieces, and fed the mice. And they all died. And they did it three times, and decided that there was something radically wrong.

Well, instead of looking at ancient mythology and the whole story of Psyche and Cupid, they went off. And one of them suddenly said,

"Of course, I've got it. I know. How silly we are! Of course, it is the one thing that we've left out and we haven't discovered: vitamins!" And all of them said, "Do you know, I've always noticed, he's brilliant. Absolutely brilliant. You see, we didn't see it. It's ridiculous." And you see, they're still doing it. They've gone from *a* to *zed*; they've gone into x and unknown quantity, and they're still looking for the vitamin. Has anybody ever found the germ inside a seed? You can't do it. You will undo casings and casings and casings.

Now you do know also this Jacques Cousteau has recently had exactly the same example and exposed it to the world. He sent some beautiful little sea horses, to an aquarium. And that aquarium was inland, so they quickly said, "These seas horses need sea water." "Oh! Oh!" said the professor, "Of course, of course." So they went to the laboratory and made sea water. And you can guess what happened, like the mice. The sea horses died. So they sent somebody to the seaside and got some sea water and the horses lived. And that's the answer.

Let us refer for a moment to this terminology that we are using about everything. Mustard. We use mustard, we use it with this; we use it with that. If you have rheumatism, you use a mustard bath for your feet, you have mustard bath for your head. And it cures it. Why? Aha. Sulphur, of course! Well, aren't we clever. Why, we've gone slap in our faces, of course. That's the whole trouble. The moment you give something a name like that you say, "Right. I've got it!" And of course you haven't.

So they go straight to the coal mine, and they get sulphur. And it doesn't work at all.

The Greek went to the *Salix*, to the white willow, and to the *Spirea*, and he got his aspirin, and it stopped his toothache, it stopped his headache, it stopped his stomachache. Because he took the white willow. So for ten hundred years, they used the juice of the white willow and the *Spirea*. And later they got bored and wanted to make some money out of it because it costs nothing to use willows, so they said, "What is *Salix?*" "Don't tell anyone. It's salicylic acid." So they went to the coal mine and made some. Now everybody bleeds inside, as you know.

All of these scientific chemical names that we give to things, they come to life in a plant in a certain moment, on a certain day, and they're there. And the next day, they're not. It may be in the root; it may be in the leaf;

it may be in the seed. Sulphur only develops in the mustard plant, when the seed, on a certain day with the Sun, develops forty percent sulphur. At no other time is there any sulphur in the mustard plant.

And this is throughout the herbs. We are always, in our ludicrousity, as our education, trying to catch everything and put it in the cage and make it static. And you can't. Therefore, you perceive that the herbs are telling us, "Look at us! Observe! And find out that you can't behave like this." They are real. They live. And you understand that no moment ever repeats itself. No day is a repetition of a day. And we're always talking about 1975, or "Well now, let me see, 1973, ah, that one." I'm awfully sorry because there's no connection between them at all. It's *perpetuoso*. And there is no time at all. For the *revolutionibus* is there.

So you see that we are hypnotized.

If you have trouble with mice, either in the garden, or even field mice, or mice in your house, *Mentha aquatica* (water mint) will drive them out immediately. Any trouble with ants: tansy. Invariably, after I've tried to give a lecture somewhere, somebody gets up and says, "What do I do about ants?!" But they are magic. Have you read Maeterlinck[3]? These incredible people with their observations of such things! The other matter about ants is that sometimes they will probably want more of your fruit than you wish them to have. Well, it's very simple. You understand, what I am trying to express to you tonight, in the whole ordination of Nature is: "I adore this! Oh, I hate that!" Black and white; hot and cold; day and night—and in the whole relationship of plants and insects and animals and birds and us is this matter. And this is knowledge. And this is what we've got to seek and observe and find out.

If you grow a *Helianthis gigantica*—the sunflower—if you grow one or two of those where ever there are ants, they will in the daytime, automatically go up the sunflower. They will all rest under the leaves. And all the little birds that you have induced in with such plants as *Senecio* (groundsel) and *Sanchus* (sow thistle), which will bring all of those birds, they will deal with the ants. Relationship and dis-relationship. For moles and gophers—endless—all the *Euphorbia* family, *Sambucus* (elderberry) in particular, and of course, *Artemisia*.

Now please understand I use international terms, but I am an American citizen. I use international terms simply because, if we go to Moscow, or if we go to Peru, they all know what we are talking about. In America we don't. If you want the common names, you must ask in the questions, or look it up in one of those good books that give them already simply.

If you have cockroaches, and you don't really enjoy cockroaches, it's terribly easy, as all of these things are: *Verbascum blatteria*, or the moth mullein. Now it was of course Helen of Troy that it is only known to us because of *Verbascum*. She had golden hair, and the Greeks did not have golden hair. And she was not particularly beautiful, but her hair was. And she washed it every day with *Verbascum*. It also attracts all the moths and the butterflies, and drives away the cockroaches.

Well, you see, all that I am really doing is, I am not giving you a lot of stupid statistics, I am opening you up the whole book of Nature so that we can say, "Is there any argument?" For instance you realize that *Petroselinum* is the very rock of St. Peter, the keys of the gates of heaven, *Petroselinum*, parsley. Even in these blasted emporiums they still sell bunches of parsley. That *look* like parsley. Why? It is so important for the whole of our nerve system, the whole of our good health, to eat parsley with everything. And yet, you've only to get some of the seed to your pet and it will be dead. And you see you take that beautiful plant *Urtica dioica*, that is the stinging nettle, the great big one, upon which all the *Vanessas*, those charming butterflies, as in those designs of the peacocks, the red admirals, the tortoise shells, and so on—those are all *Vanessas*—they all, although they are living on the nectar of flowers, they all go to the *Urtica dioica*, and they lay their eggs, because, they know, from the law of Nature, that that's what the children have got to eat. And all butterfly caterpillars eat only one vegetable. What a consummation of knowledge is in this *perpetuoso* of the fulfillment of Nature.

If you have mold in your bread or mold in your flour, whether it is there or you don't want it there, simply use *Eupatorium cannabinum* (hemp-agrimony). *Eupatorium*. There's no common word, I'm sorry, you can go on as much as you like, but there isn't one. But *Eupatorium* will even get rid of mold in bread. Aren't these incredible magics?

If you have tied flesh, dried up flesh—anybody today who uses these terrible bleaches and cleaning things in their sinks—you will have tied skin, dried up skin that splits. The bulrush or *Typha*: if you take it when it's tight, in blossom, the actual blossom when it's tight, closed up. Be very careful where you put it, because you may not know it, but before those devils invented gunpowder, that's what all the fireworks of Venice were made of. And if you put a match near that in the winter, you can blow the roof off. It is gunpowder, of a sense. You've only to undo one of those magical seeds, and you can practically fill this room with it, immediately. That will cure all tied skin, if mixed with a synergist particularly, such as petroleum jelly even, and placed upon it, two or three times.

If you wish to lose your appetite, and sometimes you should—you realize that in more religious days, with Easter, people always ate tansy cakes, and their appetite went, so all the wickedness of eating at that time was removed. Tansy will remove your appetite. If you want it back again, and you have lost your appetite, simply use the herb *Origanum vulgarae* (oregano), and your appetite is there. If, as a result of your appetite coming back you have started to overeat, and you have stomach ache, you should use cumin, and it will put you right immediately.

If you have weevils in your rice, or in your barley, or in any of your cereals, *Parietaria*, or Pellitory-of-the-Wall will remove it completely. Even in the granaries and barns, it will remove it.

I spoke of a plant just now about which there was a magical matter. I must tell you a magical matter about a little plant known as toadflax. It's one of the *Linums*, *Linaria*. This plant is a trailing plant of the *Linaria*. It's one of the flaxes (*Cymbalaria muralis* or *Linaria Cymbalaria*, ivy-leaved toadflax). It goes along and it only grows upon the sides of walls, and wherever there is a leaf as it trails, as it is a complete trailing plant, it will travel for ten or twelve feet along the walls and hang down. Wherever a leaf grows out of a stalk, one of these charming little blossoms will come on a stalk about so long. And you will immediately perceive that it is hanging over a great precipice, and this plant only grows in a wall. "Oh dear, what on Earth is going to happen!" So it blossoms right out in space on this beautiful stalk, and is a beautiful lavender-pink-mauve. And when the seed has developed, and is about to ripen, the whole stalk turns inwards, seeks a crevice, and places the seed into a small crevice.

As indeed you understand with the *Viola*, violet, the *Viola canina* (heath dog violet), it grows so high and blossoms. And then although it seeds in two ways, it does sometimes seed from that blossom. And at the moment that the blossom is over, the stalk has stopped growing.

But that area is not enough above the plant for its migration, for the plant spreads very rapidly by crown *présentement*. So what does it do? The whole ordinance of the law of *revolutionibus* then says, "Again." And so it grows that same distance again. The seed then develops twice the height, so that when it bursts, it migrates to the proper areas.

With the sweet pea: when the sweet pea seeds, it suddenly bursts on a certain day. Never is all the seed in the pod ripe, and it must migrate also. What happens is that the two halves of the pod split open like two propellors, and curl around to themselves, and then wrap each other around like that. And it is so instantaneous that you can't even perceive it, you can only hear it, as a technical click. It hurls the seeds as much as twenty-five and thirty feet, that are ripe. Those that are not ripe, before they can escape—which they would, if they had the time, but owing to the little thread holding them, they are quickly closed up and caught like that—therefore they must proceed and ripen in the proper way and fall where they should, into a new area.

And so you perceive these magics are *ad infinitum*. For eyesight there are herb cures that have cured hundreds of thousands of people whose sight has actually ceased. One of the principals is the plant *Hieracium*, or common hawkweed. The oil from the seed taken inwardly will repair, improve the clarity of all sight. The most important is *Euphrasia* (eyebright). *Euphrasia* taken as a tea, as a drink, especially from the fresh flower, and especially as an eye bath with milk as a synergist, once a week will restore the clarity of sight that is becoming dim. In the event of cataract, there is the magical matter of the one seed of *Clary*, which is a sage. *Clary*. One seed of the Clary sage, when moisture is applied to it, shoots out—unseeable by the eye—shoots out little tiny daggers or scalpels. And not the greatest surgeon in the world has been able to equal the complex procedure that this little seed operates in the eye, when it is placed in there, removing the cataract. It has been used for something like five thousand years successfully. Until the age of lunacy.

The great celandine, or *Cheledonium*, it's very important to the sight, as indeed, is the magic herb of the world, *Verbane*. And the second magic plant of the world, *Betonica*, betony. Both of those, *Verbane* (*Verbena*, vervain) and betony can cure fifty extreme disorders, bring about peace, tranquility, the removal of melancholia. If you suffer from nightmares, fifteen seeds of peony, and you will never have a nightmare. Neither if you take *Anthemis nobilis*, it will remove them. Also for good sleep, *Humulus lupulus*, or the hop. Why does everybody in that stupid old England drink beer? To go sleepy, and heaven knows they are. It used to be a practice with anybody who suffered from insomnia, to very quietly without anybody knowing, stuff a pillow with hops. And without them knowing it, they put their head upon the pillow, and the odors and the effects—note, *effects*: we must begin to lose ourselves in our observation of our inner senses in these matters—and they invariably slept most perfectly.

One of the most exquisite and perfect removals of pain and giver of good sleep with *improved* consciousness is *Passiflora incarnata* (purple passionflower). And the greatest herb of all for the uplift of the mind, the improvement of memory, and of induction of spiritual vision is *Angelica archangelica* (garden angelica, Holy Ghost). And so, I'm sorry, we could go on *ad infinitum*, I have got sixty pages. It is time for questions.

May I please repeat to you the pathways between the stars and the flowers is crystal clear and unmistakable.

Q: Can you exclude cadavers from your diet?

Yes you can. You can exclude vegetables from your diet. As a matter of fact Steiner very nearly taught me to be a complete fruitarian.

Q: There are so many little children in the world that are suffering from some kind of a deficiency disease such as mental retardation and so forth. Do you have anything that you feel, in the ways of teas and so forth that would be beneficial?

Endless, endless. Yes, indeed endless. We're onto a huge subject. You understand that what we said at the beginning is that man in his origin, his food was his physical, his mind and his spirit. Today, we stuff ourselves. Do you understand? We don't think of anything else. And suddenly we turn around to a doctor, who's had to come through the window, and say, "I'm feeling awful!" And so he goes, *psquaaak*, and he gets rid of it. But what does he do in getting rid of it? Because you can't get rid of it. Do you understand?

Therefore, this is a building. When you are resuscitated, you are resuscitated. And that in the whole build of the body are the juices, and that illness is in us all. But all influenza is a wave, it passes through everywhere; it doesn't suddenly, you know, somebody doesn't suddenly *give* influenza to somebody else. The whole influenza sweeps along; it's a wave. And according to *your* balances, so you either ride it, or fall under it. Do you understand?

Therefore you perceive where you've got to focus on this subject that your on. The malnutrition is incredible. Do you realize what's inside an egg today? Do you realize that there are no juices in anything? That the whole soil has literally got nothing in it. You can't feed the soil with chemicals. It has no textures. It has no fertility. Do you understand this at all?

I believe that. So how do we help these little ones?

A gradual—and as quick as possible—return into fertility! It is better to give a child one slice of whole wheat bread, one slice of something real that's got the juices in it.

Do you understand where the whole thing about pest has come from? Because we fed the plants upon drivel, and all the blood in the plants was nothing, so the insects had to stuff themselves silly all day long like a child does on white bread, and still isn't fed. As a result of it they get a mania and they breed like lunatics. It's what is going on in the cities.

Do you understand what I've been trying to talk about tonight? It's why you put your foot into something. If you want to put this right, put your foot there. But do it because it's good. Because it's right. Your approach is everything. Don't do it in quantity. Don't do it because they're ill. We don't want to feed ourselves because we're all poisoned. It is the beauty of living that is biodynamic. Do you understand?

You will find that the revelation into Nature will restore. The observation of dawn. Stop them looking into this giddy box. You're on a huge subject. It's the whole subject that all the world is beginning. It's likely to wobble on their feet and say, "What are we going to do now?" But they're all going to sit in their motorcars and wait for somebody to put some gin in when there isn't any petrol.

You must seek into this. You must find those herbs, those juices, those methods that are going to bring suscitation. If you would write to us at Covelo, I will try to deal with it. Other people will try to deal with it, and give you informations as much as they can. If you will write to the anthroposophical society—for I will tell you that I am not a sectarian, but I believe that almost in the whole world, there are not such deep thinkers as there are here. People who are seeking and thinking deep. This was the whole wave of Steiner. This incredible thing that he brought from there, and exposed it and magnified it.

Q: On the subject of garbage, I believe that you mentioned something about a balance, with life and death and balance. And I was wondering if you would elaborate on that a little bit?

All death is life. In the forest, all the great storms of the equinox, falling in love, breaking down the trees in their exuberance. All the boughs, the foliages, the dead animals, the birds, they're all part of the whole incredible rebirth in the equinox. And everything in Nature is this *revolutionibus*. There is no waste of anything. All the water, all the trees, all the rocks—every single thing that there is in creation—has a place, a relationship and a dis-relationship. If you wish to build your paths, you can't have enough rocks and stones in your garden. Do you follow?

If you have rubbish such as broken glass and bottles and tins, as people seem to delight in, there's nothing like it. I don't know whether you know it, but all of the great sports grounds of the world are built upon this matter. They're built upon broken bottles and broken glass and tins, because such things as are are inclined to interrupt those lawns can't move through them. And they are an excellent foundation for drainage.

Therefore everything in the garden—unless you have unrealistic things—is usable. They all belong somewhere.

On this idea that plants are the reclamation of the garbage is something...I remember reading something about that, where they cycle it, or something? Is there any good in that, any use of that?

35

Endless. You realize that you can have stagnant water, there is a pond weed that you can put in stagnant water and you can drink it two days afterwards. There are waters in which mosquitos and flies of all sorts will breed like mad. There is a plant which you can sow in that water, and every one of those will be devoured.

In the whole garden everybody today is terrified about the whole matter of aphids. The grey aphids, the green aphids, and the black aphids. There is a plant that we grow, and this is one of our many discoveries of this sort, it is of course *Nicotiana affinis* (flowering tobacco). It is so exquisite, that you would think, that with one plant in your garden, your whole garden was madonna lilies at night, so enchanting is the scent. And so enchanting is the scent and the nectar of the whole plant, that no aphid can resist it. They prefer it to everything else that grows, and they will go straight to this plant to enjoy the nectar, which exudes out of its hairs all of the time, and the moment they alight, it closes its head and eats the insect.

Q: How do you deal with caterpillars?

You deal with caterpillars by the induction of relationship and dis-relationship. The induction of birds, principally. On the contrary, there are any amount of plants, inter-relators, that you can grow that no caterpillar can tolerate. That is the reason that all the old gardens had edges of herbs: lavender, parsley, alliums, rosemary, thymus. Do you understand? I'm talking, for the first time, probably for a hundred years, about scents in the garden.

Q: Is there a particular species of Vervain *that is an herbal?*

Vervain? There is only one vervain in the world and ever has been. This was the magic herb of the Druids. It's the magic herb that has been used in every religious house to strew the water, and to bring goodwill, and happiness and peace. If you collect it in a certain way—which I'm not going to relate here because it takes a half an hour—but if you collect it in the proper way when the Dog Star is rising and there is no Sun and no Moon, you will never be attacked by a mad dog nor bitten by a dog, neither will a bad dog bark at you even. Oh yes you may laugh, but it is true. And this is the matter. You see there is a relationship between *us* and *that*. And we have got to learn reverence. And that's the point that we've lost. We make a motorcar and think that we're terribly clever.

Q: You mentioned the importance of destroying, sublimating, or some other way of getting rid of the concept of ego when dealing with the garden, and understanding these mysteries. Some first steps in that direction?

Concentro. Medito. Contemplo. To learn to concentrate. To learn to meditate. And to learn to contemplate. This was part of the whole discovery of Goethe[4], that Nietzsche[5] also delivered, and that Steiner was so engulfed in by these people. Concept. Percept. And precept. Do you understand that the whole of music comes from the intervals between the planets. This is Pythagoras and tones. That is the perfect octave, between the seven planets of the *prima mobile*. And that what this person is just talking about, do you understand that you can come *under* a note, to it, which is flat. You can hit the note straight, which is classic origin. Or you can come down from above, which is precept. Do you understand?

---

1   Claudius Ptolemy, Greek-Egyptian astrologer, mathematician and astronomer; (~90-168 A.D.).

2   This experiment by Dr. G. Bunge was written up in *The Physician and Surgeon Monthly Magazine, Vol III,* 1881.

3   Maurice Maeterlinck, Belgian author and Nobel laureate in literature in 1911; wrote *The Life of the Bee* in 1901, *The Life of the Ant* in 1930, and his play, *The Bluebird*, first performed in 1909, inspired Alan as a child to become part of the magic of the theater; (1862-1949).

4   Johann Wolfgang von Goethe, German writer, poet and vitalist scientist; notably wrote *Faust*, and *The Metamorphosis of Plants*, hugely influential for Alan; (1749-1832).

5   Friedrich Nietzsche, influential German philosopher, (1844-1900).

Everything is Governed by an Invisible Law

Urban Garden Symposium
San José Community College
April 1975

I thought first that we would talk about the productivity of the French intensive system with biodynamics. Then to talk about the approach of biodynamics, and then talk to some degree about herbs, and then you have a period of questions and answers.

In the productivity of a garden, the question, that comes up is: *What is it that we want?* We want beautiful flavor in our food; we want good color in the flowers; we want lusciousness; we want youth, so we don't have to cook anymore than is necessary, or not at all. And so, what are the ways in which we approach the growing of these matters? The French intensive system is the result of thousands of years of master culturists culminating in a whole answer of this matter, and adjoined with biodynamics, brings about a whole fruition and gives those very answers.

The primary essential to all good growing is drainage. This the ancient Greeks taught us by telling us that the finest plants grow not in the alluvial soils of valleys, but on landslides. And it was because of that, that they built landslides in the valleys, and eventually called it, like furrows: 'plowing'. We do it all today, and that is the whole reason for it. With that method came about the raised beds of ancient culture, right up to today. Through that method you get perfect drainage, and warm moist air to the roots, as well as to the foliages. For one must think of roots as leaves in the ground, and leaves as roots in the air. In this way you get a much better picture of a plant.

One must also realize that there is no division such as we make about a vegetable garden, or a flower garden, or weeds, or plants. They are all plants. You happen to cook a cauliflower, and we happen to eat the bulb of an allium, an onion. There is no difference between any of them. They are all plants. But the most important plants of all in the garden are weeds.

There is no more important plant than weeds. Weeds are origins. From the weeds, we have everything that we have in the garden: every lettuce, every bean, every apple, every berry has come from the origins, the weeds. And in those weeds are more nutriments and more total juices than any of the cultured plants of man which gradually become less and less. However, the method of the French intensive bed is now a raised bed above ground level with a small walkway around it to be get-at-able.

The next matter to consider is the word *fertility*. Fertility is not 'something'. It is a marriage of everything. It is a marriage of the matters in the soil, of de-combustion, of the production of warm, moist gases in the soil and in the air, which is what all the plants live upon, and the intermarriage of all of those matters. Therefore, it is perfectly justified to say that literally any soil is a good soil. You can grow perfectly in sand. You can grow perfectly in loam. You can grow perfectly in peat moss. Not everything, but many things, and most things. The word that we all look for, and that the whole world is looking for at the moment, in its demand, is *fertility*. And added to fertility is the magic of man's mastery of the understanding of the laws of Nature. When that is applied, into what is called the French intensive bed, you produce the very classical result of true fertility.

Texture is probably the most important matter which the world agriculturally has forgotten. Texture is entirely essential for the production of warm moist gases and for the production of the important word: *capillary*. Capillary really means, as we understand it, the rising of the waters from the deep Earth. It also has a resultant upon the dews, which you might call the compressions from the atmosphere. But in this word, texture in the soil is vitally important. You cannot have capillary if you have a seething surface on your soil, neither can you have capillary if you have a fine loose soil underneath. You must have a loose, flexible soil about two inches on the surface, and below that you must enter textured soils. That means actual roughage; and the more roughage the more down, the better. In this way you will get de-combustion, capillary, and the action of pulsation into the soil. That is breathing; that is action of the *revolutionibus*, as spoken of by Copernicus[1]: the effect of the planets and the ruling of the cycles.

When those things are interwoven, the next procedure to produce the fertility in a French intensive bed is the high culture of stratification. Is it not true to say that in the whole procedure of Nature she lays her soils in lengths? In this way, the roots of the plants and the surfaces of the plants growing, grow through the areas, which they need, in their different ages. A child begins on milk, and then goes into bread and milk, and then goes into more and more things and more things. It is exactly the same with plant life. They demand texture. It's a word we have forgotten. The idea of chewing your compost up with a machine is most developed. If you wish to use compost immediately, instantly, then chewing the compost up is advisable. But if you want compost in its true important form, you must have it as enormous texture. And you must use that compost in the form of decomposition, not as decomposed as soil. It is as the structure of decomposition that its forces play and produce the warm, moist gases, which is what all the roots and the leaves live upon.

When one talks now about roots and leaves living upon this, in the French intensive bed, you have to entertain the interplay of the planetary system, which, with its sleeping and waking, inclination and declination, does the matter of feeding through the atmosphere, so that the plant breathes in through the air, and travels down through the roots into the soil. Thus actually feeding the soils. Likewise, in the opposite pulsation, feeding out through the roots, through the soil, up the stems, through the leaves, into the air. This is a procedure, which goes on in opposition, like breathing in and breathing out, and this is the whole essential of the study of biodynamics, introducing the play of the cycles, the work of the *revolutionibus* of the planets.

Now, when these beds are stratified, with different soils, different composts, and different fertilizations, the plants are aware of this, and the planting of those plants must be placed so that they make, literally, a thermal control of their fate. That as those warm moist gases are being built up inside the bed, by decomposition, those gases are rising and are held by the foliage of the plants themselves, like a small *conservatoire*—like a small conservatory—like a glass house. Therefore, those plants need to be planted so that they cover the entire bed, or if not planted, so that they are sown, so that they cover the entire bed as quickly as possible. How superbly all Nature grows in meadows, in places where the plants cover the whole soil. How unhappy plants are when they are distraught by the inference of the elements, destroying the soil area.

That whole soil area, of a half inch above, and two inches below, is indeed the very skin of the world. It is the area of discontinuity between earth and air. It is the four elements, earth, fire, air, and water that are all the time bringing about interplay. The Sun is shining, drying it up. The only reason that you water plants is that they should dry. You want this continual change from one thing to another. It is the whole original vision of a holiday: this perpetual change that brings pulsation, inclination and declination, excitement, change.

Nothing in Nature is ever static for one moment. Therefore, the Sun dries the soil, and we moisten it. And the wind blows, and dries the soil more than the Sun does. And the cold comes, and the heat comes, and the four elements play, and all the time are destructive. But if you place these plants so that they protect the skin of the world—the half-inch above, the two inches below—you have a further control. It's like a sheet of glass with a window. The whole of the procedures that are taking place within the soil bed, and within the atmosphere under the plants is not being disrupted, but is being held above the plants by their foliage, which are not disturbed by the matter. Therefore you get within that area perfect growth control. It is only when plants stop growing for a time that they get tough. And if the collar of any plant gets tough, it will never recover in that area, and the plant will never be a good plant again.

You must, in growing all plants, think of the word 'acceleration'. From the time that the seed is born, there must be a continual acceleration of that plant. Faster and faster and faster. Therefore you must sow your seed, and get germination on a certain cycle that is going to proceed, seed, and continue ad lib. For if the plant stops, it will not be worthwhile. That is the whole reason and purpose behind the huge culture of French intensive beds. The result of the formation of that bed, which is an endless and extremely cultured work, has this result: that all the crops grown in such a bed, formed in such a cultured manner, when you take that crop out, that soil in the bed is infinitely more fertile than when the crop went in. And can this be said today about the approaches of horticulture and agriculture? This is the whole matter that the whole view of agriculture is striving and hunting for. It is the utmost importance that you improve, improve, improve. And that is exactly what this classic system brings about. It cannot be otherwise.

In the interpolation of the planting of that bed must come the study of deep-rooteds and shallow-rooteds. Now, one of the greatest achievers of Nature, of which man has no competence whatsoever, is worms. Worms are enormous cultivators and enormous fertilizers. They do both. Normally, in ordinary soil where you have a strata of compaction, which is perfectly natural throughout the world, the worms will go into dormancy both in the summer and the winter and curl up, in that strata, and merely come out in the equinoxes, and operate. The moment that you have deep-rooted plants—and *lucerne* (alfalfa) will go down sixty-two feet, rhubarb goes down fourteen to sixteen feet, chicory will go down ten to fifteen feet; there are endless, endless, endless herbs and plants that do these things—now the moment that one of those roots goes through the stratification, the worms are all delighted. They do not go into dormancy. They travel down beside the roots, and they cultivate and they fertilize to get where no machinery of man can ever attempt. For you know yourselves that four feet is about the extreme that most horticulturists and very few agriculturists ever even dream of.

Now, plants breathe out of the air into the soil, and out of the soil into the air. In this very matter, the interpolation of your plants—that is the choice of the growing of your plants, interpolated—since every plant has certain of what we would call 'chemical attributes': magnesium, sulphur, phosphorus, iron, they all have different major attributes. Silly words that you must get out of your mind because they're completely untrue. But, all of those plants do, through those very items, have an inference into the soil. So that if your soil is lacking in iron, or lacking in magnesium, or lacking in phosphorus or potassium, there are an enormous amount of herbs and plants, which if you grow, will induce that within six months, and increase it, and increase it, and increase it.

Therefore, the whole vision that leads out of that French intensive bed, into biodynamics again, is relationship and dis-relationship. So you will perceive that the course of excellent drainage, and the course of the method of planting that bed in that system, you will realize that the use of irrigation or water is literally, completely, the minimal as you would ever think of. Very, very little water is required because there is no serious drying out. There is no seizing of the soil surface. It doesn't even have to be worked. The plants themselves maintain that perfect texture on the surface. At all times, that bed is articulate breathing, and full of all the capacities of Nature, of excellent health. And now you can see the result upon the excellent nutriment and juices, that must then operate in those plants, for your soil is now the very basis of the very things that you are praying for. Therefore, you have the utmost nutriments, the utmost breathing abilities, and strength and vitalities. And this goes to show the enormous importance of the whole of that system, because it immediately undoes the words *pest* and *disease*.

Pest and disease come as a result of weakness, impure blood, poor juices, and general such matters. When you have strong vitalities, when you have strong soil which is getting stronger and stronger and stronger, you are not running into weakness and weakness and weakness. You know very well that if you feed a child or a person upon white bread out of the emporium, they will go on eating it all day, and be completely unsatisfied. And, they will get no nutriment from it; they will merely be stuffed with it. Likewise, it is true to say—and this is not negative—that if you grow plants upon extracted sub-terrestrial chemicals, you are doing exactly the same as feeding a person on white bread. The plant will fill itself, and fill itself, and fill itself; hunting, and hunting, and hunting— which is exactly what those chemicals are supposed to do—and will be full of weak juices. When all the insects, which after all are a complete ordinance of God's law, and the laws of Nature, come to feed upon the foods which are ordained for them to feed upon, they will find something which is the equivalent of white bread. And they will eat and eat and eat until they are sick, and they will breed and breed and breed until they are sick. It is exactly the same as life in the city.

And here you have the whole region in which the real words *pests* and *disease* came into agriculture. It is the result of dis-ordinance and unbalance in the cultivation, the fertilization, and the propagation of the land. When insects eat their proper food, with good food, they only need a certain amount, and then they are fed. And they have every right to have it. And the whole attitude of biodynamics is that all the insects, all the birds, and all the animals do belong, not only in Nature, but in the garden. And if we are the great administers of this world, which we proclaim that we are, we should indeed see that they are properly looked after. And if necessary, we should indeed feed them.

And if indeed you have too many birds in the garden—which is high question these days—if you have too many insects: in the whole vision of nature, is relationship and dis-relationship. Have you ever seen a butterfly, or a moth, or an aphid on *Sambucus*, that is, elderberry? Have you ever seen a fly on *Anthemis* (chamomile)? Never. You never have. I can't possibly describe all the relationships and the dis-relationships. They are absolutely complete. They are endless. In every plant is a relationship and a dis-relationship to something.

You will probably know well that *Senecio*, groundsel, when you give it to a Hartz Roller canary or to any of the finches, within two minutes, they will be singing. It is also *Senecio* that gives the softest water filter in the world, next to the *Fagus*, the beech. You would know, probably, that if you stand under a *Fagus* when there is a lightning storm, you can never be struck with lightning. No *Fagus*, no beech tree, is ever struck by lightning. It cannot be. But an oak can.

If you are afraid of bees, and don't wish to be stung, you must carry *Anthemis* (chamomile), or *Matricaria* (*chamomilla*, German chamomile), and they won't come near you. They just don't like it at all. But if you want bees to come to you, why, you must carry *Melissa*, or bee balm, and they will come to you at once. This is day and night, hot and cold, good and bad, black and white, breathing in and breathing out. It is the whole thought of Nature. And it is all operated through the arithmetic of the planets and the stars, which all revolve and move all the time.

Nothing, absolutely nothing in Nature is static, except, you might say, the law of God. That is, all the great, great botanists, and biologists, and true scientists with a knowledge of Nature, always said, when they have searched into the whole laws of Nature, they would say, "If the stars are going *that* way, and the planets are going *that* way, and it takes fifty-six years for Saturn to revolve, supposing that God decided that they should go the other way: Would they?" And the answer every time, of course, is, "Yes, they would." And there sits the whole seat of the matter.

Everything is governed by an invisible law. Invisible. And today we are so presumptuous because we unfortunately can make a motor car, and it does go along—sometimes—we think we make things. And we cannot make anything. We make nothing. But everything that we ever want is supplied to us through Nature. The big roof, everything that we eat, everything that we wear, every single thing that we do—a tennis racket—is all given us by Nature. But we do not think, it is all participant from this incredible rule of the *revolutionibus*, the revolvement.

And in this must come in somewhere, a huge vision that concerns education. We are inclined to be taught that twice two is four, and that this is this, and that is that, and the moment we regurgitate it on paper with pen and ink, or repeat it, we can get a graduation upon it, and that when we regurgitate it again and wind out to somebody else, they can wind out, and they get graduated. And so it goes on, it goes on, and goes on, and so there are libraries and libraries, of piles of books, and reams and reams, and what is going to happen in three thousand years with everybody trying to read all that, and regurgitate it all? Doesn't the forest change? The whole forest changes. Where are the pterodactyls? Where are the dinosaurs? We don't know. We're really not very clever.

Every tree that drops seed: none of the children are identical to the tree. We just say, "Oh, there's the metasequoias! They're all wearing togas!" It's absolute nonsense. There isn't any such thing. We live in an attic of words, and we believe them, intimately, and it's complete, unutterable rubbish. Every seed that is reborn in this world is new. It is not identical to the parent. It cannot be identical to the parent. The only repetition that we ever make in the garden is when we take a piece of a parent tip, and plant it. You see, we are even so statically ourselves, in cages, that we believe that a tree is a tree.

Have you not ever realized that all the buds on a tree are an enormous family? They're all really seedlings with little roots, that live through the bark into the pith of the great parent. For you can take any one of those buds and stick them into an origin root, and they will grow. And the whole bush or tree that you have done that to will be what the bud was. But if you take the seed from that tree, the origin root will have its total inference in the matter, and none of it will come true. Therefore all classic repetition in the garden in horticulture must come through seeds. Seed is the rebirth of origin. It is part of totality, and is part of invisibility.

46

All that I am really arriving at is this incredible vision that concerns the biodynamic approach, not only in living, but principally in horticulture. And it is, that behind the whole of our living, behind all the plants and all the manifestation is a spirit. Invisible. You can't talk about it, its not even tangible. And this is the precise reason why all great gardeners— real great gardeners—are really illiterates. I studied under some of the greatest gardeners in the world, and they were completely illiterate. They couldn't even pronounce the Greek and Latin names. But they were great and superb illustrators, because they always had to draw.

But, as you would know, nearly all the people who grow wonderfully, who really grew up with it, never talk. They can't talk about it. It's all invisible. And this is a very articulate matter that we have to look at: the whole incredible miracle about the very magic of a garden. All the jewels of the world, and all the maharajas put together are not the equivalent of the plants of one little backyard. They are full of the inestimable, invisible magic. Every herb—in other words every weed that grows—is related to the government of one or more of the planets or the stars. Every limb of the body—a finger, a wrist, the heart, the liver, the kidney, the eyes, the nose, and ears—are all related astrologically, as you know, to astronomy and are governed by planets and stars.

Now you will perceive why it is that within plants—as Dioscorides[2], as Pliny[3], as all of the great botanists and visionaries and philosophers realized—that there was, in all plant life, both food and medicine. And it was here that the ancient Greeks went much further, for they discovered, and knew very well, from their observance of the laws of Nature, that it was inadequate for any man to eat food for his physical sustenance. That within that food is invisible concern, and that by the adaptation of herbs with food, is found spiritual vision: uplift. That the very world of Nature, the plants, the insects and the birds can actually feed man in inspiration into vision of higher evolvement, of further sight. And that with the whole of that aspect comes perfection of health. That food is not just food, all food that we use should have it with it the herbs that are also the medicines. Therefore, in eating food and medicines together, remains perpetually, always perfect health.

You must know somewhere that the very plant *Sympyhtum*, which you would commonly call comfrey, contains in it such endless elements, that if you eat it regularly for two or three years, that is the leaves and the root and so on, you indeed have perfect teeth and bones, and repairs, and flesh and skin. And indeed it is the very plant *Symphetum*, *Symphetum* number six, that is the reestablishment of the excellence of cattle. Bones which have become solid—animals will vary upon this matter—again become hollow and beautiful as they should, and the whole structure of an animal becomes right, and the whole tremendous fat, which is issued, returns to its proper lean quantities.

You must know, and you must surely perceive the importance of so many of the plants. You would realize *Digitalis* (foxglove) is an incredible plant for the heart, and that all of the herbs are relators and dis-relators. I can give you a whole list of herbs that will restore baldness to anyone for any reason whatever. They will grow hair, however nakedly bald. And if you want your hair to fall off of your head, I will give you two herbs that will do. That if you want to stop mice in the house, or mice in the beds, you have only to use *Mentha aquatica* (water mint) and they will not come near it. You know that the whole family of *Euphorbias* will demonstratively drive gophers, and such matters, and moles from the garden.

That the most magical herb in the world, *vervain* (verbena), cures fifty human ailments, and keeps everybody in perfection. The *Angelica archangelica* and *Melissa officinalis* will lift your mind and your whole mental attitude into perfect memory, and good thinking. *Passiflora incarnata* is one of the most magical of all plants to produce good sleep for insomnia. It will always relieve intense pain, and produce a gentle sleep. And of all these matters, it does not reduce consciousness, but raises it. It improves the clarity of consciousness. Much of this is over-ridden today because of the enormous belief in the sub-terrestrials in synthetics. Everybody lives on synthetics.

Could you please tell me why does anybody grow a field of peas, and out of inner fear and terror and disbelief in the enormous law and goodness of Nature, freeze the lot on the spot, and imagine they're not going to have anything else to eat in the world? And this is the huge absurdity of the planet today. There is no starvation; there can never be any starvation. It is not of reason. There is always beautiful soil, endless fertility, endless quantity of seed. It is only our absurdities that remove it from us.

When, out of fear, we must kill something—we cannot kill something. You cannot get rid of anything. The whole ancient magics were with diseases, but you don't just—*squawk*—get rid of them, because you've got two or three more serious things at once. But you can always induce something to go from something into something else. So they always used a herb in an animal or a horse or a rabbit, as a receptive herb to that disease or ailment. They then used the driving-out herbs to lay to the person suffering, and with incantations and numerous such matters, drove the ailment into the other body. But you must realize that there is no destroying anything in this world. And indeed, Nature has no waste. Everything that is created in Nature is useful. Everything. And this is what is so magical. How absurd it is that we make all this hideous cellophane stuff and can't do anything with it; and never will, literally, be able to destroy it. Literally.

So within this view of what is biodynamics is an essential matter. It concerns the word 'approach'. Why do you want to grow something? What is the reason? Do you want money? Because any idiot can get money. You must never go to Nature and say to twenty acres, "I want fifty thousand dollars." Because you can have it. You must go to Nature and ask her for the laws. And observe and learn, and be obedient, and reverent. Because the whole laws of Nature are the governance.

And out of that observance and following and enormous provisionment—which is increased all the time—comes an enormous fruition. And from the fruition of that fertility, out of that observance, comes the most magical matter of all. And it is this: you will now receive your bonus. Having produced, through your labors, and your sense of goodness and magnification—having produced that fertility—it will rebound, in that in the ensuing circle of cycle will come new growth, new atmosphere. And in that new growth, new atmosphere will come new weeds, new seeds, that you know nothing about, that you've not seen in the area before. That you don't even know of. And will come new insects, new birds. They will all circulate and produce a further growth that you have never been able to conceive. They have come out of the invisible. And because of this, and because it is something new in your pulsation and inclination, it will lift your very *image*. Your very seed. Man's *image*, his very seed, from which he sees vision, and increases. And here Nature lifts the *image* of man, and again it rises and climbs the ladder to further heights and further procedures.

If it is not irrelevant, in the talk about herbs, we see that herbs must be grown and used *au natural*. You will probably know that in ancient days all real gardens had couches, divans, made of *Anthemis noblis* (Roman chamomile). There is a beautiful little herb—so high—that adored to be trod upon, like *Daucus* (wild carrot) do. And they grow much much better. And since it is full of enormous strength and vitality, as is *Petroselinum*—parsley, the rock of St. Peter, the keys of the gates of heaven—so they always made couches in the garden of *Anthemis noblis* and mowed them. And at all times, when feeling a little melancholia or tiredness, the thing was to go and lie upon this couch for an hour, and all of these plants with their give-off, their emanation, restore your vitality and your goodness. Is it not true that however we live, however monstrously we live today with all our perniciousness, is it not true that the trees and the plants and the grass breathe in our perniciousness? And absorb it and dissolve it and give it out as pure air again? Which is absolutely true. What an incredible magic is this!

Steiner used to teach me to lean up against the different trees and to be suscitated by them, and to feel what their give-off was. The pine tree, as you know, is dry and it effects you here. And the whole world, of all the plants, and the insects and the birds, have this relationship and inter-relationship. There is no use, no reason at any time, because you find something out of balance, to fly to a shop full of hypnotism and say, "Quickly, quickly, give me a spray, give me a powder! And right, right now! Go! Get out!" And it's all nonsense. In the whole law of Nature, the whole revelation of the stars, none of them run into each other. None of them. The flight of the birds, they never fly into each other. And that within all of that is a relationship to this matter. You've only to seek it out. You've only to find it and know it. And discover it. When you use the deep-rooteds beside the shallow-rooteds you have got your method.

No whiteflies like nasturtiums. No aphids, at all, will ever survive in a garden for long where you grow *Nicotiana anthemis* (Flowering nicotine). *Nicotiana anthemis* is one of the most beautiful plants in the garden, and it is covered, as you will know, with the most delicious nectar. It goes out of the flowers. It's nocturnal, and the hummingbirds go crazy over it. They adore it. And it will bring the hummingbird moths. The hummingbird moth flies at twice the pace of the hummingbird, and the hummingbird flies at seventy miles an hour forwards, and seventy-five miles an hour in reverse! But the *Nicotiana anthemis* is so astonishing in the garden because it is covered, as all plants are, with little hairs. And all of these hairs give off this delicious nectar. And the whole garden—at night only—when it is dusk, is filled with the scent of lilies from this plant. As dawn comes, the scent is gone. It isn't there at all. Do you understand? Is it catching?

Well, all of the aphids—whether they be green, or red, or black—absolutely adore this nectar more than any other nectar in the world, and they can't resist it. It doesn't matter what plants there are in the garden, they can't resist it. So they go straight to this plant to have a wonderful drink of death. They alight upon the hairs, and they suck, and the moment the alight and suck the hairs just close upon them and eat completely. This goes on, as you can perceive, *ad infinitum.* Givers and takers. Relators and dis-relators. Inclination and declination.

And so, this is the basis and the approach of biodynamic. Behind it, is again, the word 'approach'. Reverence and obedience for that incredible, endless knowledge which is always changing. We must not ever think that we can get hold of something, put it in the cage and say, "I've got it", because everything is changing. And all education is exactly the same. There is no such thing as knowing anything. There is no such thing as actual, no such thing as actual knowledge. It's a journey. It's a passage. And therefore it's absurd for us to create temporal things and say they are permanent and eternal. It is eternal things that we perceive, and the invisible, and then all the temporal plays itself. It's so easy.

This is the basic of the attitude and approach of biodynamic: spiritual vision behind everything that you do.

Would you care to have a short period of questions and answers?

Q: *Where is all this information available? It's impossible for me to get it all down. Is this in this book, or...*

No! I would not say so. If you would play the violin, would you get a book from the library?

As you would say, sir, "How do I find out?" What I suggest to you is this: that every area in California, as soon as possible, should be given a piece of land by the state, by the civic authorities, that over it should be a reasonably good professional classical horticulturist, who understands some of these matters, and that this person should be responsible for leading the children, the youth, and the public into the vision of those incredible matters that are our very life, that we have utterly and hopelessly forgotten. And there is no other way about it.

Where did all education come from? Fairy stories, mythology, parables, handed down from regions and regions long before anything was written in words—an incredible magic of reality. The moment that you put things into regurgitated words, you have put them into brackets of unutterable limitations. You must first know the laws of Nature, the characters of plants, how they grow, where they grow—then we can give them a silly name, and call it Hunkey Dunk, and Pliff Poff and Lady Blue Eyes. Then we can stand at last; but until then, no. That's my best answer to you, I'm sorry.

I feel that this has to be a growth of study. And it is one of those things that we have thrown away. And it must come back. There was a period when every country person understood their climatics, understood their soils, their animals, their wild plants, and knew them intimately.

What children today are really educated or led into the whole of this? There is no approach to it. It is all how to make a motorcar, how to watch a television set. If you are terribly busy with that, you can't be very, very busy watching the sunrise. And I think that that's the whole answer. And it's a huge enigma. And I don't think we ought to look at it too closely because it's rather frightening. But I think we should undo it as quickly as we can.

Q: I don't know how you even study it, if you have no authorities, if you don't know where to go to study it. You have to be able to find masters...

There are an enormous quantity of people who have a reasonable knowledge of the techniques of horticulture, of the knowledge of plant character. I am not at all refuting the enormous knowledges of universities, schools and education. I am not refuting any of it. What I am possibly trying to prevent are the hallucinations of words—that there is knowledgeability—but that we are not making use of it. We have lost our palate, we have lost our taste. Are you aware of the egg that you eat, that you would far better not to eat. The way in which that chicken is kept is absolutely monstrous. It is no connection with a bird at all. And do you realize, apparently, that had you turned to doves, or crows, and asked them to lay an egg a day they would, through the goodness of God, have done it; and that elephants would give you eight gallons of milk as a cow does, if we had asked them to do it. There is nothing in Nature that we are not going to get when we ask for it. If you want a purple pear and a white plum, it is there...in no time, *abracadabra*. It is all there.

Q: *Where are we going to learn it if it is not written down? We haven't time to go out and commune with nature as you have probably done all your life.*

How high, how high is the price of a tomato? (*Right now it costs...*) No. There never has been a price on a tomato. Or an orange. It is free. It is absolutely free. It is our incredible insanity that makes you tear all over the place so that you can't afford it, and after a short time you can't eat it. Yes, it is true. Search into Nature and be obedient and reverent.

Q: *Can you tell us something of Pan, of the gnomes, the elves, and the fairies?*

Yes! You have indeed struck an interesting matter. But again, it concerns verbosity, curiously enough. Gnomes, elves, undines, nymphs, all of these matters, of course, are absolutely real; no question about it. They are, and always have been the inter-weavers of the intermediaries. And they always are those things that are not seen. How is it that a flower suddenly opens? How is it that a seed pod will turn back and face itself in a ball? In ways ineffable, that you can't understand. How is it that a seed would even germinate? And that a plant will fall to the ground? It is the actual intermediary between the visible and the invisible. And one period of verbosity that, preceding, had to be given a name, and those names were elves, undines, nymphs and numerous others.

Thank you very much. Wonderful.

1 Nicolaus Copernicus, Polish astronomer and first modern heliocentric cosmologist; Alan's use of the term *revolutionibus* comes from his major work, *De revolutionibus orbium coelestium* (*On the Revolutions of the Celestial Spheres*; (1473-1543).

2 Pedanius Dioscorides, Greek physician and medical botanist; (~40-90 A.D.).

3 Gaius Plinius Secundus (Pliny the Elder), Roman natural philosopher; (23-79 A.D.).

Bloom and Area of Discontinuity

Covelo Village Garden
12 September 1975

Bloom, and area of discontinuity: if you survey plants, and fruits in particular, and certain flowers and certain petals, sometimes it might be more obvious than others, there is upon them a thing called *bloom*. Do you realize that the least touch in most cases, and it's either damaged or removed? It's an astonishing matter, and of the utmost importance, and hopelessly delicate. This is the reason that you have already been led into, the utmost care in your pricking out and transplanting. You realize that you prick every plant out as much as you can without touching it. This is not merely because of the endless hairs of which the plant is made up, and damaging those, but it's principally because of this bloom.

When you damage that bloom, you remove an area that is of the utmost importance to it. The area of discontinuity and the bloom connect. It is a procedure of all growth—and of more than all growth, as we'll look into it, it's in all living matters as a matter of fact—that enables a pulsation to take place: an intake and an output. It operates in a sense like an autostatic valve. You would perceive that areas often have duplications of this such as fruits do. A fruit has a bloom upon it, and a seed within its area usually has a bloom upon that, but it's not very visible. It is an obvious mistake to think that because you can't see the bloom on certain things that it is not there. This bloom is variable in its manufacture; it can be what appears to be a smoke. It can also be a type of shellac or varnish. It can also be an oil, and not only can it also be those, but it can change from one to the other.

Now the very statement that an apple swims and a pear drowns—and you realize that this is totally true: if you drop those fruits into water, the one will definitely float, and the other will definitely sink—here is concerned almost entirely the area of discontinuity and the bloom. It is well known that if you damage the bloom on a grape, you cannot get fermentation. That grape will not ferment properly. Also, you cannot dry fruits truly and well if you have damaged and removed the bloom. We have got to deal with this in discussing it, jumping about; it's so delicate a matter.

Now, take this into account. When you take a tomato, or a cherry, or a peach, or a plum, we'll take those fruits, because they're rather more the obvious, here you have an area of discontinuity; a skin, a very thin skin. And upon that skin, which are a number of skins, on the outside is a bloom, a very definite bloom.

If you want to perceive what bloom is, you should just send this (carnation) around, and any of you as you go, wipe your finger on one of these leaves, or on the stalk, and observe where you have touched it. You will see that the bloom is gone. It's obvious on the carnations simply because of the texture and the color. Don't wipe too much, or else nobody will have anything left to wipe. You all know it probably, you've all noticed it, in one way or another. It's just that it's obvious on this one.

With that area of discontinuity on the tomato, as the tomato grows, so does that area of discontinuity of the skin. In other words, it's stretchable, it's elastic, it changes. It also changes its textural capacity, extremely. It is playing a part all the time. And when the fruit is what you would call complete, that has the capacity of maintaining it in that condition for a period. Whereby you could say, if you wanted to, you could keep a tomato in a reasonable temperature for three weeks or for a month, if you picked it not too ripe, not overripe. And yet, you have only to pierce that area of discontinuity with the smallest pinprick, and within a few hours, in less than a day, the entire tomato has started to collapse. You must begin to see the enormous import that this area of discontinuity is playing.

In other words, it is like the most delicate of gardens that is capable of receiving in and of giving out and yet maintaining within it the ego of the whole matter. You will see the repercussion of this as an environmental procedure with us ourselves.

It is well to just quickly look over that and see the astonishing interplay of area of discontinuity with mankind. The moment that you have a photograph or a picture, it doesn't mean a thing if it hasn't got an area of discontinuity. It must be framed at once, or there's nothing to separate it from the room. The moment that you put a window in the wall, it's got to have a frame. Otherwise it's just anything. And the moment that you have a room, you've got to have a door. You've got to have an area of discontinuity by which you come in and out. And then you have to have a carpet on the floor, an area of discontinuity between your foot and what's beneath.

And then again, if you came, for instance, to a theater—it's very fascinating here, that you have come to observe either an ideal, or an observance, or even an entertainment. But you've got to have a complete discontinuity of the curtain, and a proscenium arch which is the division between a magical world and the general public. And when you go in, all the lights are on in the auditorium, and the curtain is down, and the area of discontinuity, the proscenium arch, is there. As soon as everybody's in, and you are going to have the magic turned on, all the lights go off in the auditorium, the area of discontinuity is removed and the lights are put on to the magical world. It's an area of discontinuity, of complete relationship and dis-relationship. It is a complete copy of everything that we are observing and living within Nature all the time. Why do ladies put powder on their face? Bloom.

So you get this interplay, and you find that it comes, for instance, to photography and drawing. The only matter about drawing and photography, is really, a silhouette. You draw an edge around something, which is the area of discontinuity of it, on the side. But as soon as you come to use color—in other words, painting—you've entered a deeper world altogether. The whole object of painting, of color, is to get rid of silhouette. And the great art of painting is to remove the edges, so that you have no silhouette. And you can go around behind something. That is what color entertains.

Now, when you begin to look into the *revolutionibus*, when you perceive that color as a force must come from the planets—and does come from the planets—and that it is not at that time a color but an energy, a power, you begin to see that somewhere this bloom, which is on the area of discontinuities, is both a reflector and a receiver.

Now it is a theory that leaves appear green, because the leaf itself— or the duties of the leaf—absorb those colors which are not blue and yellow. And a red flower likewise appears red because it absorbs all of the other rays—but not the red—and reflects them. When you watch bloom, you will see that it changes with the growth of the day, as well as

57

with the growth of the plant, and the growth of periods of climates, too.

You have heard all the ancients—for instance the Persians, and Pliny in particular—on speaking about the *Lilium candidum* (Madonna lily), that is the most ancient of all white lilies. And everybody in their obtuseness of not looking, saying that the lilies are white. But Pliny and all of the ancients who regarded the matter said, "No, lilies are gold." And whenever you look endlessly into a lily, you will perceive this. When you look at the petals of certain flowers, particularly begonias, and particularly pink begonias, because the color makes it practical to be visible; when you look at certain white petals like *Nicotiana* (flowering nicotine) sufficiently, you will suddenly see that they are gold, and not white. You will begin to see this. This is because you are looking *into* bloom, so that you are beginning to look *into* areas.

Now this bloom is utterly important. It is said that in this area is the most important nutriments. It is well known that with apples and pears, and the other fruits that you want to keep, you must maintain this bloom with the utmost care. If you damage it they will not keep, unless of course you keep by artificial means. I talk about gases and deep temperatures, and so on, as that. But to keep a fruit in its natural way, which is perfectly simple, those blooms must remain. Therefore the fruit must be collected with utmost care. Now Steiner and others pointed out at that time that it was of greatest importance never to wash vegetables before eating them. Because if you do, you wash off one of the most potent and important matters containing a nutriment which is vitally important, and that is bloom.

And indeed he taught us, and I remember it so well, that we would take oranges and lemons, and the citrus, and in the evening, keep cutting them, before using them in any way, all the seeds, the pips, were put into a basin, a china basin. They were then just covered with water, and a cloth put over the top, and put in the larder. And in the morning, the results were eaten with brown bread, with a spoon. Around all of those seeds had formed an absolute gelatinousness that was solid. The bloom of the seeds had caused this matter to take place.

It is said to be very important that if you make preserves of plums, and of stone fruits and such like, that you should apply the stones preferably into that preserve, as they are. If not, at least to take the kernels out and put those in. There is the reason behind that, of that matter. If you take butterfly wings you will see there a very similar bloom to what you would get on flowers. Then again, if you take certain flowers such as buttercups, you will see that there appears to be no bloom on the flower, but that there is on the foliage. And then if you look at a dragonfly you will find a similar thing. That there is not actually a bloom on the dragonfly as there is on the butterfly, but there is, and it is a varnish or a veneer. Therefore you begin to perceive the differences in these blooms.

I am sure that you must at some time have come to the conclusion that there is bloom on stones. And you must very obviously be aware that there is bloom upon flowers. You can't but see it every time. It is very obvious. And you see the change of it going on all the time on flowers.

Now there's another matter which concerns this that goes even further and is more delicate still. You are aware that after plants flower, the whole petal business goes, and the seed procedure takes place. You must have noticed that at a certain period of the *revolutionibus*, an entire blossoming of the seed now takes place. Often, much larger than the bloom of the flower. And here you see a bloom form in the area of the blossoming of the seed, that is unique again. For just as spiders all on a certain day, obviously produce an emanating bloom, whereby they become lighter than air and rise as a cloud. So do seeds by their manipulation of catapultation, and floating and flying, so do they achieve a bloom which becomes relatable, and beyond relatable, to atmospheric pressures and airs. They can become lighter than the air itself, and in this way, being divorced from moistures and so on, can actually take flight.

In this way, comes the view that the seed of fern taken on the night of St. John's birth[1] induces invisibility.

When you watch dawns and you watch a sunrise, and pre-sunrise and pre-dawn, you see this matter take place in the sky. You see therefore that it's not a question of light, it's not a question of the Sun, and it's not a question of dark. It's a whole wave of floatation which is taking place. You must be aware, that particularly during the night, the whole area of bloom changes.

You must now be aware that the whole area of soil has bloom. This is why it is bruisable. This is why it is damageable. Just as there is an area of discontinuity, the very skin of the Earth, so that skin, being the surface of the soil, develops—and that is the word: *develops*—a bloom. That bloom is in contact all the time with changeability of atmospherics and climatics and *revolutionibus*. For you must now be aware from what we have been studying already, that the soil of spring has no relationship to the soil of fall at all. Nor the soil of summer to the soil of winter. They are totally different capacities. Oh, you could say that's quite unstatable if you like. But the results prove that the whole matter is so.

You must also perceive from this that the whole atmosphere produces at times bloom. You are aware at certain times of looking along and perceiving things in the air that you cannot nominate either as cobwebs or dust.

And here comes very much the origin of the whole procedure of elfdom. Elfdom, as you realize, all of those names come out of the elements. Before people spoke adamantly about north, south, east and west; hot, cold, wet and dry; earth, fire, air and water; the four elements that are the intermediaries between the visible and the invisible—these are nominated, at a certain time of language, as fairies, undines, nymphs, elves and the rest. Because they bring about the change between the visible and the invisible. When people got tired of stating it was the intermediaries, they talked about fairies and undines and elves. And you will find in the ancients about the elves of light—that they actually emanate and give off a bloom that is lighter than sunlight. And that they live in color itself, and are only perceived in rays.

Whilst those elves of night, of darkness, the manufacturers of Thor's hammer, and those that lead horses astray in bogs, and catch the Moon, and bury her in the bog and release her for half the time, to shine—are all matters concerning these intermediaries.

But you will see in this matter that bloom is so important. You will see that we have bloom upon our skin. You will know it. You must know the intricacies of the effects of your hair. One day it is bright and shiny, and another day according to your mood, and what is happening, as to whether you are sad or happy, your hair is either dull or glittering. And that there are those herbs, such as the delicious *Verbascum* (mullein), that will restore that for you almost regardless of your mood. Because they have that capacity of the invection of bloom. If you look at *Verbascum*, you will perceive this extraordinary surface on that plant. It is absolutely extraordinary. You can't even find out where it begins and where it ends.

But now what are we talking about? Where it begins, and where it ends? Where does anything begin, and where does anything end? And bloom is in a sense that very matter. It's the finest entity that makes the area of discontinuity between *something* and *everything*. Therefore it is as delicate as delicate, and is obviously tremendously important. Serious. It interplays the *revolutionibus* into ego.

Out of it comes further thinkings and observations, you realize. The whole procedure of the capacity of seeing auras, which exist around everybody. Emanation. You are, I am sure, aware that are there are certain plants, certain flowers, which at certain times of the evening give off an intense emanation. You will read it in all botanical books, there's a whole list of them. And that if you observe and sit and watch, as the equinox of evening comes, you will see that you will no longer see these flowers as a group of flowers at all, that the formation, in other words the outlaying of the area of discontinuity goes, with the light, and suddenly there's a blaze of color above them. An emanation.

There are many that do it much more obviously than others, but all do it. For instance, the whole thing about peony is in this area. The peony is governed by the Moon, and therefore it gives off an emanation at night of luminosity. The whole of these flowers, if you really observe periods at night, really do produce a luminosity around them. But in actual fact it is actually very little of the flower that does it, and you are somewhat deceived by this fact. It is, indeed, the seed. The seed contains the area of luminosity. And so much so, that in the Aegean where this plant grows, the shepherds all hunt for the seeds only at night. And find them.

Do you understand this extraordinary matter about the luminous, the halo? The aura?

That when the painters came to the end of realizing that they could not paint God—deity—you will see that in all true attempts to paint this matter, they will never give you the eyes. The eyes are always removed downwards, so that you cannot look into them. Because it would be impossible. You would have to look into eternity, and that is not possible in painting. That is the only way they can do it. So, they achieved the method of the emanation, the bloom, the aura. Which was an endless shining above.

And here you begin to see the whole importance of understanding this, and perceiving it, and becoming aware of it. You realize that according to your procedure, according to the procedure of plants, in relationship to the area of the environment, so is an aura, an emanation outside of this area of discontinuity which is the bloom, which goes and mixes the two into infinity. This is full of touch, of sense. But the whole world of birds and insects and plants are extremely and utterly sensitive to this. And this is the relationship between bees, and why they either do or do not sting. Or birds and butterflies, and other matters of why they come to you or do not come to you. Of why animals and plants retreat from humanity: the emanation is not desirable.

When you are a gardener, how imperative it is to stop this word-thinking, and to be able to apply emanation. Give off and intake. The sense of reception, and the sense of infusion. Surely you must have become aware then, that this bloom that concerns the hummingbird, that concerns butterflies, that concerns plants, that concerns every living thing, really, must be a form of reflection and deflection. And here must lie a whole seat of the appearance of color, and of scent, and of flavor, of lushness, and indeed of the acceptance or the de-acceptance of fertility.

Now you begin to perceive why a particular strawberry will have an intense flavor at three o'clock and none at six o'clock. And you will say, "Impossible! The flavor's there. It's in the strawberry, my dear." Oh, are you sure? Is the scent always the same? Is the scent the same in the *Nicotiana* at noon as it is at midnight? And what about mignonette? How often have you gone to mignonette, wishing, and have nothing? And how is it that you go on smelling and not exhaust that smell, if it would be in the thing giving it off, like a juice? You could exhaust it. Do you? Do you exhaust looking at color? Now do you begin to perceive what we are talking about? Or rather what we're looking at? This incredible matter of bloom, of areas of discontinuity, and then the inner ratio, which is this separation.

Now you begin to see that all life is waves, that indeed insects and birds and plants are really not removed from each other. They are waves of forces that are governed by the *revolutionibus*, and they're expressions. And there's little removal. It is only our individual focuses of thinking of ourselves as males and females, and this and that, and knowledgeable and unknowledgeable, and twice two is four, that puts everything in categories and boxes, up in the attic in blocks. I can't really go any further than this, but to say, *open the perception, open the sensitivities*, and *open the observances*. Do not say, "I know, and this cannot be and that cannot be."

When we make a plate we take a piece of clay and we bake it in the oven. And having done so, it still has an area of discontinuity and almost—in fact it does—have a bloom. Because you see bloom is not form, by touchable. Bloom is very much what we were referring to when we said iodine is not made in the sea or in the air. It is made in the spume by the turbulence of the ocean meeting the air, in the area of discontinuity between the two.

Do you realize that you could form a water bubble on top of a water bubble, via a splash, and that that bubble would actually float on the water, and it's water floating on top of water, which according to science books is impossible? It suddenly has an area of discontinuity of its own, and the bloom of course. It must have. So I am not trying to give you anything, or to tell you anything. But it is a perception, and it's a perception of the greatest importance.

Now, you should begin to be able to perceive so much better than thinking in words what happens to a fig at a given moment on a given day. It has been full of cotton wool; you can do what you like the day before. You can take it off and bite it, and you would have to spit it out, because it is just cotton wool. It's quite horrible. You can't even swallow it. In actual fact that you realize they're all membranes, there again those electric wires going to all the seeds which are all inside the fruit this time. They're all facing each other inside, with the whole of the skin outside, but there is a little cavity in the front. And then as to allow that wasp to enter, the only insect which can enter that hole. It is the only thing that can pollinate the blossoming of the fig inside.

But at a given moment of the *revolutionibus*, the whole of the area of discontinuity and the bloom, permits of an entry, of a new issue, which was not allowed to enter before. And all of the cotton wool is turned suddenly to the most liquid, luscious, juicy pulp imaginable. The intermediaries. You could never work it out. Now you begin to see what bloom is, and how important it is. Now you can begin to see how careful you must be in touching a plant, in walking upon the soil, in cultivating the soil.

Perceive an egg: an egg has an incredible bloom upon it. That bloom is a container that the shell, which is the area of discontinuity, and the skin within the shell, which is a further area beneath the discontinuity, are all breathable, in and out, can receive and exude both. Necessitous.

Therefore, I bring the focus of bloom, which you can see so clearly on the carnation, upon a plum, upon a grape. I bring it and say: realize that this is on everything that grows, and that it is changeable as it grows and it is not static. It is one of the most magical areas of interweaving into totality. And the effect of our living, of our approach in the garden, gives off an emanation, a bloom. Now do you see why you must perceive this? Why you must understand when you put your foot in the garden bed? Why you cannot go into a field as a robber and say, "I want this and will have it!"? Of course you will. But the emanation is there; it was there with the thought, before the thought. And the whole world is conscious of it. It's vast. It's total.

Do you want to talk about it?

Q: *I understand about the grape and the plum. The bloom is obvious. But when you spoke about the orange and the seeds, that I wasn't able to get.*

You have looked at a tithonia, carefully? You have. What have you perceived? Anything in particular? What have you perceived as a shadow? Anything or nothing? Well then observe it. But I'll tell you what you will perceive, inevitably—and some of you have obviously—you will see the cerulean blue of the sky. You can't mistake it, it's there in great patches. This is a reflection of bloom. It's the recipient and the throwing off again. Here you have this with the orange. It is there for a time, and then it becomes a texture that we refer to as oils. It is no longer the powdery thing, the smoky thing. It becomes an oil.

Within the attentions of Goethe, which refer to intelligence, intellect, and reason, and *idée*, is this matter: that in the exuberance of the growth of all plants is the paraphernalia metamorphosis of all of the changes. In exuberance, in the seed, it is the minimum of metamorphosis and the total of *idée*. In the growth of a plant, it is the minimum of *idée* and the maximum of metamorphosis. You will perceive that all seed, as we spoke of the buds of trees, has an area of discontinuity around it, which is a separate to the discontinuity of the actual fruit itself. For perceive that where you have a pit in an apple, and where you have stone in a peach, you have that little seed in a strawberry—on a strawberry indeed, as often happens on others also. In the raspberry, it is each seed in a lobe.

And so you get this. I am trying to refer you to leave the attic and to perceive totality. To get out of the thinking of a pit or a seed, and to see acutely what it is. Therefore, this area of discontinuity around the seed is a different area of discontinuity, but that the fruit is the protector of that. Now you will go in circles outside that, and here you will find soil and air. And there you will find sky and atmosphere, in which the stars float. And so you could go on *ad infinitum* of course, and I can't lead you there. But that both of them have areas of discontinuity, and both of them have bloom. And if you apply them at different times, with different sauces such as milk or water or honey, you will find that they give off their invection. The seed of the citrus, and indeed all seeds, give off this enormously: tremendous vitality is given off, if you use a method of a synergist to produce its bloom and area of discontinuity to give off its secrets. Does that explain to you a little?

You must think in a sense again, and I jumped it of the buds in a branch in the boughs of a tree, are all separate entities, just like your eyebrows and your cheeks that you don't really dominate, they live in you. But what an enormous quantity of parts are a part of us that we have no concept of at all, as you found with your living this morning.

Anything?

Q: *With the drink that you had in the morning, that you put the seeds in...*

Yes, it was not a drink, it goes into a complete gelatinous solid. You could cut it with a knife and eat it with a fork. Sometimes they used lemons for a particular reason, and sometimes we used orange for a particular reason. The lemon having more procedure over certain things. It was used as an herbal treatment, and at that time we were doing endless experiments in nutrition and diet and control.

Could you do it if it was a bean seed, it would ferment...

Yes, precisely. Most enormously so. Oh yes. In different ways. Oh, this is endless. I mean, you take even the use of *Euphrasia* (eyebright), what else do you do? You take some blossoms of *Euphrasia*, which is the best fresh, and you pour not-quite boiling water upon it, you allow it to settle, and you both drink it, and use it over your eye. And its restorative powers are immediate. Is that not so? *Euphrasia* will still do wonders when you have styes and such matters.

Just be careful not to put it on the inner eye...

You are naughty. There's a more important one than that, than *Euphrasia*, and that is *Hieracium* (hawkweed). But you can't use that in the same way, it's completely internal, and this is most interesting, and this begins to apply—we're really going further than we intended to today at all—but the oil of *Hieracium* goes from within to without. It goes through your bloodstream, and it goes into your higher nature's perception brilliantly.

Known as hawkweed. Do you realize that all birds see more clearly than most other things in the world. And birds, including hawks, will go for that particular seed of *Hieracium* more than any other seed that there is. And it is said that afterwards, it has been perceivable that they are incredibly more accurate than they ever were before. But it is very astonishing, you see, you can have a hawk, literally a mile up, and it will see a movement of a shrew under leaves, it hasn't even come out. So their perception is absolutely unique. And also they have a quality of this bloom matter which is extraordinary.

And you see here again you take this matter of puffins. When the puffin lays an egg, which they do upon stones, upon cliffs, the egg, it has a bloom on it and an area of discontinuity which is equivalent to the stone and rock. Do you perceive that as winter comes certain animals' fur goes white? You must have noticed so continually how certain caterpillars are colored exactly like the foliages they are upon. You see this interplay of bloom and emanation, intake and give-off. It's so obvious.

Q: I had a couple of questions about the revolutionibus. *Do you consider the signs of the Moon at all for planning, or for sowing, or transplanting, or...I was just talking with somebody that said that was very important, and I said that I kind of thought it might be less important than the phase of the Moon, whether it was waxing or waning, and I thought that maybe you could tell us something about that.*

They interplay. The inclination and declination is what you might call the imperative issue. The other is secondary. You will lead into that in due course, so I won't go into detail.

I gave you the two intense periods of magnetics: two nights before the new Moon is the first one and is minor. The major is half Moon to full. Alright? You also understand the inference of the whole period of the inclination with the Sun, and the whole period of the declination. Other than that the ruling calendar is there, and you can survey it, and you will begin to see it, and we shall explain this as we go along. Alright?

Oh dear. Anything? Well, at least we don't end with violent argument.

---

1   The evening of June 23rd is the eve of the feast of John the Baptist, a midsummer celebration often marked with bonfires. It is one of the few Christian holy days marking a birth rather than a death.

Intellect, Reason, and *Idée*

Covelo Village Garden
1975

You must be asking yourself about what you have studied here, about what the garden has been informing you of. What is truth? Where do I find the way? You must sometimes look at the year you had and say, "What has it brought me in this?" and probably think it has brought nothing, but it has! What I'm going to try today for you will explain this and open out a new field.

At the same time, we must always say this, it has always been said to me—there is a great danger here—a danger in treating this vision. There is also a danger of taking a wrong turn. I merely say to begin with, all this focus is a vision of discovery, of escape from the inhibition of pre-formed, pre-parental, pre-educational formation—the whole of statement and verbosity. An escape from the utter invisibility it has upon us, which you cannot lift off, do what you will, because it is there, imbedded—imbedded for centuries, very often.

In this discovery nearly everyone asks himself, why is it that children have to go through such severe and painful education to come to what is called truth and intellectual capacity? And why is it that in Nature one observes a natural procedure, which seems to suit the purposes of Nature up to a point—which we feel is unsatisfactory for us? This very dominant question is always coming up. How is it that butterflies can leave Canada and get to Mexico and nobody tells them the way, and yet they all stop at the same place en route? Such things you could go on with ad lib.

How and why and what is the reason behind this, the matter of it, and why is it that we find ourselves perplexed? The more we look into it, the more we try to undo it, the more entangled we become.

Here enters the conversation that we had in the past about concept, precept, and percept. I bring it all out again. It is the three areas of intellect, reason, and *idée*. I have in the past been referring to *image*. We may reinstate that with the word *idée* now.

Before I proceed with those three, I want you to see how difficult it is to approach. You cannot approach any of these things in a direct line or you will lose yourself instantly. Take the mechanical aspect. By those words one means everything connected with imagination. You perceive how erroneous, in a sense, the whole root of mechanical aspect is. It is from outside to inside. It is always looking from outside to in—whereas all that is of creative reality is from *within*, to *without*. We see also, that in that education we are referring to in parental influence, you will see exactly the same thing. You will see a mechanical approach. It is from the external going inwards; whereas the whole of creative factor is always from inwards to outwards.

Going back to intellect, reason and *idée*. In man's journeys or what we call his imbalance, intellect undoes everything into partition from totality, because it wants to be inspected. It wants to be looked at in a total of itself, outward to inward at once. That is intellect. It divides everything up from totality to something you can put on the table, inspect all around externally. However, each individual has a different way of dividing up totality because of the characteristics of people affected by that truth: the *revolutionibus*. Everybody has their own way of dividing everything up into different areas, and having done so, nothing fits. Reason then has to be applied to put it together again. Because of the intellect dividing everything up into separate entities, it becomes chaotic, and reason is then applied to find the means to fit it back into a totality.

But do you see what is happening? The whole purpose has been one of external to internal and it is the wrong way around. You have already caused the chaotic division, but now you have developed a system of formation based upon division. It does not any more belong to total totality. It is a bogus revelation and that is what is proceeding ad lib.

If you think of the sense of movement in light of what we just said, and we then introduce intellect and reason into the word, you find the invention of a motorcar—everybody a separated movement—each person a motorcar unable to maneuver, everybody going in a separated movement and unable to comply with any total procedure. All going in different directions, in different ways, running into each other. Absolute chaos! Therefore, reason enters the scene, and straight lines are made to travel on. One that way, one that way, red lights, green lights, yellow lights—reason has entered the whole scene to put the thing into totality.

But the whole totality was based upon separation. And now you have terrific blocks. When having lost the discovery of *idée*, intellect and reason are the route to how to discover *idée*. *Idée* is that stroke, when an idea strikes. Exactly as I have said. When an idea strikes you. But that it has come about from a focus. It is a desire to strike you. *Idée* is the inert information of truth. It is so brief that with the average contact a person is unaware of the flash. It is so instant. And instantly, reason and intellect are preying upon it and it is vanished.

Have I not described to you how, when looking for the pen-stroke of the submarine on the horizon, the moment you go at it, it has disappeared? It is only when you survey with a gaze of request that you suddenly see it as you come past it. The moment you look, it is gone.

It is absolute that intellect and reason will never bring you to truth. They are, on their own, deceivers, separators, destructors. But when the balance of these three has been lost, it is only by our intellect and reason that the vision of the touch of *idée* can be found. And it can only happen fractionally—momentarily. It is that that must be sought, found out, and held.

You who have studied, fortunately, your voice and deportment, have discovered how you were not any longer aware of the muscles in your tongue, and how you had no control over your arms. Slowly, by a round-about route, you were led to use tongue muscles and eventually found them—but only fractionally in the early stages. Could you feel or sense them by intellect and reason?

When, after a period of round-about method of laughing and coughing, you were shown glimpses of a sense of that muscle—in other words, an inner focus of a sense touching that sense which is there, you began to be aware of it. The more you practiced it and held that sense and trained it, the more you became aware of it and were actually able to control it. This is what one is referring to by intellect, reason and *idée*.

Dreams are in the same area. Dreams can be full of intellect, full of reason, and are very seldom full of *idée*. Yet, in actual fact, they are based upon *idée*. The whole of truth is in *idée*, but intellect and reason are muscles and senses that plainly have balance in the matter. We have lost the muscles of our spiritual approaches and resorted, because of education and parental authority, to using intellect and reason by themselves.

Therefore, in a sense, intellect is division. It is out of balance, un-handleable, separation to look at. Reason is a reflex of that, of discovery that intellect has led you into impossibility. However interesting it's been, you can't anymore put it together. So reason comes to try to join it together with totalities, to restore a balance about and a vision. Not real totality, a separated self-totality which is a block. A complete deception.

Of course we think we see totality and we don't see real totality at all. It is a self-totality. It is only in the re-striking of *idée* that we suddenly see that total totality. And then you know that self-totality is merely a hope of that scope pulled together. Believe it. And *idée* with it aspires to enhance all the functions of the body throughout. It does not operate in the envision-ments of the mind. It operates throughout the body.

Perceive then, how it was that certain people discovered about Nature in this. But the moment you enter the world of Nature, here is the whole matter that Ptolemy, Pliny, Dioscorides, all of them are touching with *idée*. It is here, through these, that is restored for us, just as the air is restored by the breathing of the plants, what in no other way could happen—the purity of the reality of totality. So is the interplay of the observance of the laws of Nature in birds, in bees, in plants, in breezes, in the water, in reflection, so it is in these that we become informed by our *idée* observation. Without intellect, without reason, we receive the form of its performance and suddenly you become aware that you have developed the muscles of *idée*. This was the whole inner thinking of Goethe which was so great to Steiner. So great that he never let this go. He gave it to the whole world for scientific conversation. He was always aware that he could turn instantly to *idée* because it was there inside him. Therefore, when he had forgotten to live in brackets, he would revert to his garden and become advised and feel the muscles and the area to approach *idée*.

If you look at plants and their world, through roots and stems and leaves, as we call them, and you more and more use this intellect and this reason, and find *idée*, here you will see something very interesting. You will see that the whole growth of plants is very definitely an investiture relative to man's necessity. That, indeed, all of that growth thing is a phenomenon. It's full of phenomena, changes always taking place that are fascinating, demanding observation.

And the seed is the briefest of all possible phenomena, and the very essence of all possible *idée*, without becoming totally invisible. It is the entry from one world onto the other. It is this problem that we are always faced with and all these answers we try to find—how to travel from the visible into the invisible and from the invisible into the visible. This is the function of *idée*.

If you survey plants from this point of view you begin to see the whole procedure unfolding by a divine law of explanation. And you suddenly discover in the very exemplification of it that this seed is the essence of *idée* and the other (intellect and reason) becomes more and more the essence of disabilities.

You can look at the whole plant, you can look at its roots, you can look at its stem, but you can't look into its seed. You're bewildered by the tininess, and always questioning in your mind how can there be an ego in that? In this matter also understand that you may now travel into areas untold, that in the seed there is a seed within a seed. That is the seed of all of that variety.

You have seen how we have led into the fact that in an apple pit must be all the apples of the world somewhere, where it could produce any apple that has never been known before, and which has come from origin of crabs. So it has come out of totality apple and has in it totality of all apple.

Therefore, within that seed must be the seed of all seeds, and this journey now begins to come out of that because within that which is the emblem of all seed, there is a whole variety of that seed, and again beyond seed the manifestation of all *idée* of seed, not just apple. So now you begin to see that there is no such thing as an insect or a plant or a bird as an isolated entity. It is a wave of biodynamic orders which is an area of discontinuity to which we give a name, and having given it a name, separate it from totality and see it as a dragonfly.

It is an impossible subject to talk about, and it is impossible to speak it in words and try to arrive at it to place it before you. You could use *idée* and discover this: that out of that beyond, that we have just talked about, you enter into the beyond where you take all seed as whole seed, no longer as varieties. You must enter surely, without question. You enter the whole seed of rebirth, of Aurora.

You see how calamitous it is. The very scientist goes to the country; the very botanist goes to the country, and finds an insect or a bird or a plant. There is only one thing that is his real concern: "What is it?" But that "What is it?" is not *idée*, that "What is it?" is already a total separation from everything. It is a little atom trying to be put apart and then to have reason attached to it, to be put in false totality. You can only know what that is by your inner self perceiving its inner self.

Seed: The Utmost *Idée*/The Least Metamorphosis

Green Gulch Farm
11 February 1980

Since it's a vast subject, and don't let us go bounding over the fences and hedges and think we're going to discover it all. Let us talk about what is health of plants, for which purpose we must go back to the beginning of the issue where it concerns it. The huge secret. And it is a secret. You can't escape it. A huge mystery: of what is seed. This birth into the visible world from the invisible. To a degree I have talked with you about seed; to what degree you are highly knowledgeable about seed—it is endless, isn't it?

Therefore, I must first remind you, if I may, of the capacities of seeds. You can burn them, and they're still fertile. You can boil them, you can freeze them degrees below zeroes that people can't even think in their minds about, and they're still perfectly fertile. It often brings about the fertility, it cracks it. In fact in many cases, there is a ratio on seeds of how many days you should freeze, and then how many days you should apply a certain heat to bring about a quick—quote 'fertility'. Some of that is very erroneous, and it's highly experimentative.

Now seed, when she's born on the plant, is connected with a membrane, and that as the seed fulfills its physical formation, those wires, and those very soft wooly membranes, like a bird's nest, all change from the softest to the hardest. Therefore by this means, a plant, such as a scarlet runner bean, which takes no frost at all—the whole plant will go black with one degree of frost—stalk, flowers, leaves, the lot, except that one bract from which the beans hang, all the way up, they hang. Those bracts of beans will turn slowly from a beautiful lush edible bean, into a canvas with shellacs with steel casings. And they can hang there the whole of the winter through, but if it goes below zero, not one touch of the four elements can interfere with those seeds inside. Can't get in.

You can actually make raspberry jam, with raspberries, you may throw that on the ground, and in cases there has been germination.

The whole story about the most beautiful cooking apple in the world, Brambley's seedling, there was a farmer called Bramley, and his wife made him an apple tart on his birthday, because that's what he always liked. She threw the remnants of the tart on the compost heap. And up came a bunch of apple trees, and amongst them, one, that left the others, like the Eiffel Tower, sitting. They were so struck by this performance, that they marked it and kept them, and carefully propagated them. And out of it came an apple this size. The one, of course, out of the one.

And so you see this capacitous-ness of seed. Now when that seed is born you must think of it as an egg. You see in an egg is the chick, surrounded by the embryo, and that is surrounded by skins, and then there is what is called the 'white', which is a larder. Then at one end there is a skin running across which leaves an air pocket, and that air already is not the equivalent of the outside air—it's a *conservatoire*. Now, from the moment that that *revolutionibus* starts propagation of the embryo, the white is absolved by the embryo, and as the white is absolved, the skin falls in and the air from the outside comes through the shell. It's entering that way through the area of discontinuity, and so, it is being eaten up at a certain ratio. And this is indeed exactly with seed, that they have within them these casings, endless coverings, but that they all have around what they call the cotyledons or those formations, the same thing as an egg white. They could be oil matters, protein matters, some of them eat it up instantly in the fall. Some of them keep it for years. I was participant in the raising of the lotus seeds from the tomb of Tutankhamen. Over three thousand years. The plants did propagate, but of course they were so weak, they didn't exist, it didn't continue.

Now, you must think very clearly about this matter, about this seed. For you must see that Goethe's statement is very remarkable: "The seed is the utmost *idée*, and the least metamorphosis." It has in a sense then—to wickedly try to translate that further—it has the utmost of the invisible world, and the least of the visible. To be able to sit on this Earth. Whereas the plant growing, pursuing at all times, whether a plant, a creeper, a shrub, or a tree, becomes the least *idée*—but the same *idée*—and the utmost metamorphosis. Which is endless. It appears in the physical world and can flow into that ad infinitum, until the whole world almost is absolved, in one seed. Do you follow?

Now when you grasp that you will realize that a seed produces a plant with the *revolutionibus* at a certain moment: the Moon, in position of the planet, each night getting preparation, in inclination says: *clap, clap, clap, wake up, wake up*. The next night more: *I said: wake up*. Half Moon: *wake up!* Next night: *bang, bang, BANG! Wake! Pop*. The Moon, with the moisture, has split apart the waters that have opened up the canvasses and shellacs of the seizure of that seed. The seed itself has not done it. And now the two ways up and down are released together. And so you have that and that (root and shoot growth).

Now perceive that there is an area of discontinuity here, what you might call the negative soil, and the positive air. There is a throat matter to the plant now, and that this one is going down, hunting the warm moist gasses; that one is going up, hunting for warm moist gasses. But there is a connection in the middle. And there is the whole *beauty* of what we live in, the atmosphere of the world; so is the skin of the Earth the area of discontinuity of the plant, in its two areas. Now perceive you, that what is in the seed—we were talking about the embryo, utmost *idée*, and you begin now to inwardly perceive without verbosity the meaning of this *idée*—that is voluptuous apparently, and cannot be put into the scales of quantity and quality. It is unique in that. It is beyond quality or quantity. And that the amount of root that goes down, and the amount of top that goes up, has no inference, it is all led by that *idée*.

Therefore comprehend this. A lie that Darwin said, is that the crown *présentement* is the mind of the plant. And of course he had to say that because he was only seeking in the mind. Now, here is the whole matter which brings it to the clarity of your perception. So long as in those soils there are the requirements of that plant, and so long as in the airs above there are the requirements to be sought of that plant, the joy, the linkage and the friendship of that ego will remain together. In other words, let's call that matter which was in the seed, let us call it the 'protein', because it is quite a good word. Now so long as that remains linked together—understand that it's expanding, the plant is growing, and therefore this growth of this ego which is obviously expanding—so long as the fortifications, the health, the fertility of the soil and the atmosphere both are capable to fulfill its necessities, its desires, it will respond in this in remaining amicable, beneficent and will keep in touch with each other. That protein will not be divested. If there is, however, a want, a shortage of that health virility—and again we are talking about the proteins now, that are in the plant, in the soil, and in the atmosphere—so you have got it in the soil as well as in the plant, and if they are not there, what does happen? A little microbe of that protein runs out into a leaf and misses touch with its connection, with the rest of the protein. The moment that happens, the four elements become *animos*, unfriendly, reverse—call it any word you like, it doesn't matter— and you have disease, illness at once. Before that the four elements must obey, and are beneficent. Now they are malefic, as you would term it, and here enters the whole scene of health and disease.

See you therefore that it is not a question of the prolific-ality of your seed, of your plant, of your adjustability to an area. It is in all of it combined, the attitude of fertility, that there must be this beatific interplay and that it can't be let hold of. Are you able to follow this?

Now, there is a further matter connected with that, that the beatific flow also becomes a spreading beatific. In other words, it's catching. We mentioned in a degree how an opening carnation made the others open, and a dying carnation made the others die. Do you see the purport there? When that protein has separated, and you have lost contact, you have a vital force let loose. Dangerously. And that that malefic not only becomes the word 'disease', but it is a spreadable disease. It is a catching one.

Now then do you understand the attitude of the biodynamic and the French intensive? It studies the behavior of man's destiny of being conductor of the orchestra, and seeing that the control of fertility is correct. And it is terribly easy. For all of the life given to us for it, all of life supplied for it, operates it perfectly. It is a matter of conductorship. Have I explained that to some degree of graspability? You see it's very difficult because we've really gone out of language.

Composting

Covelo Village Garden
13 April 1977

We're on the subject now, this morning, of composting. And, I would like to treat the subject, as absolute basic clean, to the dawn. Which means that one must state quite clearly, the moment you mention certain words today, a whole procedure of monstrosity in the mind enters. You see, the moment you enter *food*, the whole mind is consumed by man and his want. This physical, horrible, selfish, destitute, thinking of want. It's unfortunate that when the organic grower mentions compost, the whole thoughts are arranged around the requirement of utility: "Of what use is it? Is it really of use? And how much do we get? And we must make all we can. And the plants will grow on it." It's an incredible, mad, already insane utility. So for goodness sake discard it, because it's absolute rubbish.

It's a law, and a system of Nature. It comes out of the provisionment of the four Archangels. Having said that, one has put it immediately in the air, without a foundation, where it should be. So let's begin.

Some periods ago, for instance when the American Indian dominated these lands, and some period ago, when our histories are reasonably written in idiotic verbosity, that we all pretend to hold true, you found that people lived almost entirely on meats. And that the animals that the people lived on, lived on vegetables. Of course. But that was a procedure that went on. That doesn't mean to say that the providence of divine law was such an institution. Therefore you've got to think of past, present and future as though it were, indeed, a time element. You have got to think of what you are doing at present, of what you were not doing a thousand years ago, and of what you would really like to do in a thousand years' time. That's very important. What would you like to be eating? And how would you like it to be grown? And how would you like the *environnement* to have become because of their attitude. That's what we're really talking about.

In a sense, when the great French and Italian epoch came in, of vegetable culture, it was the beginning of a pathway to that. It was a religious uplift. And religion and philosophy undoubtedly enters into the whole approach to this. Steiner then leads into the attitude of fruit eating. There you see a huge difference, again.

The whole concept of this matter concerning composting has got to be placed, not only in plant issue, but in climatic issue, because that's its greatest representative. There undoubtedly was a period when humanity lived in a subtropical climatic, and that that is a fruit area. When it came to live outside of there, the fruit procedure, not only diminished, but vanished. So I am saying at this moment that climate, and soil, and the four elements of an area that we live in, are what we've got to begin to look at.

The whole of this issue demands an obedience to the observation of the laws of Nature: humus, health of the soil, and the manipulation of human beings as a participant of Nature. In Nature and with Nature. *Not* in domination of, making use of Nature to a purpose. It means that man here has a destiny in that he is an agriculturalist. It is demanded of him by Mother Nature herself that he do so. And that when he does so, he will be provided. And when he does not do so, he will not be provided. This is what the industrial revolution brought about. The industrial revolution broke up the home, in the family, in the garden. It brought about living in vast quantities of over-civilized birth in small areas, demanding that country areas that had capacity of over-providence, by the huge productivity of Nature's benevolence, could grow the produce, and ship and train and truck it in to the limited tiny separated areas in which civilization had barbed-wired itself in.

The whole of Xenophon's[1] explanation then, of *eco-nomia*, was wiped out. A person washes, and what they wash with, is not waste. A person eats, and what they eat is not destroyed. And a person breathes, and what they breathe is not destructive. It belongs in the area in which they live and express and reflect. When you get a million people living elbow to elbow, that procedure does not take place in any natural form at all. In Nature there is no waste—it is all re-delivered—life into death into life. The plants take the acid of the dead foliages, of the humus, and turn it into sweet, into sugars, into oils. And it goes back into death into acids. This the bee does likewise. The very blood of the bee is acid. But its juice that it puts into the nectar—for it is the bee's juice of spit that it puts into the nectar as honey—so it regurgitates it as a sugar, with the love of the flowers: honey, nectar.

What I am referring to right at this very moment, is the key of the matter, with our present position. It is impossible for any family, any small group of people to live in any other way than the rebirth of their wastes, of their greens, with an area of Nature, in which that multiplication of arithmetic is the law of Nature. The moment that that is undone, an unbalance is in, and providence does not flow. In that word 'providence' you must not look at what is looked at today by the government, which is quantity. It is *quality*. And that's only a term again, in which there is enormous depth of meaning.

If you look then, at human being, and its performance in its creativity, in its reflection of the way we live, and the area in which we live: that give and take is an interplay of reflections. It is exactly the same, then, with the livestock that lives with us. That too, must have its proper interplay of its waste, being re-formed into life. And in no way must that be meddled with. Neither can the sex life of plants and flowers be interfered with for the purpose of the advantage of utility of civilization. And again with the animals, and again with the fruit trees, likewise, their areas, and the necessity of the interplay of areas.

What Mr. E.F. Schumacher from England, who came over here recently, whom you all know, is talking about small area, "Small is Beautiful", is this issue: *Eikos-nomia. Eikos*: the home, the family in the home, in the garden. The interplay of the fruitiousness, the fertility, of man's *image* as a leader, director, within Nature. As the Sun's Sun guides the Sun—and we do not see the Sun's Sun, for it is too vast, too black—but that as the Sun guides and leads the planets that dominate this Earth, so is that leadership reflections. And this is a participle of the arithmetic of destiny.

Therefore you will see, that if you endeavor to take an area that is outside the scope of your interplay, there is no replacement of the law of Nature. It must become defunct. Arid. Sterile. Not fertile. In other words, it becomes less all the time, not more.

The enormity of the leadership of humanity in Nature is beneficence, warmth. That, if you may say, is a view into the future. Someday it must open out into totality, perhaps. That's beyond vision, surely, at present. You may say, if you like, that it is change, and not enlargement, and that's perfectly clear. And simple.

Now. Let us begin to come down a little more then, into what you would call factuals. The contents of matters, the color of flowers, the scent, the value of the give-off of trees, of plants that restore all the perniciousness of atmosphere that is made, back into purity. *Fresh water. Fresh air.* What is fresh water, fresh air? What an incredible thing that you go from one place to another and you think you've met it. And suddenly you go to the Himalayas, and you breathe the air at eighteen thousand, and you realize that you have never breathed that air or such air before. Neither have you heard the sound that you have heard of that sound before, ever. And then you hear the stars for the first time, because there are no other earthly sounds to destroy it. And you begin to realize that there are extremities beyond extremities, of Suns beyond the Sun, that lead this onwards. That therefore, in the contents of these plants, is something of the *image* that is in man in his destiny behind this.

That the contents for the requirement of food in vegetables, is obviously only in the very leafy stage. Even the birds and the insects of the apples, only rarely adopt *that*. The real tea is the tip of the camellia leaf, not the camellia root. Now they put the sticks in, and I believe the stems too.

Now I'm going to delve further into the compost then. Since it's the young vegetable which is more delectable, more flavor-able, and requires no cooking—and cooking is again, is it not, cultivation in the kitchen of the Sun? It doesn't matter what you cook by, there's no other cultivation in the kitchen except Sun. Oh gas? I'm sorry, but it's the Sun. The electricity? You know it's the Sun. And the coal and the wood. It's fire. Prometheus brought it. There isn't any other. But it gets worse and worse as you muck it about. And much more impossible, and divorcing in its appropriation, until you have destroyed your beautiful food that you have produced by a false cultivation. It's perfectly obvious, the less you cook, the more cultivation you've done in the garden, where it should be.

Now instantly, that's led you to something. You must see the huge difference between dead matter—which is not really very pleasant to eat—and very live matter. There's a total difference between a compost heap made of dead hay or dead straw or dead leaves, and, in fact, there's no relationship almost at all between the young leaves, green. And then again you can go much further, to tips. And then of course, you will go into something which I'm not going to touch today: seed, which is the furthest of them all.

Now, we'll deal with this compost again in a minute, and we'll deal with it just technically as to how it is best to go about it. But let us re-look at the matter that we brought up a little while ago and re-establish it. There are words today which are negative, and they exist: *pest* and *disease*. They are rife everywhere. The matter then of pest and disease concerns the word *balance*. If, out of the scientific laboratory of man's mind of connivance against the law of Nature, you will invent a destruction against disease, and not against the person, as it should be, you will wipe out life, energy. And this is the procedure of the governance of agriculture: *Wipe out the whole of life, so that you may have it for yourself.* But you wipe out the life that is in the thing that you want. The energy is gone. The whole of today is a provocation of hypocrisy: something that looks like something, that is not. We have acted tirelessly throughout the municipality of Nature, and we have got a case left, without a soul.

The whole maneuver-ment of the law of Nature in growth is the operation of the four Archangels in their duty. Handing from one from the other, from the center of each period of the quarter, the goblet of the energy, to the next. That is non-static: movement, rotation, cycle. You may look at it which way you will, but you have to perceive the enormity of it. When you look at the fields at this moment, and the reflection of the Raphael, rising out of Gabriel, you cannot mistake what is happening. And then we will see, this warming look of Uriel, looking at us as we are overwhelmed by the production of Nature. It rises up and faces us.

Plants are an angelic force, likewise. The whole mantle of the world is foliage-ing—a whole angelic force that operates the play of the energy of the Sun, demanding the physical energy of the Earth to come out and marry it and make heat, warmth. The life force takes place in this most magical place in the world in which we live: atmosphere. The very brief little area which you refute.

The plants are carrying out what you could easily call, if you like, the battle of the four Archangels. Oh yes, it is. Michael does descend with a sword of iron into the Earth. Therefore, it is forever a waging of forces, and that if you cessate that waging of forces, you'll have cessated life, energy, and you have a shell left. It is absolutely essential that what we call disease and pest is totally existent, and it is existent in all of us. We have every disease, every one of us. And there is every pest in the world, and there ever will be, and nothing can be exterminated. Nothing. There is no extermination in this world. When you eat something, you do not dissolve it into nothing. It is re-issued in different forms of reflections. And that's all that happens with anything, ever. This is what plant life is doing, and it must have the issue of death to re-form life.

That reformation then, is a participant of that cycle of the four Archangels, of autumn, winter, spring and summer, again into autumn. The non-static perpetual, never the same acute rotation. The mathematics of the planets and the stars interplaying, making a different canvas for it to work on each time the cycle reappears and re-forms. That therefore, this whole procedure of the living of plants, can only be health: disease can only be held in balance of joining of health. Pests can only be held in balance of life entity of insect, of bird, of animal, of human. If the providence and the law of Nature are fulfilled, and are fruitious, and develops into a fertility of magnification which is an increase, the moment that it is attempted to be defiled by exemplification in other forms, such as chemicals, the whole system is undone, and must go into deformity to produce eternal death. That it may re-form into construction, out of a greater destruction.

That you know full well now, having looked at it in the garden, that both leaves and stems and hairs and fruit, are covered with bloom. I am referring to that astonishing thing that when you wipe, for instance, with your finger, the leaf of a carnation, it has completely changed color and form. Instantly. That bloom is what? Emanation. Aura. It is the receiver and the giver: this procedure of inclination and declination. It is a vast protective. That bloom cannot exist on that fruit, on those plants, on those hairs, but from life into death. If it is there by artifice, it has no strength, it has no quality. It is not a protective anymore, it does not prevent the Sun from burning it. It is deformed. It is going downwards into a destructiveness.

This reformation, then, this re-forming, is assisted for us by the manipulations of the laws of Nature, and there are three enormous attributes in this. These are all overlooked today in agriculture. Those three may be termed worms—and with them then you can apply a whole bunch of others, naturally—tree roots, and deep-rooted plants.

It is well-known, that in the ordinary systems of agriculture, mechanical in particular, worms are destroyed, wiped out. They are the horticulturalist's, the agriculturalist's, greatest of all friends. They both aerate and manure, and they co-operate, as man is meant in Nature, with the deep-rooted plants. Now you know that worms, of which there are something like forty-eight variety, there are only two variety which do their duty—their lavatorial—on the surface. And those are the annoyance of golf linkers. The other number, probably in the nature of forty-six, do their duty, like many birds and animals do, in certain areas of their tunnels. They have apertures like ants do. Like goats they go to the toilet all the time. We forget the enormous fertilization that a multitude of worms produce in the soil. In adjunct to that enormous fertilization is the most astonishing and bewildering cultivation of little tunnels. Just the right size to suit and make enjoyment and health for the plants. Not like gophers. Well, we need say no more.

These deep-rooted plants—this does not necessarily refer to trees, it refers to plants, deep-rooted plants—there are many that go down to sixty-two feet, and the quite normal procedures of things like rhubarb and such plants will go down usually from twelve to sixteen to eighteen feet deep. Now, you know that there are no cultivars that will go into those areas, other than explosion. And that's liable to compress rather than to decompress.

Very quickly I have to remind you about the four Archangels and their duty. And this is *revolutionibus* also. The whole interplay of the law of the stars, of the planets, their givings and takings; inclination and declination; beatific and malefic: they're so important, you see. We always pretend there aren't any bad fairies, they're aren't any naughty dwarves. Hmmm...don't tell the good fairy if they're weren't. She would become like the luciferic and disappear in the imagination.

So, one has to go back quickly and look at the duties of the four Archangels, which are cultivation. Cultivation, a word that we have made, which means the interplay of the four Archangels in the very soil which is life. As the plants are life, the soil is even more life. The more interplay there is in the soil—and now you see the importance of escalating beds on mountainsides, that you get this interplay, not only down, but from out of the side and underneath—the more interplay that you can have in the soil of the four Archangels, the more response is there. So that even a plant in a pot will do better than a plant in a bed, as regards blossoming, and as regards fructification, should we say. And that is why the Hanging Gardens of Babylon were such an example of this. Complete operation of the four Archangels, of *revolutionibus*.

Now I am beginning to point at the whole issue of compost. The whole operation of compost would be useless without deep cultivation. You would merely have a hypocritical pretense of the surface. You would induce something that could not be continued by the root-ism, the ahrimanic. It would all be luciferic and no ahrimanic, total. Therefore, the cooperation of deep-rooted plants is a fulfillment of those angelic qualities of the Archangels. That those deep-rooteds—don't worry at the moment about the worms—they simply say, "There's no water up here. I haven't got what I want up here. I'm going down forty feet." And down they go. And as you know they begin, even in their very first year, many of them, to go down ten and fifteen straight away. The moment that they bore through what is called the 'compacted', which is the swinging of the Earth, partly, that holds the magnet force of the physicality of the Earth from being thrown out by the Sun saying, "Come world! I'm going to destroy you!" "No," says the Earth, "You're not. And I'll only let my vital strength go through, and hold my ego in." Oh dear.

So you get these roots that go through that compaction, which is preventing the Archangels from total operation, if you like—you must forgive my words, re-form it—and so, they go down and break through that compaction, and have begun a release.

Normally, as you know, the worms, because of summer, roll up and sleep on the edge of the compactment, and in winter, roll up and sleep on the edge of the compactment, and rather like some of the members here, they sleep most of the time; and just a short time in the spring and the fall they come out and get on with a little bit of manuring and then get back again.

The moment that the roots go down, the worms begin to operate all year round; their beatific swells, and they have great joy and excitement in living. Down they go, in the regions that were un-educated, un-fertilized, and un-cultivated. They begin to cultivate it, and open it up. And so it begins to breathe. And so it becomes fertile. The foliages improve, and the young growth increases.

The trees do likewise, in the fact that they are the re-formatives in the whole of Nature of barrenity, of barren area. The seeds of trees in the forest gradually spread, re-form, and always give more than they take, after their children. As they begin to grow up, they replace much more than they use, and the insects, and the birds, and the plants make joy of it. And they add to it their qualities, but retrieve from it their quantities. So you get a reimbursement of certain areas that are taking and putting. This is going on all the time. This is the application, then, of man's ecology in his destiny as a horticulturalist.

Therefore, in order to bring this about, the old system of agriculture was to produce a certain ley crop, which would give us, as the forest is a giver in manufacturing new soil, and relieving desert into beauty, so there are endless plants, as there are in human beings, as there are in birds, that give, to what we would describe, more than they take. Everything in a sense gives more than it takes, but in some it's malefic, in some it's beatific. These plants then, in particular, are chosen for these purposes, particularly the deep-rooteds. They would be sown in an area that requires an introduction of fertility, an increase of fertility, which has become primarily malefic, barren. And that if you were to turn that into the soil, it would indeed increase the product and the operation of the soil, by opening it and causing the capacity of the four Archangels to operate more fully, and become more fertile and more beatific. But the operation of turning that green matter, of death, of what was life, into death, causes the life energies which are already in that soil to be occupied by the manipulation of nitrogenic fastening, as you might call it. Turning death back into life. They would have to use their forces to do it. Therefore it is better to remove that, and place it in what is now termed composting heaps. Whereby, the manipulation of the elements—warmth, moisture and combustion—nitrogenic manufacture will operate in that heap. If it operated in the soil, it is like the whole of Nature which is content with what it has got, because man does not prolific-ize in it. But the lone mad man prolific-izes in it, and his *image* enters it, a new attitude of reflection appears, and grows, and is requested in destiny.

That the procedure of all animals—in the ordinary procedure of Nature, of throwing the dead leaves, of throwing the manure—is within a balance, but it is not a production of man's requirement. Therefore, it is required that the manipulation of that manure of animals and birds is adopted in the balanced equivalent into that compost, that it may not be ejected into gaseous matter, and deposited over the oceans and other countries and other people's gardens ad-lib, but should be an ecological compaction in his *conservatiore*. This is the waste into life of the area in which man in the home in the garden must embellish and become fruitious.

Therefore, a quantity of the utmost green herbage is placed in a certain quantitive—not turned into the soil, but taken out and placed in heaps—with a certain quantitive of the animalistic and birdistic compost; which is what manure is, and human compost likewise, in less a degree, which is what it is. There is much more roughage in all animal compost, and human compost is very uneducated these days. Therefore it is a quantitive required to begin to place. Now if you place green herbage all together, you will get a nitrogenous combustion, but it will not be the same combustion as the balances put together. If you're going to be a fruit-eater in a thousand years, your attitude of change is going to change out of that, into something else. That you've got to permit. You must not cage it. It will be led, and the keys will be there.

When you place all those animal manures, because you are not thinking, and not appropriating to the balance of Nature, but appropriating to the necessities of your labor of your machinery and what you think you want, you will place it all in a great heap so that you can use it when you want it. It's completely lunatic. That great heap cannot possibly interplay in the way in which Mother Nature destined that manure to fall out of the animal in a little pat, and the animal to go on it. It was not meant to stay on it. It is well-known that all animals have a great dislike of eating the herbage that grows around their own pat. They don't, they move on. Sometimes they prefer the growth that comes from other procedures, in fact, all things do.

You will see this whole law in what I've told you about the carnation. If you pick a carnation in a bed when it's all coming into bloom, the one carnation, the others won't come into bloom except much later. And if you have left the one carnation, other carnations will come into bloom quicker. Likewise, if you leave a carnation to die and perish, the carnations around it will also die, and not only the carnations around it will die, but even the buds opening will die. They follow suit. They cause emanation. That is why *botrytis* spreads so vastly in little tiny seedlings.

Now, the whole of this combustion, which produces what we call a certain *heat*, is brought about by this inter-placement then, of these balances of natures. It is found generally that climatic has an enormous control over this combustion of turning life-into-death-into-life. Wind is utterly destructive. Rain will destroy a temperature after a certain quantity of cold-th, of cold rain. Warm rain will increase it. Therefore certain protectives in certain areas are necessary. When you make compost heaps in the sub-tropics, where you have a beautiful equilibriate maritime climate, you need no protections of any sort. You want to expose it to the total because you have got everything there, complying to what is required to bring about life-into-death within two months. But when you have an extreme change of climate—where you are not meant to live, but have but decided to out of your own invention—there you have already disobeyed the whole principle of law. Which has revealed itself to you, and you have decided to do otherwise.

And so, you must use tactics that must control those elements. Therefore you must dig a pit, and you must place the stuff in those pits. And those pits need to be certain sizes; and they should always be oblong. And for the matters, where you have a thoroughly sound climate, two-foot is enough. But if you wish to use light manure, human manure, then you must go to four feet down. Four feet is a requirement. And you must, indeed, bring to a temperature, that compost, in order to bring about the destruction of destruction, to a temperature of one hundred and twenty to one hundred and fifty, really for twenty hours, but by law of the health department, whatever idiocy you call it, two weeks.

Now all of those manures that we're talking about, no matter what they are, in summer months can be can be completed in three months, and in winter months, generally, in four months. Normally speaking your manure of animals and birds to green matter should be one in four, can be one in three. The moment enter you enter night manure, you must go one in six, one in eight. That those applications should be applied in layers.

Turnings are a matter of decisions and thinkings, but an end of a first month's turning is generally advantageous, but these pits can be so made that you do not have to turn. It's a very big labor to have to turn compost heaps, especially considering that each one should contain three and four tons. It is a very considerable job. There are obviously—and you've got to think into the whole future here, again— enormous devices that could be achieved, to make a turning of such a thing really very simple. And there is always a device that could be found for such a matter. I am working madly on winches for plowing, for deep, six foot plowing. That with a winch, do you realize that, well, I myself have moved a seventy-eight thousand ton ship with my own hand, by winding a winch. If you had a heavy machine winch on a line, that you could wheel down the side of a field, and simply by operating the handle this thing would ride through the soil on a countervane, keeping it to a certain depth. I won't go on with that. You must draw it out and design it afterwards.

This compost, then, is a balance. Out of this compost is life-into-death-into-life. It is from this that you are going to get bloom on your plants. That bloom is the refuter and accepter of life forces. It knows its own operation; it can't be interfered with by man's thinking, and can only be fulfilled and present by its own growth. Just as a tree grows and the wood stays together, and you can make a table leg out of a piece of tree, and it stays together for hundreds of years. How much more intelligent is the growth of that beautiful tree than churning up the wood into sawdust and then trying to bang it together with some chemicals to make it stick together again. It's a little insane. The whole of this is done for us in revelation, and this is what we have to look at.

Compost then, is replaceable into the soil at that period. That when it is replaced into that soil—into all soil—after a certain period the soil itself changes in each cycle of the Archangels, and becomes more beatific and more fertile. In saying it becomes more beatific you must realize it also becomes more malefic, in balance. The two go in balance. Therefore you have got to have fungus, pest and disease in the soil, or the trees and the plants will not be strong and able to contend. That is why man must not hide himself in a monastery, and refuse to look at the people in the world, and leave them to destitution. Oh dear, I'm getting very much off, aren't I?

The preponderance, then, of this attitude is that a family, a group of people, a village of people, have a devouring, a certain proportion of requirement, and a certain proportion of exudance and waste. That is both physical, mental, and spiritual. And that this fits an area in which he lives. You will see that this rushing about the world, collecting trees, and plants and seeds from all over the place, and bringing them back and crossing them which each other, has resulted in a huge disrupt of origin. Of course, you see it in the minds and the lives of people, likewise. One is saying here that the whole of Nature is the law, and that there is a balance in that law that is irrefutable, and very full of secrets and invisibilities. It cannot be calculated; it cannot be added up and subtracted. As the golden age of the Greeks said, the whole attribute of living is to be a reward and a fulfillment of the creator, creation. And to be obedient to the law of the elements would be providence, and to be disobedient to the law of the elements would be no providence. Destruction. There doesn't seem to be any argument. There is no argument in this matter. You either do or you don't.

Plus, the domestics that go with the garden, with the produce, follow the same principle. And so they have bloom, they have fervor, they have coloring, and they breathe and fulfill in the same way. And their give-off, their waste, their emanation, both physical, mental and spiritual, is within an area; and that area becomes a fertile operating.

I felt that this approach to it is probably more of a key for us to have a view of what this word compost has become, since we specialize by trying to take something out of the box every time, and separate it, and place a huge anchorage of utility around its neck. This cannot be done with the attitude to commerce. From there, we can go into endless panorama of different vegetable compost, different fruit compost, seed composts, multiplication composts. I have taken what you would call, just the general attitude to compost heap, which is the revitalization and reformation of soil, with which there is always perfect health and balance in pest; the coming back into animal, bird and insect, ad lib.

Do you want to discuss it?

Q: You mentioned seed composting.

According to the quantity seed that you are doing. Of course it's much more than usual. The whole entity in this—and I can see what you are aiming at, and I'm not going to tell you. You've got to find it. But I give you the whole key to it. Of course, Goethe gives it to you—seed is the utmost of *idée* and the least of metamorphosis; a plant is the utmost metamorphosis, and the least of *idée*.

Do we need to say any more?

If you look at what has just been raised, it was an attempt, somewhere, of probably the fault of increase. But you see, if you take such things as bone meal, if you take such things as wood ash, it should not go into the compost ever. You must always realize that wood ash is one of the greatest and quickest of all fertilizers. Why? What did we say? You go in the kitchen and cook what you've already cultivated in the garden, you cultivate some more in the kitchen and then you're able to swallow it. Because it's a bit too much because your digestion is weak and lousy. Wood ash is very identical. You should never really have to burn anything. If you do burn, you can burn anything. You can burn a seed. You would get the utmost of utmost. Oh yes, you would. But you would have destroyed the utmost of *most*.

The instantaneous result would have been absolutely enormous. It would kill most plants on the spot. Indeed all wood ash applied to seed boxes and seed beds kills them the moment they germinate. Much too much. And of course it's like lime. Lime, as you know, is fired-off chalk in the kiln. Ash is very much the same. Ash is the Sun, working at a hundred times the speed, on some wood and some roots and some old paper, and God knows what you put in it. And simply devouring it up at a colossal pace. So that what? All the flames and the smoke go roaring in the air, and you have destroyed the rubbish. Drivel. You can't, absolute nonsense; you can't destroy anything.

So what's happened? Well the flames that went up, were what? What are flames? The energy of the Sun in almost compacted *idée*, and they're going to do *that*. Spread out like lightning. Lightning's going on all the time, leveling out, total. That's what Nature's doing; that's what the four elements are doing; that's what the Archangels are doing. And smoke is going up. All being moved out. And when the rains come it's all going to fall down on your neighbors and your beautiful farms over there, and Mr. Snodgrass, who pinched your cow. You're not going to get it—or very little of it.

But the ash that remains is still a consummate for remnant of multiplication of what was a huge quantity, is now an alchemist's reduced quantity into total quality. If you had manipulated, as Steiner taught me—and we will do—the burning of all that rubbish, so that none of it flamed, and no smoke came out, but smoldered for a very long time, you would end with all those gases in the heap, in the ash. And so vital and virile is that, the moment that you put it on the soil and put water on it, it goes *pwssst* just like lime does. It will explode! As the Sun would do to the world if it got the chance. It would absolutely explode and does, and boils—and you will blister yourself as you do with lime, when you spread on your skin with water. The elements are restoring it to totality, instantaneously. Therefore, what we are talking about is very dangerous. That's why we're not including it in the soil. Seed compost is already too, too vitally centralized. Not to be touched; it is the secret. It's a huge secret. The one element that none of us can have any conception of, is where does life come from to a seed. And it is very clear, different stars...well it's no good talking about that, because we'll have to go to Kew Gardens to learn that.

Does that answer your question?

Q: You mentioned animals have an aversion to eating the herbs growing from their own pats. Is that a consideration in our relationship to our own waste in composting?

Definitely. Very much so. In France it was found very, very deleterious. And all manurings. It's exactly what the whole of the French intensive system did, very stupidly. It became commercial. And what did they do? They didn't worry about the law of Nature anymore, about animal manure and quantity of balance. They worried about the money they were going to get out of the market, out of the sale of the goods. And so what did they do? They used more and more manure, and less and less green matter until the whole thing was a filthy, dirty manure drink, when you ate a lettuce. It had no taste of the lettuce at all, and somebody said, "But this is a cow pat!" And indeed it was.

You don't seem to have picked the key up off the table. It is an uncalculable—but very clear—perception, a law of Nature, of balance. A person, a family, living in an area, and quantitives—do you see? Again, there's got to be the channel of perception into fruition, into fertility, that's going to change this too. That's why I mentioned to you—very rudely—that Steiner taught me that fruit eating was a whole vision of the future. And you see the orchard, in a new vision entirely, is a different thing altogether. Fruit growing, and becoming ripe in its different periods, is totally different to plant. And that probably plant would seem to belong much more to animal. Do you see? And now you begin to see things forming again into new pockets, but that's a long way out of the window.

Q: Is idée *ahrimanic and metamorphosis luciferic?*

Nincompoop. You would say so if you like to invent it.

Do you see? It is this madness perpetually, the statement that God lives within Himself, but that everything that is born has an ego, it is true. Light and shadow. But you can't talk about ahrimanic and luciferic unless you talk about the four Archangels. Do you see? The four Archangels override, utterly, the whole power of the ahrimanic and the luciferic. It is participant. Do you comprehend?

You must never talk about the beatific without the malefic. Just like Findhorn always aggravates me to a degree of insanity. They're always talking about the good fairies. They will never talk about those wicked elves which I met on Skye endlessly, and caused me many a nightmare.

Q: The garden is now just beginning to enter into manure composts and the different ways of handling our manures. I'm wondering now with that lead-in to the young plant compost with manure in the amounts...

Today I talked just generally about compost heap. Do you understand? About the balances that exist in our present latitude that we live and think in. But I've wanted to get up to the next floor, the next floor.

I still say to you—and I take the instance of the potato. The potato came into culture from South America, and it swept the world with its beatific quality as a food, and it became dominated by industry and commerce to make money out of. And they fed it, as the French did, as all the growers did, with more and more manure. Now where it came from in the Andes, the animals were very scarce; the herbage was very vast, and it wasn't used to manure, in its origin. And it's still in origin, it's a young plant in the world. That therefore disease, unbalanced, appeared on it like mad. It got scab. It got disease. And the plants even—as I have told you so clearly this morning—went into destruction, into death. Famine struck Ireland, so they had nothing to eat for two years, and whole parts of the world went into famine, because they had relied upon this potato and its beatific qualities, "And now the blasted thing misbehaved and failed and disease came in! And the whole world was full of the filthy beast of nature, misbehaving." *Mon dieu!*

So, what do we have to do? Doubleday research? Organic? You saw what the problem was. They said you can't put this manure into the potatoes. You must grow it on pure vegetation compost. And *Symphytum* (comfrey) is the ideal. It will show you. So for a hundred years, they did it. Now they grow the finest potatoes in the greatest quantity and the best quality, and the most beautiful flavor, in perfection, that is possible. You restore the issue. Now you can go back, if you want a little more quantity, and a little more quality perhaps, you can go back to a small amount of manure again. But don't you go and commercially overstep it, or you'll go into destruction again. Malefic will overtake.

So now you must understand that I am saying to you in this garden, in particular, which is to be an example of this matter. We have got to have compost heaps made of *specialized*, special herbs, that are applicable to special plants, when we begin to understand the planets more, when the herb garden has taught us many lessons. Do you follow? In the meantime, we will operate our manures more intelligently, and our human manures, with our ordinary compostings. But you will still have to use, on your much more *religious* plants, much more *saintly* plants, you will have to use discretion. And on your fruit trees.

Q: Lets get into another area. What I would like to lead up to is, what Steiner was pointing at, with the preparations. We're in an area that we can think about this, and there are people that are doing it.

Yes. Oak bark in particular, *Urtica* (nettle) is very important in it. Valerian. The seven (biodynamic compost preparations). However, I had a lot of practices in my younger days on all that, and I must say I found other things, you know, since, much, much, much more. You must be careful not to ever become (place) somebody on a pedestal, static in the cage, and that's the—what's their names are.

Q: I have one more question, since you brought it up, about the potatoes and Symphytum. *The Symphytum breaks down so fast, with so much moisture, I was not able to tell, or be able to explain to myself, whether it was the fire that was breaking it down, or it was the moisture.*

Neither. It's the Archangel.

.

---

1   Greek historian and philosopher; friend of Socrates (circa 430-354 BC).

Energies and Elements

Covelo Village Garden
May 23, 1977

This is a summarization of a whole series of lectures we've been having together, and a survey, a finalization, of what you might call one motif of the symphony which will proceed again through the ensuing year. Because it's the last lecture of that summarization, there are lectures, or talks, to follow. One of them, which concerns a reflection of this study today, will be on the purport of art and craft.

I have been giving you some oddities recently about how to cook things, and how to use the herbs. Here's a little one about young cabbage. You know that the English are renowned for ruining cabbages, so I go to a Scandinavian recipe, which some of you may know. You take your cabbage, try not to wash it if you can help it; chop it up fine, placed in a braising pan either with drippings, or olive oil and butter, whichever you prefer to use. Cook the cabbage thus, without a lid, for a very brief time, turn it—chopped fine mark you. Put no condiments in at that stage. After a few minutes, you should add a required small quantity of either cream or fifty/fifty. And now you should place your condiments of whatever you use, salt and pepper—there's no need to use herbs in this, you should not; salt, pepper, and of course I always recommend paprika, *capsicum*. When that has cooked, gently, for a little while, a very short time, add one-third—supposing you are cooking that dish for two people—of a freshly grated nutmeg, and don't cook, merely stir in. It is a Scandinavian dish. Sounds very odd, and is most attractive. Far better than something that I had in Le Havre once that was raw spinach and peppercorns.

The subject then this morning concerns energies and elements. Cold air descends, hot air rises. We take the whole thing for granted, just like this garden, just like all the roses in bloom. "Oh, they're in bloom." And it's all accepted, for nothing. That's the way we've become: capricious. Here is one of the most astonishing and remarkable happenings, which is a mystery. And you must understand that we only refer to now in this moment in the idiocy of verbosity, 'hot air' and 'cold air'. What is it? We have talked about fresh water, fresh air, and with it, fresh food, fresh living and fresh thinking. It's movement, of course. Non-static, *revolutionibus.*

Cold air collects in depressions and becomes stagnation and static. The effect at sunrise is a static. The effect if that same procedure has movement and is not static: the effect is stroking. The ordination of the leader, the sunlight at dawn, demanding its energy flowing, demanding the ego energy of the magnetic earth to come out and meet it. Demanding it to, and marrying, making what we call in verbosity 'warmth'. We are around the whole of that subject again. And now we have got a lot more to look at, and to understand, of what actually happens, how and why.

Why does a bracken (*Pteris*) cover on a bed protect the plants? When there is a severe frost, those plants under the bracken are protected. "Oh, because there is bracken on them." Rubbish. This isn't so at all. And why bracken, and why not something else? Well, numerous things do, and numerous things don't. The bracken has a uniqueness of receptivity; and what it actually does, is that at that period it holds in the warmth that is in the soil, and protects it from the cold, which is advancing from the descending air of cold from above, and prevents that marriage until the Sun comes.

The balance is concerning slopes and flats. The higher the temperature, the more rapid the chemical change—I use the word 'chemical', you understand what it means—in plant juices. To the degree that it is perfectly feasible to say—that indeed the director of Kew did state, one time—that every rise of ten degrees Fahrenheit doubled the change in the juices causing growth. Doubles every ten degrees. The lower the temperature, the less those changes are able to take place. The higher the temperature, they also cease to take place. But that in all cases, plant life, shrub life and tree life is more adaptable to high temperature rather than low. A vast living on the side of high than on low. When one talks about the chemical change, this is something we must now look at carefully. The effect of heat and freezing and normality upon plants also concerns moisture and dryth. The marriage of the four elements are combined in this matter, and cannot be separated.

The short light in what we call the spring, the dominance of Raphael, the short light, the angle also, is a constitution of leaf growth. But as the light, the marriage, increases in its energetic velocity, so does leaf growth cease, and blossom commence, and so intercede. In each of those cases within the plant, the juices are changing completely. In the early stage during the light, when it is shaded as you might say, shadowed, leaf growth takes place. I refer here to the woodlands where plants like nettles grow. Well, all of the plants which grow in woods have much more leaf than blossom, than those that grow in the shade. All of the plants in the valleys are much taller, with stems and foliage, than in the mountains, the same plants. And that in nearly all cases, the plants in the valley are more inclined to annual, and the plants in the mountains are more inclined to perennial. That in all cases, as you ascend, inclination of altitude, the foliage decreases and the blossom increases. So do the water juices of the foliage change also from the valley to the altitudinal rises. Those water juices are very much reduced even at three hundred foot altitude, and have already become the constituents of what you might call severe acidity or severe sugar.

These matters are completely interwoven, applicable, manageable, to change to climatic. They can manage cold and heat. The water juice cannot. This is somewhat difficult to handle, as you realize, and you must follow it as we go along. You will see that in the spring those water juices flow—it's part of an inclination—that then they change with the Archangels' changing, and they turn into something else.

I refer to this in seed again. You will realize that if you take a scarlet runner bean, in growth, it cannot take one degree of frost on any of that foliage at any time no matter what is happening with the foliage. In the spring, if that bean has come up, and there is freezing, that bean will surely be wiped out. If in the fall a slight frost begins to occur, gently, that scarlet runner bean will not be hit, but will survive for a period. On the contrary, the seed which is formed inside the pod, that pod will change its constitution completely, with Archangel Michael taking over, and will become hardened, completely, into waxes, glazes, and securities. And the seed itself will lose those moistures, within the cotyledon, and will turn to sugars and oils, leaving the moisture only at one-tenth. In other words, you have gone from plant, utmost metamorphosis, least *idée*, into least metamorphosis utmost *idée*. Now you have absolute jurisdiction over the four elements. They cannot touch it. They can hang there throughout the violence of Michael into Gabriel, and nothing can harm them. They're protected.

Changes of juices: I'm trying to get us out of our illegitimate acceptance of verbosity, and find and perceive what is true, and what is truly happening.

One has now said that freezing can be handled by plants themselves. What will kill a plant when it is born will not kill a plant at another period. The administration of the cycles, of the change: all of this is most important that you try to marry it in your mind, for it is going to be the key to the whole of your techniques in the garden. Out of the attitudes of the opposites, then, out of the attitudes of the opposites, I refer to the young weak juice of spring, which can be destroyed by any ill-tempered element. It is delirious in its birth.

Now, perceive you, what I have just talked about, that I have said that that seed in the pod—mind you in the pod—that also the seed has cases that are pods. And all of these cases are cases. There is no what we call embryo. There isn't any such thing. It floats through emanation from one into the other, visible into invisible.

But if you will look at that seed, that then is one-tenth moisture, to put a stupid statement, and the rest is oils and sugars and acute acids. That it cannot be touched by frost. But the moment that you apply moisture to it, it is absolutely adaptable to the least frost and will be destroyed instantly.

Now you understand why I spoke to you about soaking seed, how delicately this matter must be approached: where you soak seeds, and what the climatic is, and how the controls are going to be. For if that seed is to be soaked by the four elements in marriage combined, then there is an interweaving. But if you have taken one or two of the elements, and applied them to bring about an earlier procedure of awakening, you have got to make sure that the other mathematics of the elements are in line. And that is not very easy for human beings.

Out of the young, weak juice of the green shoot, delirious in growth, in birth, out of the center of that comes the necessity as the change of those four Archangels one from the other, handing the goblet, comes the necessity of utter hardness. For the elements are flame, and the consciousness is inside, and it strives at once to make what is called hard wood. Hardest of hard.

You see the same thing in your soil. The young tilth, the beautiful young tilth is delirious with growth. And the elements, capable of attack, and fear, inside—I use the word 'fear' for what it is—and out of that gentle and extortionate growth of the *revolutionibus* flowing in that beautiful tilth of open soil comes the requirement of seizure, to stop it, to prevent it. And the seizure takes place. It's alive.

So out of the center of each quarter appears the next.

Then look at inclination and declination, and the two intermediaries of the two equinoxes, which are opposite each other, dawn and *even*-ing. It is there you will find the same thing.

Now in a glass house, where you place glass and put false heat, you don't put false light. So you have got this matter, it is chiefly used during that period when the light of the Sun is at its lowest demand of the marriage. In other words, the energy is at its least. But you have increased one element: the warmth. And since the light is not, you have got a false ratio, and you have got a false growth. And if you add moisture as if the light were there, you will get *Botrytis* (grey mold).

This brings you to the focus of what is called climatic. Warm moist summer; cold dry winter. And the in-between twos: the equinoxes, the gentle equilibriums, the subtropics of Cancer and Capricorn.

A plant then becomes resistant to over-cold and over-heat by lessening its water content. I am using a term there, do you understand, I am talking about the wateriness of the young juice. By lessening that, and increasing the change into acidity or sugar or oil. Therefore you could very well say, normally, that the early spring is a water juice; the early summer, acid is beginning to flow into that water; that summer, the water now changes into the first stages of acidities and sugars; and in the fall, develops totally into acidities and sugars and oils, and exudes the waters. Not to be left.

Now, those changes that we are referring to in plants from the water juices to the sugars and acidities are an actual change, just as a leaf is a change to a flower, and a flower is a change to a seed. Now that change is a procedure. It does not in any degree comfortably go backwards. If the change has been induced by the Archangels' law, the procedure must take place, and the following will happen. The moment that water juices are invited to flow, the procedure is flow, and you cannot stop it. This is where the positions of false climatics are malevolent, for they will destroy. The plants cannot go back on what they have done. The same with cold, and the worse with wind.

Frost, water, wind, heat: change of temperature, and also moisture, changes the juice structure flow, acid to sugar and vice versa. All frost procedure descending, lowering the vibrations, will be accentuated to the utmost and last degree by wind, adding destruction to destruction. That high acid and high sugar in a plant or a tree will avoid low freezing, but be fatal to severe freezing. Those juice changes then go with the inclination and the declination. They change easily in that procedure with it, but not against it. And not at all easy, to any form of reversal, backwards.

Now there are many plants, many shrubs, which are called half-hardy—and you understand what that word means, somewhat. Now those particular plants and shrubs, if planted in what you would call a light sandy soil, in good drainage, will ride a severe freezing, and even wind with it, whereas those same exact plants, if planted in a heavy soil, in a clay soil, or any soil with a bad drainage, they will inevitably succumb, at exactly the same climatics. Now you begin to see that we have not got a static matter concerning plants. It is all related.

Now it is time to look at this extraordinary matter, not of inclination of climatic, but incline and decline of the mountains having four sides, which interweave, that make them not four sides. You must begin to look at what takes place upon that angle, that in the dells, the pockets, you have what you must look upon as a stagnant collection that is going to refute marriage. That in all cases on incline and decline you have got non-static. For the colder it gets, the more it will descend, and the warmer it gets, the more it will rise. You have got movement all the time. That is what the French intensive bed is built upon.

I am going to go back to what I was talking about earlier, with the plants that grow in the valley having long stems and a lot of foliage, and not very much flower, and being largely annuals. And on mountainsides, on rises, slowly, as you go up in altitude, less and less foliage, and more blossom, and more seed and shorter; closer to the ground. This all points to certain matters. Again, you begin on the low and you go out to the high and you go below both. You realize that all areas below sea level are obnoxious for growth, and all areas beyond a certain height of altitude are obnoxious for growth. Well that isn't just plants. No, because waters from mountains from over a certain height are extremely bad for plants, and so for the animals. Now you begin to see this amalgamation of matters, at least I trust you do.

When we said less heat, why less heat? The point is, that those leaves, at those altitudes, because of the angling slope, because of the movement, do not need a vast period of the water juice. They very quickly turn to the acids and the sugars, and are complete. And they therefore, containing more acid and more sugar immediately, have the capacity to ride either severity of climate. That is a whole different view to imagine, that it does not freeze, or there is not cold, on escalating beds. It's a capacity of plants in a different realm of growth; such as we are talking about spring and fall. And you have got a totally different plant of the same species at totally different altitudes.

Now you realize and know that there are varieties of different plants: what you call hardy, half-hardy, and tender. Those varieties are, because of that matter, according to their water juices thus to the elements. It is those that have less and less water juice that go into the hardies. And indeed you could go to certain mountains, such as you get in the Cape of South Africa, you go up those mountains and you find all the different varieties of lobelia, of lilies. All the different varieties growing at every different hundred feet that you go up. Covering two thousand five hundred feet. Nothing but stratas of different varieties of the families of the plants. Therefore, you must see that your structure in the plants on altitudes changes.

Now do you remember about livestock, and that your livestock should breed at certain altitudes, not in flat lands? Now do you understand? Do you see? It is not merely connected with the angle that the cow might be standing.

Here you also have some attitude to young, middle age, old in capacity. Remember that higher temperatures can be borne with more than low, and that cold descends and heat rises. Now you will understand that up to a certain point, the higher the altitude, the better the components. The lower, to the flat valley, the more danger.

Realize that there are waters, snow, glacial, that are beatific and malefic. One is inclined to think of all water as beatific. Very far from it.

Shade, evergreen, and deciduous, and the word 'shelter': quite different. Shade to all plants, and all animals and birds, and us, is obviously essential. What a mystery that there is, what we call in stupid words and take absolutely for granted, deciduous and evergreen trees. It is incredible that all the leaves suddenly fall off of a tree, and it has none. And the others sit there and are covered. Can you explain it? "Oh yes, of course, easy. It's all in the laboratory." It's a complete mystery. And that mystery is part of the performance of the Archangels.

Therefore, with the discussion that we had about the roots of trees, and the performance of trees, you must look at the importance of using and operating in the farm and growing evergreen and deciduous, and the implementations. But much more important, you must look to the word 'shelter'. And now, what did we say? Here is the most extraordinary matter that nobody looks at today in horticulture at all, or is talking about today at all! We are talking about shelter! What is the huge malefic appropriation of descending cold? It inevitably comes from a direction. And you know that if you have got a seething, biting cold wind that you are walking into, you turn around and go back and open up an umbrella in front of you. Or if you are on a bicycle you hurry up and turn around and go back the way you came from.

That is exactly what the whole articulate approach to using escalation is based largely upon. It is an enormous shelter, that does not face into the malefic. The malefic slides off of it, as a sloping. And just as you have that protection in the winter, for all of those crops of some delicacy—all the young vegetables and plants—so in the summer you have the malefic of the over-heat. The two periods are enormous in sleep: summer and winter. All the plants go to sleep in the Sun in the middle of the Sun, the day, noon. You're going to look at that with *Nicotiana*, and see what happens at noon. And even those that blossom in the daytime and sleep at night, they all are completely recumbent at noon.

Where you have over-cold, you face your south, during the over-cold. And where you have over-heat, you face your north. North, south, east and west; earth, fire, air and water; hot, cold, warm, wet. And so you use those slopes that are angled away from—again you do not face the abortive, the malefic. With the angle as you know how we discussed, it does not enter but is ricocheted off.

I want to describe here about the system of fruit tree. The more green wood, the less blossom; the less fruit. And remember we noted the principle—you can't escape it now—shade in a wood produces green shoots, not hard wood. Green wood. You will never get within a wood, hard wood that you get outside, which remains green wood, and is full of green wood. And its appropriation is the water juice. All the fruit is connected to sugars. Therefore, the more shade: the more greenwood, the less hardwood, the less blossom. Now do you see the fallacy of orchards all blocked together? You have got the utmost shade. All within the trees, under the trees, and around the trees, and trees to each other, all shading each other. So you've got green wood, and not blossom and fruit.

The more light, the more demand. As the Sun demands, as the leader, the energy of the Earth to come out and marry it, so do we with each other and everything else, and so does fruit, and so do flowers, and so do foliages.

Therefore the more light, reduced during the less light period of less green wood, less green wood. But always in the spring the Archangels bring the greenwood. But with the more light capacity, not shady: the least green wood, the more hard wood, and therefore the more blossom and the more fruit.

If you will look at the system that we follow here, you will perceive that that is a following affair, fundamental. At the same time it must be noted that light and shade must be married. How interesting it is that in certain fairy stories and in certain myths suddenly a person has appeared without a shadow; now that is always a mystery beyond mystery, full of fear. How interesting that when a leaf falls off of a tree, it comes down and meets its shadow, and they both disappear. Oh yes, when looked at in words it means nothing.

Therefore you will see that such crops as rhubarb, asparagus do much better if during the over-heat period they are shaded, because they can take rather more cold than a lot of other plants. They should have during the summer some shade, therefore deciduous trees enter the scene. Also realize why we've blanched the endive and the celery. It's the same reason. Because light will turn the juices into sugars and acidities. So the pulling up of the earth stops the light getting to it so that it remains delirious. It does not go into the structure that it wants to, in order to hold the great stem that is going to hold the very blossom like a timber tree.

Now we can look more at these escalating beds with their walls, with their drainage, with the interplay of *revolutionibus*, with perpetual movement in line with the whole *revolutionibus*. You will see that you have entered a sea of culture. And this is why we grow plants in pots. A pot is a little escalating bed. It's raised. It has beautiful drainage, and the *revolutionibus* can enter through the pot to all the little roots. Just that much. Sometimes it enters too much. That is if the climatic supports. And you have to use something else about the pot.

You must know the principle of growing strawberries in barrels. These are indeed tubular raised beds. You simply bore holes in the barrel, and you plant the strawberries all in the sides. And since a strawberry is an acute Alpine, it very much responds, it says, "O that's wonderful! I'm nearly home again."

You can say, "Oh yes, we understand that perfectly." But you can't *understand* it.

You realize that when growing grapes, get a cold house, and you always put the roots outside. All these things implement the same thing. What are we talking about? Acutely, alchemistically, we are talking about, in escalating beds, raising the vibration. And to a certain degree, in flat hollows, you are lowering the vibrations. Now when we say raising and lowering we are also pointing to those two appropriations to the four Archangels, the ahrimanic and the luciferic. So the more you sit in the dell, with the cold air descending, the more you are approaching the influences of the ahrimanic. The more that you are approaching towards the stars, you are of course, in raising the vibrations, approaching the luciferic. And we have said, have we not, that all plants and trees can tolerate the luciferic more than the ahrimanic, by saying, 'heat more than cold'.

Regarding livestock: the balanced diet of livestock is a disease of man's mind. The balanced performance of the manipulation of soil is a disease of man's mind. "Within the infant rind of this small flower, poison hath residence, and medicine, power." (*Romeo and Juliet.*) You can't have one without the other. The idea of wiping out the insects, the birds, the slugs, the dry, the cold, the heat, of wiping it out, can only create fear within us. It cannot create anything else. In the procedure with livestock, it is compliant today that the balance of the diet is worked out as necessitous to the animal. It must be perceived, now that you have discovered and studied your herbs and plants, that the animal, like the plant, like the area, comes under the constitution of the *revolutionibus*, which is perpetual change. At no time is the diet of any animal exactly alike, and at the different periods of the four seasons, the changes are enormous. We can hardly take these things into account, and certainly we cannot measure them. And the thinking that we can, is full of dis-ease.

If livestock is not granted its authority of palate, it must instantly become pregnant to disease, by not being self-reflective to the law of life through its palate and through its senses.

I bring up again the ancient Russian story of the bashilik[1]. Here was an emperor and a princess and a prince. The prince falls in love with the princess, and the emperor agrees that they should be married. And very suitable they are. When the prince has married the princess, and he is living in the emperor's palace, the emperor and the princess have to go on this journey. And as always in these narratives, they give to the prince—the princesses' husband—the hundred keys of the hundred rooms. Ninety-nine you may, one you may not. But the hundredth key is there. And the prince agreed to *yes*, and to *no*, that he would, and would not use the hundredth.

And away the emperor and the princess went. The prince went through the ninety-nine rooms day after day, in ecstasy, growing more and more with the enormous smile of Uriel, was overcome by it, was overwrought, and could not resist the disobedience of the one hundredth. And when he had unlocked the door of the one hundredth, there in the middle of this great room of stone, was encircled in all the bands of the metals of the world: bashilik, this incredible being of the utmost of dragon in human form. And chained with every metal and chain existing in the world to the center of the room.

And when bashilik perceived the prince, he motioned from the fountain for water. And the prince was overcome with bashilik, and could not form his own views at all, in any way whatever. And went to the fountain and brought the cup of water. And bashilik drank, and ordered a repetition, and drank, and ordered a repetition and: every chain was broken, every band was gone, and Bashilik had wings and flew out of the door, seizing the princess who had now returned with the emperor and vanished over the mountains.

A huge bunch of laws there so I won't discuss it. But remember the one hundred keys were on the ring. And out of the greatest fortune— closest of all, hand to glove—came the greatest misfortune.

Of course the prince as you would realize later, goes out into the world, and since he was kind and generous to Nature, had received gifts of a feather, a fish's scale, an ant's fiddle and numerous matters, which when he required them to chase bashilik, they all came and joined the battle, and eventually...

How much is all always taken for granted? We look at all the roses come into bloom, and we say. "Ah, at last! There they are, about time too! They are beautiful aren't they, yes wonderful, well let's have some celery. Oh, there are the strawberries, they're arrived, they're blooming all aren't they?" And everything is that.

Always rebirth, every dawn everything is new. No strawberry ever tastes the same. Not that strawberry with that flavor, ever is that flavor of that strawberry the same. Everything is new.

Only some of the contagions of mechanization could be said in any way to be static at all. We rely on that static, until we press the start of the car and it doesn't work. Never anticipate. Never expect. Never know that the next season is going to be the season because it won't be a season, it isn't. It's something you've never known. Something none of us have ever known. Every seed comes out. We've never known it, we've never known it before. It's all utterly, utterly new. Our whole approach to life must be this.

Believe in spring; believe in summer, but do not *know*. For that knowing is an anchoring that is not true. It is connected with verbosity.

The reflections in Nature are never static, never the same repeat. Only our words. Further to that, added to it, Nature is total. All of us have a pre-sentiment that we think of insects, birds, fish, plants and trees. "Oh yes, yes. That's all a part of Nature. Now we must get on with life." You see, you can say what you like, there's an abyss there, a tremendous abyss of enormous depth that you can't really see the bottom of now. And that the whole performance of human beings is a destiny the same as birds, the same as the bees, the same as the plants, and this is what Pliny and Dioscorides were saying when they said the plants contain something in their life which is inexplicable to us. They cannot show us the human root. But in showing us their obedience to the root, in some way leads us to discover our own, in common.

All the roots of every living thing, all roots, growing, are beneath us, are one focus energy, one radii, all like radii of reflection out of the One. It is pre-eminent that we arrive at this, that we become absolutely compliant with the obedience, the reverence, the destiny that we are, being born. For what miraculous things go with creation and reflection! What miraculous things take place in that beautiful garden among the beautiful plants and the trees!

And now when one states that, do you perceive how now this shines out of all humanity through each individual as a reflective entity? It is only through each individual that the new birth of man's garden, connected with Nature, and that to a degree unknown in the future, it is only through the individual that the miracle of seed takes place through the miracle of man—a man, a person, a woman, a child. It is that child, that woman, that man, living in a garden that becomes the consummation of a reflective marriage, that is spiritual, that produces the ordinance of seeds in plants. And these are new angels, and they are a beatification. This matter that I am referring to has never come about by a mass approach. It's never come about through a laboratory. It's *in* to out; not *out* to in. Can only come about through the destiny marriage of an individual in the garden with Nature.

As one spoke about in the glass house, the reduction of light being the reduction of energy, you had weak plants. Weak plants out of balance that were prone to insects; insects have to eat a lot more of false juice, of weak juice. That is why pests have come about, because as you know in the agriculture of today, with the false juices in the plants as a result of artificial fertilizers, they're full of weak juice, and all the poor insects have to eat fifty and a hundred times more. Just as the wretched child in the city, goes on eating white bread all day, and has no sustenance at all, but only constipation.

This is the creation of pest. If you look at plants like that, and what you call the diseases of pest, which is unbalanced, we must look at us. That if we have, and do, live in an unbalance, we have a weakness. And that if we don't live in the day and sleep in the night, and if we do not observe and comprehend the dawn, and the evening, we are broke, we are not righting. This is a destiny, and our comprehension of living in, with, summer and winter and the two equinoxes becomes a participation that we are living with the four Archangels, marrying the procedure, and we become reflective to the leaderships. And our energies come out and meet those leaderships and are married.

Do you want to talk about it?

Q: Alan, you once mentioned that you had germinated seeds from Tutankhamen's tomb, and you germinated them. Do you think you could talk about that?

Well, of course. It was done through Wisley. How it was done? Ordinary propagative methods through an intensity of controls. Inside controls, following the whole formation of the seed. To a last degree, of refuting argument of the elements. And they germinated... I've forgotten all of the details...it's very interesting, except it was also uninteresting, of course, because the seed was modified, and had to be cracked from the mummification. And, as far as I can remember, it was seventy percent that germinated, but of course the ancientness of the procedure in the plant had become so ancient, that as a plant it couldn't grow. They did rot, some of the seedlings, but they also didn't grow, because they all turned out to be other than they expected, it was a lotus that was no longer known. Merely a matter more in interest than any sense.

Have you come to an understanding now about the enormous danger of wind? Concerning freezing and concerning moistures? You see now why I am always so on my toes about when there is wind in the orchard. That the wind, more than the cold, removes the liquid juices out of a plant, takes away the vitalities, and takes away the virtuous juices and blows them out. Therefore if that plant is positioned where there is wind, not to open its pores with moisture—in other words to be dry—the wind will have less of this advantage. If you apply water when there is wind, the pores will open and the wind will take all the insides of the plant and remove them to another area altogether.

It goes further than that of course, because then the wind, having removed those juices, those juices cannot turn into the sugars and acids which they will need for future occasions. They are delinquent. It becomes a mathematical conglomeration, more and more. Do you follow?

Likewise when there is wind with freezing, the whole of the freezing is trebled to what the freezing alone is. As I have said, upon dry soil, sandy soil with excellent drainage, a plant of that same nature will survive, where in a heavy wet soil—the same temperature, the same climatic—will destroy the plant utterly, and does.

What one is very gently saying here is that there are no extremities whatever that the entry of man and his destiny can bring about regarding protections and controls and changes. It shows you that nothing is a fixation. That in truth, it would seem to be believed—believable—that the whole visible Nature, to us, is a reflection of our behaviors, and our living. That includes their capacity, of course, of resurrection and forgiveness which the whole plant world, as you already perceive, is packed with. You have to put all those together and marry.

Now here is another matter which is interesting. And it's one which is highly questioned—even here I've heard it questioned. If you grow a half-hardy plant, in only a hardy area—that means unsuitable, you understand?—and you manage to achieve it within the more genial climatic period, you take the seed, you have not changed the constitution of the issue of those plants to any other plants taken from any other area, as regards that capacity of dealing with the element. Do you understand what I am saying? That is a whole key that needs to be looked at. It means that there's nothing static. Do you follow?

This does not mean that you cannot bring about a change, but it does mean that the change as Bach (of Dr. Bach's Flower Remedies) says is not to cure an illness or a disease but to cure the person. Do you follow? So it is not the plant that you change—which is what they are all trying to do today—but the relationships.

How fascinating it is that in all the variety of plants, they all have these capacities of managing here and not managing there.

You realize that in the whole procedure of crab apples, there's very little season. They're all just crab apples. They all happen in August. The moment that man's *image* came in, we had a different apple, not a little round green one, but a long red one, married with the *Malus sylvatica*. And out of that there was an *idée*, well that's enormous. "I would love one in January." "What did you say? You shall have three wishes because you're good. What are they?" "Oh! An apple in January!" Abracadabra! Born, just like the motorcar, just like the expressway, just like the office, just like social security. And so are gardens.

Out of the whole of that are tinned strawberries, and chrysanthemums all year 'round, and frozen peas. I spoke of birth, everything fresh, never anticipated, always exceptional, new. The whole thing in the concept of the reflection of the human is born. They eat tin strawberries all the year. They have no desire, when the beauty of the Archangel says, "Perceive!" They don't perceive and they don't want. And they go on stuffing themselves with tin strawberries, until they have an apoplectic fit.

The seasons and the compliance of the obedience to the law of the rotations, produces early potatoes—those potatoes in that frame are now ready; they will be the most delicious potatoes. You can't have any! That the potatoes then come in the middle season, they come in the late season. Now the late ones you can store—if you try to store these new potatoes we are going to raise, well you wouldn't have a chance of course, but they wouldn't be protected, they would go rubbery in two weeks. But the old, the big potatoes—you see how full of words we are—what we are talking about is the Archangels; they have blessed this matter. Do you follow? Now do you see what we are talking about?

There are apples you can put in the store, and you must pick them at a certain time. You mustn't pick them when you decide you will. It won't work. Do you follow? And you must put certain herbs with them, not what you think you will, "Oh I like this. It smells nice." Won't work.

---

1 Alan's pronunciation of what is usually called a 'basilisk' is obscure, possibly conflated with the French word for basilica, *basilique*. Equally arcane is the origin of the Russian tale of one hundred doors, of which one is to be unopened. There are variants on this theme in the *Thousand Nights and a Night*, and in the Grimm Brothers.

King of the Golden River[1]

Carmel in the Valley, Virginia
October 26, 1979

Good morning. You won't need any notebooks. Just make yourselves very comfortable.

In a secluded and mountainous part of Stiria there was in olden days a valley of the most surprising fertility. This valley was surrounded by great rocky mountains that rose up on all sides, jutting right up into the sky, and whose very summits were always snow-covered, rising amongst the clouds. So that being with snow upon them, there were flowing great streams that fell in cataracts over the precipices.

One such rode to the west where it came out onto a precipice, and fell from a great height in a great waterfall. And such was its position that from the whole area, up from this valley, that when the whole valley was in the darkness of evening, or the darkness of predawn, that the Sun would strike this cataract as it fell, and the whole stream would appear to be gold, and was lit up, and thrown up by the ways of fire of sunlight all around it. And so it stood out long after the rest of the land was all in shadow and darkness. So it appeared with its rainbows over it, linking it to the mountains. It appeared completely brilliant, and became known as the Golden River.

It is very strange that all of these cataracts and this golden river did not flow into the valley itself. They always flowed into the other side, where they flowed away down the mountains into the plains and away over the lands through the cities towards the seas. But, so beautiful were these mountains and the great peaks covered with snow, that they drew the clouds at all times of the year. And that even when the whole of the rest of the country around was dried up and arid with heat of summer, so the rains would fall in this valley most beautifully and gently.

Therefore, in this valley so great were the crops, so high the hay, so red and rosy the apples, so blue the grapes, so rich the wine and so sweet the honey, that it became known as Treasure Valley. It was always called by everybody the Treasure Valley.

Now this valley was owned by three brothers: Schwartz, Hans and Gluck. Schwartz and Hans were much the two elder, and they were really rather gauche and angry creatures—they were very enormously built, they were very strong—but they had very bristly eyebrows that they always forced down and looked out from under, so that you couldn't see into their eyes at all. And yet you always felt that they were looking rather too far into your eyes. They were also, of course, farmers. They farmed this valley, and they farmed it very well indeed. For they destroyed everything that didn't pay for its keep. For instance, they shuffled the black birds out of hand, because they ate the fruit. And likewise the hedgehogs, less they should suffer the cows. And of course they wiped out all of the grasshoppers, less they should get into the grain, and the cicadas, because they would be annoying and sing all day in the trees.

Of course, also, they had never known to be charitable. They never gave anything to the poor, and they certainly never went to Mass, and they objected to tithes. They also treated their work people very harshly, and gave them as little as they possibly could, and took everything from what they earned. And so, amongst all of these people they became known as the Black Brothers.

Likewise of course they were very clever. Because during the period when the rest of the country dried up, and the crops were poor, this valley was always of course a treasure. So all the people from all over the vicinity came to the farm. And of course they had to beg, and they had to pay. And they went away cursing the Black Brothers. So it was assumed that they were very well named.

Now the other brother of course was very young, he wasn't yet fourteen, but he was of an entirely opposite nature. He was very generous and very, very kind-hearted to all living things. And as you can imagine, of course, he didn't see eye to eye with his brothers, and of course certainly they didn't see eye to eye with him. So that he was continuously rained with blows, had his ears boxed, and was generally deployed for everything unpleasant. Had all the household duties to do like scrubbing the floors, cleaning the food, preparing the food, cleaning the boots, for which of course he got endless cuts and curses.

Life went on like this over a number of years. And so it happened that one year was particularly bad, and the whole of the vicinity had had heavy rains throughout the summer and that all of the crops had failed. They had not been able to reap the crops in before the rain came, the fruit did not ripen, and the hay was all ruined. And again they had to come to the Black Brothers' farm, and again they were met with the same treatment: extortion. Even to the degree that those who were absolutely starving were left at the door with nothing.

It was on such a morning and on such a day, which followed, that Gluck had been left to look after the house, with the usual provocative warning to let nobody in and to give nothing out. That the doors had been closed and a cold winter was setting in, and Gluck was sitting by the hearth, very close to the hearth, for the walls were rather damp and running, stonewalls.

He had been sitting tending a leg of mutton, on the spit, which was turning over the hearth. And it was just beginning to smell rather delicious and looking a little bit brown, and he couldn't help thinking in his mind's eye—his sparkling blue eyes—he couldn't help thinking how pleasant and different it would be if only his brothers realized how delightful it would be to ask a lot of the neighbors in to share this wonderful piece of mutton. When after all, everyone else was living on terribly dry bread, whilst they had such incorruptible supplies, and this beautiful piece of mutton, which they couldn't possibly divest of themselves. Just as he was thinking thee things: *knock knock* on the front door. "Gracious me," Gluck thought. "That's very strange." And yet it was a very soft *knock knock*, as though the knocker was actually muffled. Then again, he thought it must be the wind, for who would dare to knock twice on their knocker? He was just thinking these things when lo! It was not the wind, there it was again: *KNOCK KNOCK*. But now there was no question about it, it was as though the knocker was in a great hurry. So he jumped up and ran into the wing of the house where he could open the window and look out to see who it was.

Gluck saw the most extraordinary man he had ever seen in his life. There, standing at the door, was a little man with a very long nose—almost the color of brass—with very gay eyes, twinkling out of behind long lashes, hair down below his shoulders, like mustard and peppered silk, and two moustachios, which came out from either side under his nose, and twirled down like a couple of corkscrews, and seemed to go down into his pockets. He was not above four-foot-six, and he was dressed most extraordinarily. Somehow all his clothes ended at the back, sticking out like a swallowtail. And over the door was a great cloak, which normally must have been six times too long for him, that the wind, which was blowing enormously and was carrying out behind him right away into the bushes and trees down the farm.

On top of his head pulled over his hair was a hat going up into a point that was at least four feet high, which was as high as he was himself. And out of that going on up was a black feather at least three foot more, that, out of wet and rain and wind, was somewhere hanging down beneath his swallowtail like a beaten puppy dog's tail. Gluck simply stayed motionless, gazing out of the window at this extraordinary little man. And so he just gazed. And so it would have just gone on.

But the little man, having knocked another concerto very rapidly, who was aware that his cape was flying around some trees in the back, and turning 'round to take in a few turns of the cloak, perceived Gluck's face looking out of the window. So the little man said, "Hello young man. That's no way to answer a knock at the door. Let me in. I'm wet." Gluck simply stared. The man said, "Did you hear me? I said, *let me in!* I am wet." Gluck said, "I am very sorry sir, I can't do that." The little man said, "Can't do that? Why not?" Gluck said, "It would be the death of me. My brothers would kill me! They'd beat me to death when they came back. I am not allowed to let anyone in." The man said, "I am very wet, and cold. You've got a wonderful fire dancing on the walls in there, I can see it. I need to dry myself. Now let me in."

Gluck, who'd been leaning out the window for some considerable time, discovered that he himself was very wet and very cold. He climbed back through the window and closed it. And then he noticed the mutton, and then he noticed the fire. Then he noticed the fire playing on the walls. And he thought of the little man wet at the door. "Oh well, it doesn't matter if they beat me again. I've had enough beatings, haven't I?" So he ran to the door, and he opened it. And at that moment, the little man came in with such a swish, a huge gust of wind literally shook the walls, the whole roof reverberated and even the chimneys rattled. He closed the door quickly. The next thing was, the little man was sitting by the hearth very comfortably, but of course he had to put his hat up the chimney, because it didn't fit in the ceiling.

So after a few minutes silence, as Gluck was expecting the silence to be broken by the visitor, and finding it not so, he said to the little man, "You will soon dry there sir." He went on turning the mutton, and sat by the hearth also. But as Gluck watched and turned the mutton—and didn't like to stare at the man, of course—he was aware that the little man was not drying at all. That water was beginning to run between all of the cobbles of the stones of the room, up the kitchen. There were streams, that were beginning to grow into almost rivers. And that when he looked at the little man, he saw that this water was pouring off the hat, down over the shoulders, into gullies all down his cape. And what was worse, that there were two spouts coming out of these corkscrew mustaches, which were whirling around like two fountains into his pockets, and bubbled out. Bubbly water spilled all over the floor and produced these enormous streams. And Gluck said, "Pardon me sir, may I take your hat?" "No thank you."

He turned the mutton. Now his feet were in water. He looked all around, he said, "Excuse me sir, but can I take your cloak?" "No thank you, I am perfectly comfortable." "Could I do something to help make you dry?" "No, no, perfectly comfortable. It's all right." "But it's not all right. You see, the whole place is swimming in water." "Good," said the little man.

Gluck said, "Well, excuse me sir, but you see, if my brothers come back and find you here, they really will beat me to death." "Oh, I'll see to that," said the little man. "Oh sir, please no! You mustn't talk to them. You mustn't wait until they come. You must go before they come back." "Oh," said the little man, "is that so? How long can I stay?" "Well...not long, as soon as the mutton is done, you must go. The water, you see..." "Oh," said the little man, "It's perfectly alright." But Gluck said, "It's not alright, you see. It's all wet!"

There was silence again. After a little, he tried to take no notice of the water, and turned the mutton again, and it really was brown and smelling very delicious. And the little man with twinkling eyes looked at him and said, "Couldn't I have a little piece?" "Oh impossible, sir!" "Oh, but just a little piece. If you took it off near the knuckle." "No sir, indeed sir. That is...I couldn't do that. They would really kill me by beating me if I did that." The man said, "You see, I'm very hungry. I really am very hungry. And I'm very old." Gluck said, "Well sir, tell you what, they did promise me one slice today. You could have that." So he went and warmed the plate, and got the carving knife and fork, and he cut a nice big slice out, by the knuckle.

Bang! Bang! Bang! at the door. "Oh!" Gluck quickly put it back, trying to fit it so as it would look like as if it had never been cut, and fit perfectly. And then, as he rushed to the door, the little man swirled off of his seat into the middle of the room, and started twirling 'round. Gluck rushed to the door and opened it, and in came Schwartz and Hans. Schwartz drove his umbrella straight into Gluck's face, and Hans butted him on his ears, and said, "What the devil did you keep us waiting at the door for all this time, when we knocked? Can't you let us...bless my soul, who the devil is this?" Gluck said, "Well, brother, excuse me but um..." "Excuse me nothing," said his brother, "What do you mean by it? Who is this? Who are you, sir?" The little man said, "A very good morning to you, sirs," and started bowing with his great hat and twirling his feather up and down extremely politely.

Gluck said, "Brother, please, you see, he was very wet, and cold, and at the door and so I..." At that moment Schwartz picked up the rolling pin and went to hit Gluck on the head, at that same moment the little man interposed his long conical hat. At the very moment the rolling pin—which alighted, of course, on the hat, and not Gluck's head—water squelched like an absolute cataract in every direction, and at the same moment the rolling pin turned a fast series of summersaults throughout the air, flew into the corner, against one wall and then the other, and fell down in the corner on the floor.

There was some amazement over this. The brothers quickly recovered, by Hans coming to, and going up to the little man, and said, "Exactly what are you doing here? Explain yourself." The man said, "Well, you see, I was very wet and very cold, and I asked your brother to let me in. I wanted to get warm." Hans said, "Well, you have your clothes on, your hat, you've got a great feather: go out! Walk!" Schwartz also inter-joined likewise. The man said, "Excuse me sirs, but I am also very hungry. I am also very old." At each of these comments they interposed, and told him to get out. At which he became more polite, and more begging, and pointed out to them the deficiencies of his age, and of how wet he really was, and that he had not eaten for days, and was indeed wanting food.

And at last, since he did not move, Hans went to him, and said, "Are you going to get out?" and went to seize him upon the collar to throw him out, where upon the moment that he touched the collar he too did a fast series of summersaults twirling in the air, struck the corner, one wall and then the other, and then fell down on top of the rolling pin. Schwartz was en-livened by this, and rushed at him enraged, and said, "How dare you treat my brother…" at the same moment, as he was about to strike him, to carry him out, he likewise did a vast series of summersaults, went twirling through the air, flew at the most horrific speed into the corner, and fell on top of his brother, where they sat in consternation.

Gluck stood with his mouth and eyes wide open. The little man meantime, in the center of the room, had started to rotate in the opposite direction, so that the whole of his costume began to wind around him. He then seized his hat, with its feather sticking stout straight, and with a very gigantic bow, he said, "I wish you good morning, gentlemen. I will call again at twelve o'clock tonight. You will understand that after the hospitality that I received this morning, that will be my last visit to this valley."

Schwartz and Hans both attempted to disable themselves from each other's mix up. And with gaspings and groanings and furious ejaculations, were about to rise and curse, when a cloud evolved into the middle of the room, and the door banged. And the cloud passed the windows, and it seemed to go into the most extravagant shapes, floating down amongst the bushes and trees of the valley, and disappeared over the horizon.

They picked themselves up and approached Gluck. They said, "Well, what do you have to say for yourself?" And of course Gluck made no reply. Whereupon Schwartz said, "Very well. Mutton. Let's serve the mutton." So the mutton was brought and Schwartz took a carving knife and fork, and of course, "Ah, I see. So, it's already been cut. By you?" "Yes." said Gluck. "I see. So that you would get the biggest helping and all the gravy. Typical." *Bang-bang, bang-bang*: box on the ears. "Time to go to the coal cellar and stay there." Gluck retreated to the coal cellar where he stayed. The two brothers ate themselves silly, put away and locked in the cupboard what they couldn't eat, drank themselves thoroughly, and went to bed, having shuttered up the house.

So the hands of the clock went round, and acutely at midnight, the most incredible commotion of noise, like an earthquake. Schwartz and Hans sat up on their bolsters in bed. This incredible noise. The whole place shook, everything was in water, the stars were above them, and they were sitting on a bed in the open. At that moment Schwartz managed to ejaculate on sufficiently waking up, "What is this?" And suddenly, in the middle of it all, seated on a revolving cushion as it were, was the little man, completely dressed with this hat on, smiling on his cushion. And he said, "I am so sorry to discommode you, gentlemen, but you will remember this morning that I did say that I would visit you at midnight, and that it would be my last visit. Well I would recommend you, for if you look at the floor and you see that you have no roof, you will go to Gluck's room, where you will find that I have left the roof on for him, and that you would spend the rest of the night there, perhaps." At that moment the cushion began to spiral very rapidly, and in a great commotion, swept away and vanished into the night.

When the brothers did wake up in the morning, and looked about, they looked out the window, all that was left, literally of the whole cottage and building was just the one room with the roof on it. But when they looked out of the window there was the tragedy. There was not a tree nor a shrub nor a plant in the entire valley. The waters had swept right through. And there was nothing but a red mire of mud throughout the whole valley. They searched the house, there was nothing whatever left of the house or in it their possessions. Everything was gone. All of the crops, cereals, even the pile of gold, which they kept, locked in a room. There was only one thing left, the kitchen table. And on the kitchen table a small white card. And on the card in rather spidery scrawl was written: *Southwest Wind, Esquire.*

Well, Southwest Wind was as good as his word. For not only had he ravaged the entire valley, but also his connections with all the other winds—in particular the west winds—had all come to agreement on the same matter. And of course they did not visit. So that now from then on there were no rains in Treasure Valley at all. No rains whatever came. And as there was no river, there was no moisture. And the whole valley was from that time onwards a desert.

The brothers had nothing to farm, there was nothing they could raise, they spent what little money they had left, and they had no means of living or existence. So they decided on a profession. They decided to go to the city, and since they had stowed away some ill-gotten treasure in the way of gold ornaments, to which they had invested their ill-gotten gains, they decided that it was a very good knaves' profession to become goldsmiths.

After they talked it over, they decided to proceed with this, since they had all these gold objects. And so they hired a furnace, and set it out. So they turned the gold objects of their ill-gotten gain into salable gold, and made money. And the unfortunate part of it was that they were—in the middle of a knavish practice—they were stowing into the gold, which was sold, mostly copper inside. When people came to know that, of course they didn't deal. And there was another matter, which again disapproved the whole issue, and that was, although Gluck worked the furnace, and attended the operations very satisfactorily, that all the gold that was sold, they spent as money drinking and eating, and looking after themselves. So that they very quickly spent that gold issue, and had nothing again. Nothing whatever. Except one last item. And that one last item happened to be an extremely valuable gold mug, which belonged to Gluck.

Which Gluck was extortionately fond of it, for very secret reasons. Not that he drank anything particular out of it, other than water or milk, or such things, but because of who gave it to him. It was an old uncle who told him a very fascinating story about it, and also it was solid gold, that it was incredibly valuable, and most exquisitely wrought. And Gluck had always been very, very, very deeply, secretly fond of it. However, the two brothers, as you can imagine in their manner, merely laughed in his face, seized the mug from him, and tossed it into the furnace. They went out to drink, and left Gluck to attend to the melting of this pot, until it was ready to be poured into a mold, so that it could be sold.

Gluck was very upset. He went to the furnace; he opened the lid, he looked and he saw this beautiful little mug. It was really a very large mug, and it had always been, even with his brothers, extortionately admired, for whenever they drank their Rhenish wine from it, they had always found that this curious design on it, and its molding, had a reaction. For the two handles that were on either side were in the form of the most excruciatingly delicate woven silk golden hair. And that made the handles. That hair flew up and turned around, and came down and joined under a face. A very curious face that was both frightening and yet beautiful. And that that face was hardly visible in the molding other than two eyes, which seemed to glint. The curious thing was that when you drank out of it, you were always caught by your eyes being caught on the glint of these two eyes on the side of the mug. And that after a period they seemed to weep. So it was very, very strange all together.

So it was that at looking at this again, in the furnace, and seeing it begin to melt, that Gluck was very upset and disconsolate. He then he looked and he saw that the nose and the molding of the face was beginning to run and turn into liquid gold. So he closed the lid and walked away from the furnace, towards the windows were it was cooler, where he could sit and contemplate, for this window looked right on to those mountains that I told you about.

He looked right up at those great mountains, rising up into the sky, snowcapped, and it was evening time now. The furnace was molting the gold into this crucible. And he looked up into the mountain and he saw the whole beauty of the evening. The whole valley was in darkness; the rest of the countryside was all dark. The stars were glimmering out and yet where this water shot over this precipice, this exquisite gold was shining. This golden water, all sparkling, throwing up the most incredible light.

And he couldn't help thinking out loud: "Oh dear, if only that river really were gold. How nice it would be." "No it wouldn't, Gluck my boy!" said a voice right at his ear. Gluck jumped up. There was nobody there. He looked all around, kept turning to the back, but there was nobody there. He looked under the table, but there was nobody. He couldn't make out what...

He went and sat down again and looked up, and was again caught by the exquisiteness, which nobody could evade, of this waterfall and this gold, which was now more brilliant than ever. But now he thought, but not out loud this time, he thought silently to himself, "It really would— if you come to look at it—it really would be nice if that were gold." "No it wouldn't, my boy!" said the voice. Gluck really now couldn't make it out. He jumped up, kept twirling around to see if somebody was hiding behind his back. He twirled. He ran to the door. He looked up the stairs, he went to the basement, he looked down the stairs. And then suddenly, there was the voice, going: *la la lily lily la, la la la lily lily la, tra la la lalala*, rather like a kettle on the boil. Wherever he went, he couldn't find out where it was. Seemed like an echo. Then at last he was quite sure it was nearer the furnace. He ran to the furnace. *Yes, it was! It's coming from the furnace.*

So he opened the furnace door, and out came the voice. Then he opened the crucible, and the voice stopped. And then in quiet clear tones came the voice, "Let me out." Gluck was quick to slam the door. He went back to the window and stood with both his hands to his jaw, in a real fright with his mouth open, and his eyes literally falling out. "Gluck, let me out, I say, I'm ready." Gluck rushed to the fire, pulled the crucible out, and unstoppered it. And now it was pure molten gold. There was no mug left. But instead of reflecting Gluck's face, Gluck was looking into the face that was on the mug, which was looking straight into his eyes. And again Gluck was so terrified that he backed straight to the windows. And again the voice came to him, "Pour me out, I am ready." No move. "Gluck, I said, pour me out, I am too hot." No move.

"Gluck, look, be a good boy and pour me out." Gluck eventually managed to pull his nerves together, took the crucible, and tilted it to pour the gold out. Instead of which, what happens? Out comes a pair of legs attached to a body, two arms, a head, and there is a little dwarf a foot and a half high, dressed in the most exquisite shining gold raiment, with the most articulate, incredible, and terrifying eyes and expression. Beatific and malefic, connected to the last degree.

Gluck simply stood aghast. Whereupon, this little one and a half foot dwarf tries his a arms, tries the movements of his head, and then, stretches one leg out straight in the air, and brings it down—rather like a ballet dancer—and bangs it on the floor. Having made quite sure that everything was in good order, approaches Gluck and says, "Nothing to be alarmed about." And so Gluck not knowing what to do, said, "No sir, of course not." The little man now takes three steps of at least three feet, poising his feet in the air, and bringing them down, and then turns and comes straight up to Gluck. And says, "Do you know who I am?" And Gluck can't answer.

So the little man turns away and takes six steps at least six feet long, and points his feet in the air, brings them down on the ground, and then comes and stands flat in front of Gluck, as though expecting him to say something. And as Gluck does not say anything: "You will be surprised to know that I am the King of the Golden River." And again does one of his six-foot stampings, up and down, and then again faces Gluck again. Whereupon Gluck, who feeling as he must come out of an idiotic silence, says, "I trust Your Majesty is very well."

The golden dwarf took no notice of this remark whatever. He said, "Yes, I am what you mortals call the King of the Golden River. I have been, as you have known me in the mug, for a long time, by enchantment. And it is your actions, and what you have done, that have liberated me from that enchantment. And because of that, I am glad to and prepared to be of service to you. Therefore, *attend!* Any person who will take three drops of holy water and drop them in the source of the outflow of the Golden River, up at the cataract, for him, for that person, the river shall be turned to gold. But nobody shall make a second attempt. And anybody who drops three drops of unholy water will be turned into a black stone."

Without another word, the little dwarf pirouetted, walked straight into the furnace, turned red, then yellow, then white, and disappeared. Gluck ran to the furnace and looked in, looked up the chimney, and he ran to the window and looked up at the mountain, and he ran to the furnace. And then said, "Oh dear, oh dear, oh dear, oh dear! My mug! Where is my mug?"

At that moment Schwartz and Hans came in, in no good mood. And indeed of course when they found what had happened to the mug, that mood changed to black anger. They pounded Gluck for his prevarications and lies, excuses, for there was no answer as to where was the lost mug. Having pounded him for a quarter of an hour, 'twas night time and they all went to sleep.

What was a surprise in the morning when they approached Gluck for the truth, and he held steadfastly to the whole story which he had related to them, concerning the dwarf, the King of the Golden River, and the prophesy. For he related it acutely word to word correctly, and he could not be lying. Whereof they were both very excited and elated about such a possibility, and started an argument as to which of the two brothers should be the first to go and try the gold of the river. And this argument grew into a quarrel, and this quarrel resulted in drawn swords, and a fight took place outside the house. The neighbors rushed in, and unable to separate, called the justice. Hans ran away and hid, and Schwartz was captured. Taken, tried, fined, and as he had no money to pay the fine, was put in prison. This greatly delighted Hans as you can imagine. Hans immediately decided to take the opportunity and be the first to get the gold.

The question of course, was how to get the holy water. However, he pretended to go to evening services, and in doing so, stole the water from the font, and put it in a phial. And so the next morning, long before dawn, he prepared a basket, plenty of food, bread, two bottles of wine, and of course of all things, hung at his belt a phial of holy water.

It was a beautiful day. The sky was blue, the sea was exorbitant. But somehow he had a great worry on his mind. In any case, he had to go through the town on the way to climb the mountain, and he passed the prison and looked in through the grill and laughed at Schwartz.

He then went on, and started to climb. He looked up and he could just see, in the vagueness of the morning light, the great cataract. And he entirely set his whole thinking on that, so he didn't observe the beauty of the day, but only one thing was in his mind. So he set out at a very incongruous pace, and climbed, and suddenly struck a glacier which he hadn't been aware of before.

And he found this glacier almost impossible to cross. It was full of jaggedness. It was nothing concerning ice about it: it was almost as though it was full of human incongruousness. All the time there were voices and creakings and crackings of the ice that were not like ice, but like humans in dissipation. This caused a nostalgia to creep all over him. And he slipped, and fell and cut himself, and hurt himself very badly. And shortly he lost the basket with the food and the wine. He managed for several hours to literally creep on all fours across this glacier and threw himself on the turf on the other side, where he was expecting a better route.

However, when he had recovered sufficiently, he realized that he was extremely thirsty, that his wine was gone, the basket of food was gone, and that there was nothing to resort to, but to suck some pieces of ice. And this he did. When he looked at the path, he realized that it was not the beautiful path that he anticipated, but it was all slime. There were no plants, there were no flowers, there were no insects, there were no trees, it was terribly steep, and he slipped the whole time. And it got worse, and it got worse, and yet as he went up it got hotter, and the Sun scorched and burned. After an hour, he couldn't tolerate it, because he was absolutely parched. And still he was trying and pressing on with what strength he had.

And he suddenly thought he couldn't go on any further, without something to drink. Then he bethought of him of the phial of holy water, "Well, there's quite a lot there. It is only three drops that I need. And if I don't get there, what's the use of the three drops anyway?" So he thought that out, "I'll have a sip." So he took the phial from his girdle, and at the same moment lying almost at he feet, that he hadn't noticed was a little dog. And the dog was paralyzed, unable to move, at the last stages of existence. Ants were crawling over its tongue. At the same moment, his eyes flickered and looked up at him, into his eyes, and to the flask. He kicked it with his boot, out of the way, so he couldn't see it, and took several gulps, recorked the flask, hung it on his belt, and climbed better.

But the way got harder. It became more dark, more purple, and there were clouds collecting. And yet, the Sun, the heat of the Sun, became hotter, and he became more and more exhausted. He tried to hurry and couldn't. And after another hour, it was already well past noon, he was struggling on, and realized that he couldn't possibly go any further, but what he must have water for his throat.

At last he gave up struggling and stopped, and took the flask again and when he looked at it, there was plenty to spare, to have a good sip. So he uncorked it. And at that moment there was a child, almost the same condition as the dog. Its eyes actually opened and looked into his eyes, and looked at the phial. He quickly turned away, so he couldn't see it, and took a long drink. And corked it up.

When he looked up, he saw that he had not so far to go to get to the cataract, and so he climbed on grabbing with his hands. Now it was harder than ever it seemed. And a thunderstorm came up, and was building into great darkness, and he became frightened in himself. He was only five hundred feet below the cataract, looking up at it, and he thought he couldn't even make that. And so he looked at the phial, he saw there was still enough to spare, to have the three drops, and that he would at least have the power to get there. At the same moment, there, stretched over a rock, was very, very old man, almost breathless, who groaned, and glanced at the phial, and glanced in his eyes. And again he turned hurriedly away, and there was a violent flash of lightning, and the thunder roared. It became extremely dark. Purple clouds set over everything. In darkness, he became bewildered with fright.

He hung the phial quickly at his belt, and struggled on up, and grasped the rocks, and pulled, and each one was harder. And he groaned and screamed, and pulled, and eventually, he was right beside the roaring torrent. Standing on the very edge, and there was the water swirling, gushing over the cascade of the precipice, with this great cataract. He was about to turn the whole thing into gold, and he took the phial, and there was a great crash of lightening and thunder. He flung the three drops in the phial into the great river, and there was a terrifying shriek and a flash, and he fell into the water.

And there was a great black rock with water gushing over it. A shining great black rock.

When Hans did not return, Gluck was very frightened. What might have happened? And eventually he went to the prison and told Schwartz. And of course Schwartz was extremely happy and glad, but pretended to be upset. He told Gluck that he could not possibly go on while in the prison, and that something must be done to liberate him. So Gluck promised, as they had nothing whatever, that he would go to a goldsmith's, since he knew something now about furnaces and smelting, he would go to a goldsmith and hire himself out, and raise enough money to liberate Schwartz.

This he did, and worked hard and diligently, and was poorly paid, but very quickly had enough money, and he went and paid the justice. Schwartz pretended to be very grateful indeed, and was liberated. Immediately Schwartz thought in his mind of what must have happened.

He felt that the only thing that could really have gone wrong—for he knew Hans' strength and capacity—was that he had been probably turned to a black stone because of some misdemeanor over the holy water.

So Schwartz took some of the money and bought from a bad man, holy water. He put this in the phial in his girdle, and early the next morning he prepared for the journey. He took also with him a basket, with the loaves and the bread and the food, and the wine, and set off. And again it was a beautiful day. But again this man had the one thought in his mind. He looked up and saw this cataract, and that that was the whole of his goal, and that was his attainment. And he too likewise climbed too fast, exhausted himself, and found the horrors unsuspected of this glacier, where he also fell, where he also lost his provision.

Schwartz just managed to get to the other side and fell upon the bank, and used the ice. He then too began to climb and found it more difficult than he had ever known or expected. It was all slippery and slime, and there were no plants, nothing to hang onto—no bushes, no trees. And after an hour, he couldn't tolerate it any more. And he had the same thought as Hans, and he undid the phial from his belt, and looked and said, "Well, I have ample in here. At least I can moisten my throat sufficiently." And at the same moment, in opening the stopper, perceived the child, and the child immovable, in the throws of death. The child's eyes opened and looked into his, and looked at the phial, and he too spurned it and turned away, and took the drink. And restoppered, and as he restoppered, it was as though a cloud came over the whole setting.

He became terrified and frightened inside. And that fright spread through his veins, and it was harder and harder every step to climb. And after another hour he couldn't go on any further, he was exhausted and terrified. He stopped again and looked at the phial, and was about to unstopper it, when there was the old man even beckoning for a drink. And again he turned away and spurned, and drank. Stoppering up the phial, he climbed again, and he too eventually reached, in the last extremities of his capacity, five hundred feet beneath the cataract. And he realized that by some means he could get there. He looked at the phial, and to be sure to get there, he only had to have a sip. And as he unstoppered the phial, he thought he saw Hans, and he laughed in the gurgling dryness of his throat, and said, "Huh! Do you remember when you looked through the bars of the prison? Did you ask for water then?" And he kicked with his boot, and he drank, and he climbed.

Again the storm came, and the lightning and the thunder, and it became black, and pitch. Eventually he was on the edge of the great cataract, with the stream tearing by with its crystal clear waters. And he knew that in one moment he was going to turn the whole thing into gold, and this enormous crash of thunder and this great flash of lightening, and he quickly threw the phial into the water, and the whole sod fell away from under him, and with a great shriek, he was a black stone, beside the other.

For a long, long time Gluck was terrified. He couldn't imagine what could have happened, and had all sorts of terrifying thoughts. And so he went and worked, and was very poorly paid with his goldsmith. And during that time he cogitated, and he kept remembering what the little dwarf had told him, how friendly and kind he had been and seemed. Eventually he was overwrought by this and felt that he must make an attempt. So he went to the priest and asked if he might have, and the priest gladly gave him the holy water, and he prepared the phial at his belt. He did take some water and some bread in a basket. And very early in the morning, a most exquisite morning, full of sunlight arriving, and the stars were disappearing, he set off and started to climb.

As he looked about, he found it very beautiful. And he climbed. And when he came to the glacier, he was indeed very frightened, and was alarmed at these extraordinary sounds that were more human than natural. But he plucked up his courage, and eventually crossed. But in doing so, he too fell, and hurt himself badly, and lost all his provender. Eventually got to the other side and rested. And he used the ice to suck, to recover.

And then he looked up, and he bethought him of what he was going to do, and he was hoping to restore and find Schwartz and Hans, and all of the other things that were in his mind. And as he looked at the path, he saw that there was grass, and that there were little plants, and they had flowers, and that there were butterflies and dragonflies about, and there were roots to hang on to. And as he climbed it got a little easier, and each climb got a little easier, with more bushes, and more stepping stones and rocks. But after an hour, he too was exhausted by the energies, and couldn't go on for being absolutely parched, gasping in the throat. And he too thought of the phial, and he too thought whether it would be reverent or not to do such a thing. And then he felt he would not be able to attain his goal if he didn't do this.

So he took it, and as he was unstoppering it, an old man with a staff came 'round the corner of the path, and begged of him water. And Gluck looked at him and shook his head, but the man looked into his eyes. And Gluck unstoppered the phial, handed it to him, and said, "But be careful! Only very little. Very little, please!" But the man drank fully half, and thanked him, and as Gluck looked around, he saw him hurrying down the hill.

Now as Gluck turned, his throat wasn't dry, and he was happier. He thought what a beautiful day it was; it was one of the most beautiful days he'd ever known. And the plants became more and more enchanting, and he enjoyed them. And all the colors as he looked up, and the sky was blue, and he began to enjoy it and adore. So he managed another hour, but then he too was parched again, and literally couldn't move, and felt paralyzed all over. And he took the phial and looked at it and saw that there was still half, and that three drops was what was wanted.

And so he pulled the stopper, and at the same moment, he saw out of the corner of his eye, stretched on a rock, the little child, in the last throes. And that the eyes met his, and looked at the phial. And he went up to her, and opened her mouth, and poured in all except three drops. And as he put the stopper back carefully, he saw that there was enough left, he hung it at his side, and as he hung it at his side, he saw movement. As he turned 'round to see what the movement was, the child was running down the hill. And he found that he wasn't dried up and parched, and he could climb a little more, although he was suffering greatly.

And so he set off. The path was easier now. Everything was brighter, and birds were singing, and he even felt happier somehow, inside. He climbed a little faster. And then he got to that position, when at last, he looked about him and there at that position five hundred feet above, was the cataract, with the water falling over. And yet, he literally couldn't move, he couldn't stir another limb. He couldn't even make an ejaculation from his throat. And there, as he looked at the phial, and saw only three drops, he realized he couldn't move any more.

And there out of the corner of his eye on the left now, he saw the little dog, lying prostrate. And it looked into his eyes, and it looked at the phial. And he turned away. He tried to walk. But he stumbled. He couldn't move. And he turned, he looked at the dog, and he tried to turn away, but couldn't.

Suddenly out of his cracked, parched throat: "Bother! Bother the King of the Golden River! And the gold too!" And he seized the stopper, pulled it out, and put the phial in the dog's mouth and poured it in. The little dog jumped up on all fours, and then it stood up on its hind legs, and its tail disappeared. Its ears grew longer, and longer, and longer, and vanished. And quite suddenly, it began to turn into a dwarf. And in three seconds, standing in front of him, very erect, very severe, was the golden dwarf, King of the Golden River.

Gluck realized what he had said. And the dwarf shook his head. He said, "Don't worry." And Gluck said, "I needed the three drops..." And the King of the River suddenly looked totally different. He looked more severe and more stern, to the very rocks in the mountains in their severity. And he said, "Your two brothers have been turned into black stones." And Gluck jumped aside and said, "Oh, but you couldn't do that! So cruel." And the King of the Golden River said, "Do you think I am allowed to permit such behavior?" Then he grew more stern still, and he said, "When the water of purity is refused to the weary and the dying, it is unholy, even though it is blessed by all the angels of heaven. And when the water of charity is given, it is holy, even though it is defiled by death.

At which the golden dwarf stooped, and plucked a lily, upon whose three petals were three crystal drops of dew. These he shook into the phial which Gluck was holding. And thereupon said, "You will take these and drop them into the river, and then you will descend on the other side of the mountain. And Godspeed." And in a few moments, he had turned through gold, to red, to white, and thus as he had been a rainbow. The King of the Golden River had vanished.

Gluck took the crystal drops in the phial, and climbed, and he climbed and he reached the side of the river. And there it was flowing, in its crystal water. He was full of *elixir* and happiness. He threw the three drops into the river. And then he stood in astonishment. For it had not turned into gold. Indeed, it was strange, that the level of the river even dropped, and seemed to drop into a hole. With a beautiful musical sound.

But again he was obedient, and after looking at the mountain, he traveled around the peak, and traversed downwards on the other side of the mountain, as told. He eventually came around towards the foot of the mountain, and suddenly had a view of Treasure Valley. And now he saw what had happened.

The Golden River, still cascading over, had also dropped into the ground, and was coming out half-way down the mountain, and turning into a cascade in the valley for the first time. It was running in rivers into rivulets into streams throughout the valley.

He waded his way, down the valley, to the home. And in a few weeks and months, all the grasses had sprung up, and the plants, and the weeds; and the bushes and then trees. He propagated the crops, and he lived in the house. And everyone came to the door and was received. And so, the whole valley was again a garden. And what had been lost by selfishness was restored by devotion.

---

1   This story was written in 1841 by John Ruskin (1819-1900) and published ten years later under the title *The King of the Golden River or The Black Brothers: A Legend of Stiria*.

Pudleston Court, Herefordshire, Alan Chadwick's ancestral home. (Peter Whatley)

Alan Chadwick (R) in *She Stoops to Conquer*, 1954. (Courtesy of the Centre for South African Theatre)

Alan lecturing at UC Santa Cruz circa 1972.
(Courtesy of Paul Lee)

The Admiralty House, Simons Town, South Africa,
in 1975. This was Alan's first garden project 1957-8.
(Terence MacNally)

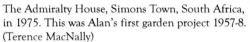

Overview of the Covelo Garden Project in California, circa 1976. (Richard Joos)

French intensive double dug bed at Covelo. (Courtesy of David Field)

Alan demonstrating raspberry pruning at Covelo, 1977. (David Field)

Starting a bed in Carmel-in-the-Valley, VA, summer 1978. (Courtesy of photo archives www.backhomemagazine.com)

The garden at UC Santa Cruz, circa 1970. (Courtesy of Paul Lee)

Alan talking with a student, Carmel-in-the-Valley Garden Project. (Courtesy of photo archives www.backhomemagazine.com)

Addressing students in the Covelo barn. (Courtesy of David Field)

Sunken herb mandala, Covelo. (Courtesy of David Field)

Alan had a deep mistrust of automobiles, calling them "exploding boxes tearing about everywhere". (Courtesy of Paul Lee)

Drawing by Margot Bergman of Chadwick's conception of a Sanctum Sanctorum in the center of the garden. (Courtesy of Margot Bergman)

Alan receiving a tussie-mussie. (Courtesy of Paul Lee)

Alan with students at Carmel-in-the-Valley, his last garden. (Courtesy of photo archives www.backhomemagazine.com)

Ley Crops

Carmel in the Valley, Virginia
April 1979

I have done a switch today because of a question that was very wisely brought up by one of the great moguls of the manor house, on ley, and I felt it was a very, very suitable thing to focus upon. So this begins our focus upon composts. We'll be focusing upon certain plants regarding ley.

I beg to remind you of the importance of the word *conservatoire*. And from the point of view of that, banks, dug up with ditches on either side, turned into hedges, surrounding all the different paddocks, and fields, and areas, making separation, so that you make *conservatoire*. That *conservatoire* is not merely to keep a cow in the field, or to keep sheep or pigs from getting into a wheat field, it constitutes much more than that. It constitutes *conservatoire* of atmosphere; *conservatoire* of prevention of wind from disrupt; area of protections; therefore think of paddocks and small fields rather than large fields, and think of them surrounded by hedges on banks with a gate leading into them.

Therefore, the hedgerow, you must understand, also contains not only all the shrubs that are so important like *Crataegus* (hawthorn, thornapple), hawthorn, bullace (wild plum), sloe—which is hawthorn—and numerous trees and shrubs in it, but it also contains all of the blackberries. It also contains an enormous quantity of the very plants that grow on either side on the banks, that make such superb cutting three or four times a year, that make the most exquisite and beautiful composts, and are a breeding ground in their own natural performance. So that plants can propagate themselves. That's very important.

Then you also must realize that all those hedges, which correspond and lead into copses and woods, are also the homes of all of the hedgehogs, the shrews, the birds, and those matters that are so paramount and important in relationship and dis-relationship.

Now when you asked yesterday, "What is ley?" you must realize that a balanced sense of constituent in this matter is, that whether you are

133

calling yourself horticulture or agriculture—you can call yourself a farm, a small farm or a big farm—you should consider that two-thirds of that area should be ley. Especially in the early days. Later, it could possibly be reduced to one-third. One-third is a minimal. Two-third of the size of the whole area is an excellent constituent.

In looking at ley, you must realize that in the whole of the families of plants—and I suppose you could use the weeds, the word 'weeds'— there are the givers and the takers. There are those that give utterly, and literally take nothing—and we're going to look at some of those today— and there are those that take everything, and literally give nothing. You've got a very excellent performance, really, in maize. Maize is a terrible thief. It absolutely ruins the soil in no time, the herbage from it is almost useless, unless it is burned—in which case the wood ash is of some value, but not very much—and as a forage, it's destitute. So you've got a terrific thief there, in a sense.

Then you can look at certain trees like the eucalyptus and the *camphora* (camphor tree). Although they are highly medicinal, and a great value from that point of view, and although they do give honey to the bees, they are total scavengers of the soil, driers out of the atmosphere, which sometimes of course is an advantage and a necessity, but they are acute thieves, from that point of view. Of course you see this in the whole of Nature, and you see it utterly, incredibly, in humanity.

Now, of all of them, one of the most astonishing is this matter of grass. We just say to each other, "Grass, you know, the lawn," or "Grass: the field." One little realizes that grass hardly produces any seed, and when it does, there is only about eight percent germinate-able. And that here is one of the incredible magics: that it produces both in the atmosphere and in the soil, a fertility which is almost incomparable. And that when you grow certain plants with grass, the grass is even added to in that performance.

Grass is making compost all the time, and its roots are making compost in the soil as well as the grass in the atmosphere. And you noticed how much it breathes, you watch every early morning, this incredible surface upon it. And it's doing the same with the soil. So two inches in the ground to two inches above, you've got a loam performing each year. Turf loam is one or the most exorbitant of all compost matters and soil producers.

When you grow clover, forty percent, with any of those grasses, all of the grasses grow better, and all of the clover grows better together. Where you grow ranunculus, the buttercup, with either clover, which doesn't grow with it anyway, or grass, both of them deteriorate, but the buttercup takes over, and slightly wins, *totem*. It's very necessary to look at all of this. You understand that ivy, creeping along the ground, flat, cannot possibly bloom, must never bloom. The moment it climbs a tree or a wall, it will blossom. It is one of the laws of the plant. You realize that the whole family of *Scrophularia* (figwort), you have a performance of a plant which is unhappy on its own, and loves society. There are plants which are social, then plants which are ego, and there are those which are intermediary in that matter.

So you must look at all that, and you will see everywhere, this matter of the equator, and the two equinoxes on either side. You'll find it in everything.

This *Scrophularia* that I speak of will only go to run to bloom and be happy if they are growing amongst other plants. Then there's a whole bunch of plants which only grow with one other particular kind. We'll deal with those much later. They're of great interest.

Today we're going to take the whole background of the vetches, the *Vicias*. So we're just going to check over them and we're going to discover the huge area of the most incredible gifts, that are beyond, beyond all imagining, and have all been discarded for bags of chemicals.

I trust that that's given you a brief resumé, as an interlude into where we're going to go.

When I talked about the compost and the takers and the givers, you must realize that *Urtica*, *Urtica dioica* in particular, the stinging nettle is more beneficent to you in the spring, if you eat the little shoots and the leaves as a spinach, than any spinach. It has much more nutrition in it, shall we say. And, that that will break down, and can be actually used as compost, if you make it in a certain way, in four days. It is broken down into gaseous deterioration.

Symphytum (comfrey) likewise, in six, eight, or ten days, will perform the same issue. Some foliages will take three months, and some foliages will take four days. And you've got this enormous change. Therefore, do you see this pedantic attitude of looking everything in the face, similarly?

Plants or weeds. A vegetable garden and a flower garden. You see it's all monstrous ludicrosity. We've got to get back and comprehend *totemism*.

Then we're dealing with the *Vicias*. Amongst the *Vicias* is one called *Lathyrus* (sweet pea), and that's the plant which you would know as the 'everlasting pea'. It is by rights a perennial, and there are four members of it—of no importance in this discussion—*pratensis* (meadow vetchling), *sylvestris* (flat pea-vine), *latifolius* (everlasting pea), and *maritimus*, which is *Pisum maritimum*. That is the little bunch of peas that grow very much after July, on stalks, and they're either cerise, or cerise and white, or white. They have a rather silvery curious-looking foliage, and prefer to creep along the ground around hedges. You rather see them creeping all over the ground over banks.

The *Lathyrus sativus* (Indian pea), which is a separate one altogether to those—I will refer to it at the end, but it is the only truly poisonous one, of great danger, which I will refer to. And it is known as the poisonous barberry throughout the world. It caused much consternation and problem in history, and had to be dealt with by monarchs, and even the pope.

Most astonishing of the whole of this group is the member *Ornithopus* (bird's foot). *Onobrychis*: and another name for that, which is perfectly simple to refer to and look up actually, is sainfoin, and you would translate that: *foin* is hay, and *sain* is saint: 'holy hay'. It happens to be true. Just as *Angelica archangelica* is an angel. So don't mistake it.

This plant is a little bit similar to alfalfa, except that is has a very, very different performance. And here is one of the utter givers, and literally no-takers. Now you may sow this as a seed into a plowed field as a ley. It will come up incontrovertibly, whether it rains or whether it is hot. It will germinate. You can, if you are careful in cropping it, grow it for forty years without any declination, and you may take six and eight crops a year of herbage, constituting as much as forty and fifty tons per acre from this plant, per annum.

It makes a root something like the alfalfa—the alfalfa will go down to sixty-two feet, this plant goes down anything from twenty to forty. It literally prefers to grow—and you see a huge pointing here— it prefers to grow in arid soil. As gravely as you like, as clay as you like, as monstrous in its performance of clogged up, ill-consumed, un-irrigated, destitute—the kind of thing that they have made with the bombs—here is the one plant that is going to restore the whole issue. And can restore it in fifteen years completely. No matter what pernicious performance humanity has made, here are the angels waiting to come in, and will, of course. Therefore, you see indeed, it is holy hay. It's an incredible plant.

And here is a plant that every inch of it is the most exquisite cattle fodder. There is almost nothing to equal it. It is also one of the most consummate compost creators, to make soil.

Now, here is a huge matter. That when you sow a field of that, and you've got nothing—you couldn't grow potatoes, do you understand, you couldn't grow cabbages, and you certainly couldn't grow cereal, you'd have to pour stuff onto it—you will sow that seed, and if you want to in five years, you could put the plow through that field, plow up the *Onobrychis* and you have got a fertility equivalent to garden soil, created. The roots have gone down, they've gone down into the subsoils, they've unearthed the irrigation, they've created irrigation, they've created worms, and they have already created a soil compost on the surface of so many inches deep, and the whole thing is underway. If you leave it for ten years, so much the better; if you left it for fifteen, you have got about your utmost, that it will create on its own.

Therefore, the whole attitude of this plant is of course bewildering, and incredibly overlooked, and was never overlooked until the coming of the physicalist age.

So we'll leave sainfoin there. Don't overlook it; it's too terribly easy to overlook.

Now let us look at these *Vicias*. These are the vetches that you see—they grow in woods, they grow right up the trees, they grow all over hedges and cascade; they'll grow in banks, they'll grow under the hedges, and they will grow in the open fields, and they will certainly grow, excellently, in the plowed lands, the cultured lands. The *Vicia sylvatica* (wood vetch) is the great one that hangs in bunches of vetch, and will go up twenty and thirty feet up trees, and hang off boughs in the woods—you have probably have seen them, I imagine, here in the whole of these Appalachians. There must be an enormous quantity of this sort of thing in the forest and the woods. It is indeed a monstrous soil builder; it is the most exquisite of bird foods in the seed, and it is every bit of it supreme fodder for animals: all animals, all.

That is merely a woodland one, and it is very difficult to propagate, and is often attempted by the seed to propagate it and is generally a failure. But, since it is a perennial, it does of course spread from crown *présentement* and by spreading and rooting itself.

There is *Astragalus* (*adsurgens*), which is a milk vetch, which is not an animal forage, but is an excellent compost maker. There is *Anthyllis* (*vulneraria*), which is the kidney vetch, a little low-growing one that makes an enormous bush. There is the lotus, which belongs to the trifoliums. This little lotus—you must all know it as Lords and Ladies, or Lady's Slippers (*Arum macalutum*)—a little low-growing plant, no higher than that, with a little trifoliate foliage, and suddenly, in June, all of these stalks, with these bunches of yellow Lady's Slippers with orange on them, and apricot. You know what I am referring to. This is what is called the lotus.

Now all of these, every one of them we are referring to, are smothered in bacteria on the roots, and are therefore colossal soil builders in the soil alone by root performance. And that that bacteria, as you know, once becoming in the soil, spreads in the soil, breeds in the soil, and pursues for eight to ten years after you might take the whole crop out. That bacteria lives in the soil, and this is what the Greeks considered the greatest of all of fertilizers. This is what is utmost on the *Vicia faba* (fava bean). Therefore, the little lotus, as indeed you must know the *Medicagos* (*Medicago sativa*, alfalfa), that are similar to the lotus, but that they mostly have one little yellow blossom, like a little tiny fermosa ball, with the trifolium foliage, and have those very annoying seeds, like a little snail, that when you tread on them you go bathing in the river or pool, you half a dozen sticking on the ball of your feet, and are most uncomfortable to walk upon. Until you are home, the foot is covered with them, of course you don't know anything about them.

Vicia cracca, it's the tufted vetch, and is a perennial. You'll see a lot of differences here: there are annuals and perennials, almost nothing biannual and triannual. They are either annuals or perennials. And this is a hugely important note because of your ley performances. I'm going to pull all this together, don't worry, it sounds a little bit loose at present. And I'm giving you the names—which I know worries some people intensely—you mustn't worry about that, because the names at this stage are not that important, but that they do have huge inference in this matter.

The *cracca* is the tufted vetch, which grows enormously all over Asia—it simply smothers Asia—it's all over, you must have seen it at times. And is one mass of blossoms of purple, purple blossom in bloom. Very beautiful. It's extremely nutritious to both cattle and birds. They cannot and do not live without it.

The *orobus* (wood bitter-vetch) is a perennial. It is whitish with purple streaks. Now there is another member of that which has chocolate upon it and is very obvious. This one blooms in May and June. It's whitish to cream.

There is *Ononis (repens)*, which is Restharrow, which is more like a pea than a *Vicia*. There is, as I say, the *Medicago*, particularly the *Medicago sativa*, which is the equal of clover. There is the *Melilotus* (melilot, sweet clover), which we spoke of yesterday, the *officianalis*, the *vulgaris*, and the *arvensis*. Those we dealt with. There is another one that I mentioned yesterday: *Trigonella ornithopodioides*, very small. *Foenum-graecum* (fenugreek) is its true name. It's an annual. We're going to grow it enormously. It is forty percent protein.

Now beware, forgive me for using this word at all. Do you see we are into the world of absurdities? *Protein*. And I do warn you of this, you must forgive us if we have to use words for reference, but you see I am referring to the values in eggs, fish, meat, and now in a plant. So these are kind of relationship values. The reason I warn you of this, is that we can be vastly deceived. We can use the word protein and pretend in our conniving mind that we completely comprehend what we are talking about. But if you suddenly look at *Trigonella*, that protein up there wouldn't mean a thing.

I must warn you because of the perfidy that's going on here. I mean one of the huge performances in this place is the adoration of cellophane bags, the use of cellophane in this place—they're absolutely crazy about it—they've done all the doors with it, they've done all the windows with it, they use it all day long. They cover everything in the larder with it, they put all the vegetables in it, they put all the fruit in it, the refrigerator's packed with it. I believe they go to bed with it. You realize it is one of the most terrifying, it's one of the most filthy inventions that's ever been. And you realize that we're going to invite here, Professor Paul Lee, to come, in front of our faces, to the whole world, and say, these people tell you not to make this damn stuff! Don't create it and don't use it! And we're going to sit there and say, "Hooray!" and all the time it's being used like a shuffleboard. Do you see what I'm alluding to? We're not looking at what we're doing. We're pretending today, we're full of hypocrisy. Well that's enough of that.

The *Trigonella*—since it's said to be forty percent protein, and alfalfa is likewise, and *Onobrychis* is likewise—this incredible value *in*. And you see when I spoke now of protein you will remember my reference about health and disease, and the protein in a plant, which begins at the birth of seed, which is the energy from the other world, coming into this with life—expands in the plant as a metamorphosis, and that in a sense is that protein that we're talking about. And that according to that seed, and the other world, there is either a plus or a less of that energy. Do you follow? Do you understand what I am alluding to?

Somewhere connected here again, is something connected with origin. I can't give you the key of that, of course.

Then there is the incredible plant, the *Vicia faba*, which actually comes from Egypt, and of course was grown there enormously, and was a constituent of the fodder for all of the animals, and the food for the people. I better give you some remarks about that whilst we're there. Well, it's vastly concerned with the Greeks. The Greeks, you know, both Hippocrates[1] and Pythagoras[2], you will read endlessly statements about not eating beans, particularly the *Vicia faba*. There was some consideration that the soul of humanity goes into the bean at death. Now you are also aware of, are you not, that the *Vicia faba*, and many such beans, such as eating asparagus, are very destructive to the eyesight. I mean instantly and immediately, they affect it. And you realize of course that there are likewise, all of those other seeds and plants, that immediately restore it. For instance the seed of pumpkin. If you eat any pumpkin with asparagus, it will have no effect on your eyesight at all. And again you see the *Levisticum* (*officinale*, lovage) affects the eyesight very much; very, very much indeed. In fact that's one of the reasons they say it's a love plant—it affects the appearance through the perception. Oh dear, I'm getting a little bit lost of course.

However I must also refer you not only to that matter, but to two other matters. One is this: that during the time of the blooming of the *Vicia faba* and some of its other constituents, the natural timing of the ruling, there is much more prevalence to mental alienation than at any other of the seasons of the year. It is said to be due to the scent of the plant. Which you understand, the two top petals are black, absolute ebony, death black; and the other is white, and there is that vein. So it is extraordinarily, in a certain sense, a prophetic funeral flower. Do you understand? And, of course, it's the most intrinsic of all aphrodisiacs. I used to go and visit some friends in Pinchbeck, New Holland, Lincolnshire, which is all fens, and dikes. And there they grow during the period the *Vicia faba* enormously for the London market, which is extremely popular. And this household in particular that I went to, they told me to use the back door—all the doors are locked, during the next ten days. All of the *Vicia faba* fields were in bloom, and they all had female servants. And they wouldn't let any of the servants out. They go to the village you know, and never come back. They would have you know that they just took a sort of a walk. This of course is utterly true. It is of course the most incredible aphrodisiac imaginable. Walk past a *Vicia faba* field in the evening, and you will actually swoon. It's the most incredible matter.

There is also the fact that during that period, as I say, mental alienation, is known throughout—you know how sophisticated the world becomes by taking statistics about mental derangement and so on, and that there's no question for that period. Of course, the suggestion is that it's really the cosmic area, when the mind is loosened. So it could be partly that, however, there is the lotus, there is the *Vicia*, which is *Lathyrus sativus*, which, throughout the whole of history of civilization has been denounced by all the monarchs, by all the governments of countries, for this curious plant, looking much like many of the others, but growing and producing seed. Every pigeon, every bird, every animal that eats the seed, loses the use of its limbs. Almost immediately. There's no sign of pain, there's no sign of approaching anything, and all of a sudden, they double up, and have lost the use of the muscles. And they just collapse.

It's a very much entirely connected with muscular, and is obviously a cosmic connection.

And that at certain times, because so much was used in the *Vicia*—as I will speak in one minute, in other reference—so much was used in *Vicia* in the making of flour, and cakes, in the past centuries—all of these were ground up—they very often got this plant mixed in, with its seeds, and incredible setting in of the limbs, unable to move, and actually the monarchs and the governments had to actually have this plant pointed at as a plant that absolutely must never be seen, must never be allowed to be propagated, and must absolutely be eradicated. So, that is *Lathyrus sativus* and is known as the poisonous barberry.

There is *Vicia hirsuta*, which is the tiny Hairy Tare. It's a strangler: if it gets in the wheat or the cereals, it does strangle. But for all of that, it's a super-abundant plant, of the utmost nutritious compost value. And one seed, in one season, will produce a thousandfold. A tremendous colossal abundant fertility. That applies much to all of these *Vicias*.

The *Vicia faba*, as you know, has the most, utmost preponderance of the bacteria upon its roots, and is a colossal nitrogenous manufacturer, and has this enormous growth of composting. And you realize that when you shuck the bean, the enormous quantity of shuck that there is to go in the compost heap. And the incredible gift of the whole of this plant is just enormous, and it is an utter disinfectant against all fungoids, as indeed all of the propagation of the bacteria is.

In India grows in the desert lands in the sand a plant, which when there is no new movement in the air whatever, suddenly all of the leaves, of one certain position of the plant, do *that* (move in one direction). And ten minutes or twenty minutes later, they all do *that*. The whole field moves. It is one of the most bewildering and undoubtedly miraculous things to observe, because there is no breeze whatever. There's nothing to cause the plant to move, it's its will's procedure, connected with the cosmic. Its name is *Hedysarum gyrans*, (*Codariocalyx motorius*—telegraph or semaphore plant) from which comes the word 'gyrate', and it is looked upon as one of the great mysteries of the world.

The gum tragacanth, (*Astragalus tragacantha*) which is far better than gum arabic (*Acacia senegal*), comes from one of the great soil builders of *Astragalus*, in the Cordilleras (Baetic Cordillera, Spain). Annually it has been observed there, as in Sicily, the wheat plants will make mounds of compost four and five feet high in one year. Some of the thistles do this here in America. In Green Gulch, when I was there, I very much took note of an occupation that in certain dells in the hills there, where the thistles had taken over and even the cows couldn't enter because the thistle was so thick, they had actually made ten foot of the most exquisite compost, all out of thistle. So this mad thing of *get rid*—do you see what we're doing? We get rid of everything, and then we say, "Now, what do we put in?" And we bring a bag of something, which constitutes literally nothing. But an end.

So let us go very quickly then, at this bunch of the most important. First of all I'll begin at the end and come back to them. Do you realize that out of this family is *Herbam lens* (*Lens culinaris*) which is the lentil. And here again we are lost in the vulgarities of verbosity. But of course this was what Esau sold as his pottage[3], for his birthright, you realize, that this very plant was that. It was the red meal pottage that he made. It was *Herbam lens* which is the lentil. And of course the only reason it is called lentil is that it is eaten, as you know, in the religious procedure in Lent. And so it became known as Lent-til. Probably out of the word 'lens'.

Now. *Vicia cracca*, which is one of the *sylvaticas*, and plus the *Vicia sylvatica*, as a fodder, is supreme. It is known, well-known throughout the whole history of farming, that when cattle are at all starved, or weak from lack of nutritious feeding, to immediately introduce them to this plant. It advances them instantly above anything else that is known in recovery. Their recovery is instant, immediate from the moment they start on it. They adore it, and it is obviously a whole secret fodder of reconstitution to the opposite of starvation. And this applies to all of these likewise. But those two in particular: *cracca*, and the *sylvatica*.

Now we've saved the *Vicia sativa*. Here is your annual. It's the charming little one that has the one, cherry-cerise bloom, little sweet pea, on a hair stem coming out of the grass, as it were. You must all know it. As a fodder it is incomparable. Until one hundred years ago it was said, that not one-tenth of the cattle, in other words nine-tenths of the cattle of the world were answerable to this plant. Nine-tenths of the cattle of the world. Cut green, it will re-form five or six times in a year. And that in all cases, the growth of this plant—unless allowed to go to seed, but in all other cases otherwise—will take no exhaustion from the soil whatever, but create soil all the time. One of the most monstrous and enormous givers. Only if allowed to go to seed, could it be said to partly take a partition of what it gives, and that negligible. The most incomparable, to all cattle, poultry, birds, wild: everything.

The reverse one to that—now that one blooms as you know in May and June—is the *Vicia sepium* (bush vetch). This is a perennial. It is the earliest and the latest: the earliest to rise and the latest to bed. Incomparable. It is utterly green in any reasonable climate—just a reasonable climate—I'm talking about ghastly England in February. The cattle are radiant upon it. It is the earliest, and last and latest to bed in the Autumn, in November and December. Again, five or six croppings a year, and produces seed that all birds and poultry and livestock, and pheasants and partridge and pigeons, are simply crazy about, and restore their plumage when they've gone 'broody', and have molted. These are the kind of seeds that restore their nutritious matter in their feathers and their bones.

Therefore you have got, amongst the greatest and most supreme of all, as a fodder, *cracca* and *sylvatica*, and amongst the composters, and the fodder, *sativa*, which is an annual, and *sepium*, which is the perennial. Now I'm not going to give you any more of that because the names and everything will tie you up. I trust that you will see from this that this is just the beginning of a huge list of the great givers of the weeds. When we study *Urtica dioica* you will come to understand, it can take over two thousand acres in three years, if you wish it to. And will cover the whole of that area. And that you could cut that twice, and get hundreds of thousands of tons of soil from it, and every bit of it is a disinfectant as well.

Do you want to talk about it?

Q: I was wondering, if these Vicias *would destroy all these thistles that swarm over our fields in the summer...*

No, on the contrary, do you see, most of the *Vicias* like to climb, and they invite other plants in a certain sense. They are not—there is the one that I mentioned with the tiny hair, *hirsuta*, that is a strangler. If you want it to eradicate thistle, that would help. One of the best ways to eradicate thistle is simply to plant the whole area of course with *Symphytum*. *Symphytum* will even eradicate the whole of the *convulvulaceae* (bindweed) in two years. Do you understand what I am referring to: *convulvulaceae*, the root that goes down six feet, the convolvulus. Convulsion! You see nobody knows what they are thinking of or talking about today. But it is the whole word 'convulsions'. And that the more you dig convolvulus up, six feet into the ground it will come up, every bit if it, from every little bit of root that you chop up, and every little bit of stalk, and every seed will germinate. It's a most colossal performer. You can't possibly deal with it on ground that has been plowed in England, in proper countries of agriculture. Any farm that has convolvulus upon it at all cannot be let or sold, and comes out of a government jurisdiction, that in so many years, this will be absolutely clean, or it is removed from the owner.

Well the thistles that grow here so much this summer, take over, that all of our neighbors complain about growing in our fields, those are not harmful?

Oh, to them, because of the way they run their agriculture. But, if you want to produce soil, they're wonderful soil producers. They're wonderful honey producers. Oh, you must look at it. I'm sorry, but what is your *Carduus*? Of course it's a thistle.

And many of those thistles, according to the ancient Bohemians, the Gypsies, the Egyptian, Bohemians, take the young shoots, and just peel off the outside—incredible food—like asparagus. Incredible.

Oh, the monstrous mentality of humanity. Everything becomes an enemy. I'm not suggesting, now I'm not suggesting that when you have a paddock for cattle, or pasture for your cattle—I mean, actually, you don't want your thistles coming up. I mean they're obnoxious to the cattle. They stop them from grazing, and you must keep your land clean. Do you understand? Yes, you must take them out.

Anything?

Q: Which is the dangerous one? You were talking about the dangerous thistle.

Oh sir! I do beg you! I am a horticulturist of a type! But if you want the names out of eight hundred thousand plants I must go get a book.

Do you understand? I don't carry it in here (points to head). It is a *Carduus*. Do you understand? And it is the only one that has a lateral root, very much the same as *Pteris* does. *Pteris, bracken* grows that way, but then sends up a stem that has the frond. Do you understand? Now that *Carduus* does the same thing. Now any part of that root—any part of it, or the stalk, cut up—every inch of it will grow. Do you follow? This does not apply to any other *Carduus* or *Cnicus*. And the whole of that family you understand, the botanists will chop each other's heads off of which is a *Carduus* and which is a *Cnicus*. Do you understand?

Do you require the name of that plant? Yes, then I will bring it to you. Do you understand? And I will demand of every one of you—in one year—when I ask you—you will come up with it!

If you tax me like this, I'm going to tax you for a change! (Laughter.) I spend all my life these days—well, I've worked all my life in a garden and loved it. Now I spend my life in a box, looking all this up, to be sure that I don't make any mistakes in relating it to you. That's my life now...

---

1 Hippocrates of Kos, "The Father of Western medicine"; (~460-370 B.C.).
2 Amongst the many things Pythagoras of Samos is credited with introducing to the West is metempsychosis, the transmigration of souls; (~570-495 B.C.).
3 *Genesis* 25:34.

Irrigation

Covelo Village Garden
30 March 1977

I'm going to run over some herbs, with notation for you that you begin to invent upon them, use them, prepare the preparations, and get on with it. Lobelia is dangerous, but a very important herb, for rectifications. We are going to deal with it in the very near future as an herb. The gentian is extremely important. The *Gentiana* blue has skin disease eradication. Sunflower seed oils, and juices are extremely important for the eyes. And for digestion generally, but the eyes in particular. The oil of the pumpkin seed is vitally important for all glandular procedure. No Balkan or Hungarian person has ever suffered in any ancient age from glandular trouble, for the simple reason that they have never ceased, in centuries after centuries to occupy this method.

The echinacea for cleansing the blood stream: nothing to compare. The meadowsweet for beatification. The *Polygonatum* (*odoratum*) in the form of the common known Solomon's seal, to repair bruises after quarrels and fights. The *Tragopogan* (goatsbeard) for all form of putting right to repair after illness. Digitalis, not any longer in particular, to put our numerous hearts right, but principally as a soil preparation against invasion of slug and matters. Absolutely harmless to plant life and probably would absolutely refute them. The ashes of burned *Pteris*, *Equisetum*, and sunflower stalks—*Helianthis giganteus*—particularly as a potassium, but more particularly as an anti-fungoid. So I've just run over that list to start an infusion of these matters, to regurgitate them.

The subject this morning, because the educative staff has said that it is high time that I am going to lead into the whole of the irrigation systems for the garden, so, the subject is that this morning. However, before that, if you'll forgive, I have some what you might call some introductions. And the less said about them, the better.

The most wonderful journal that came out in England, partly through Schumacher—well, Schumacher was merely a descendent of the whole issue—but he was, as you know, the president of the Soil Association—this journal is a participation, the journal of the Soil Association in Great Britain, which is now almost defunct, all those people having become aged.

Rachel Carson[1] said in 1963: *I truly believe, that we in this generation, must come to terms with nature, and I think we're challenged as mankind has never been challenged before, to prove our maturity and our mastery, not of nature, but of ourselves.*

A little paragraph; how it should be done upon agriculture. The opposite pole to the attitude of government advisors and tycoons, is that of Laurence Easterbrook. Speaking on the BBC program on "Your Farm" on the nineteenth of February, he discussed the various aims that a farmer *might set himself: An ideal might just be, to become the best farmer in the country, or to breed the best stock, or to have a farm that gave you the least worry, or the most contentment. When I started, I thought about this a good deal, and came to the conclusion that I would take health as my ideal. I hoped that this would mean that other desirable things, such as profit, would automatically follow, if I could succeed in creating a healthy farm. I think after some years of experience, I think one could do much worse than take health as a prime objective. It means that you develop a habit of considering first, the welfare of all the living things in your care. Healthy animals. Healthy plants. And healthy soil. And the soil with at least a couple of million living organisms in every spoonful of it, is the most living thing of the whole lot. Shamefully little is known about the health of the soil. When it comes to animal health, I am in a one hundred percent revolt against the current theory—all too common in medicine as well—that life is an obstacle race with the bugs, and the most you can hope for is to squirt enough dope into them to hold disease at bay. I believe that living things in a healthy state have a natural immunity to disease.*

He goes on a little further, but that's the gist.

Albert Steffen[2]: *With this experience, it clearly began when strange plants fascinated me. I started a herbarium. At that time, I was taking my first lessons in Latin and assuredly it was no mere chance that I began to dry out the plants, just as I was learning the dead language. That I was in danger of rooting up my own instincts along with the plants eluded me at first. As I began to use the microscope, laying out the plant preparations on the rectangular slide, in order to study the cell structure, I noticed, for the first time, that I was becoming estranged from nature. The harm I suffered was revealed to me in a curious way.*

One day, as I went out of the laboratory onto the street—I hadn't passed my examinations in the meanwhile—I felt compelled to look for the wrinkles, warts, and all such disagreeable things in the faces of the people that I met. I bethought me involuntarily of various noses, blubber lips, and jaws with more or less decayed teeth, as they would appear under a magnifying glass. What use to touch or delight me escaped me now. The blue of the cheek, the violet of the eye, and above all: the spirituality revealing itself in gait and gesture. My barren soul was no longer aware of these things.

As Mr. Bailey[3] and a number of other people would say as regarding irrigation, I can't tell you the system in words.

I want us to discuss right now the matters that concern the key of the whole of this so that we look at it. There are many aspects that we are not truly conscious of, as Mr. Steffen describes there. We are focused out of line because of our own ordinations of focuses which are not in line with Nature's. I go back onto some of our previous studies, and I draw your attention to something, and will leave it right there. We spoke of the energy that the Sun, as directed by its great leader— another Sun—directs its energy *at* this Earth. The energy comes out of this Earth, of the magnetic energy of the Earth, a separate volley, and meets it, and creates what we term, in language, 'warmth'. Growing in the heat.

That is land, that concerns Earth. And you've already looked at some degree of the mantle, the clothing of the Earth, of this angelic procedure of plants. That informs an intermarriage-ship with the marriage-ship. Yes. Alright. So what happens in the ocean? As it were, the opposite of Earth. Now you begin to have a perception of what we're talking about. Variation.

There you have the huge manipulator. It is, as it were, that the ocean is the opposite of the Earth, as the Earth can almost be described as the opposite of the air. Indeed you ought to look at this in a minute. So now I simply place this before you, and you must use your own scales of balances, and imaginations.

Reference then the dawn, and the coming of the Sun, and the land. "Com'on. All of you. Out. Meet. How are you this morning? Well, you're well, I'll tell you that. So you're going to be well." And it does the same to the sea. And when it does the same to the sea that it does to the land, in the same area conjunct, you get the word 'maritime'. A marriage-time. Not violent either. A what you might call—to use horrible words again—a temperature equality. The oceanic reply to the Sun's energy, and the Earth's reply to the Sun's energy are two opposites, but where they're married they make a Cancer and a Capricorn, areas of equilibrium.

You leave the oceanic area, and you go over mountains inland, and that maritime becomes an abeyance, left behind, and now it is land replying to the Sun energy. And that is quite different. It is one-sided, so to speak. If you were to go a little further, would you not come to a wide river or a lake? And now what happens? Here is not salt water, with salt plants; here is sweet water, land water, with land water plants. They're quite different. But again, you achieve a semi-maritime, outside the Capricorn and Cancer area, halfway out again, each way. A balance, but not as balanced as the coastal.

And here you find, as you get day plants and night plants, the variations of plants which co-habit in that angelic prevalence of distribution, their application. And their performance. They create the atmosphere. Where there is no river, no lake, no pond, no mire, no bog, the land issue is it own domination.

At the University of California (Santa Cruz), the professors who came to the garden to help the students to find out what to do—which of course was bound to be reversed—in the garden, the one thing that they always said was: "I really don't know anything about gardening, I confess it, but, I'll do the digging and I'll do the watering." Of course we said, "Now please, for God's sake, leave that alone and do some gardening and then we should be safe."

I want us to look at a further partition of the opposites we just referred to as regards ocean and land. We've put into groups those four Archangel performances that we nominate—let's put it simply—spring, summer, autumn, winter. Now you make those same divisions, you must. Those seven variations to begin to understand this matter of the application of water, and the way in which Nature appropriates it, and that's what we've got to follow. Nothing else.

Therefore, that *divertissement* is different from what is imagined, what is thought in the reason and intellect mind, which, don't forget, is very precise, and predominant, and false.

Let us begin in winter. Because the winter is essentially more dark than light, we will refer to it as 'night'. Out of winter let's travel into what follows in the cycle, spring. What happens in the spring out of the middle of what happens in the winter? Does not light increase out of an over-formation of night? In the whole of winter you have the absolute, total holding of darkness, over light. It is predominant. In the spring, you work out of that predominance—but still within the predominance of dark—into light, until they are equal, and you pass out of it in to the reverse. And so you must send night into day, in the spring. And so you enter the summer, at which you must say, the whole of the period of Uriel is the predominance of light, and therefore it is utterly dangerous. For it is going to run away and blind. And then you enter the period that reverses that, in the opposite direction. That is what is complicated for us to understand, because it is utterly natural, and not connived. It is a very reversed happening.

Now if you put a motorcar into reverse after going forward, you're not doing that at all. And in all our machinery, we don't do that at all. And so we are stuck. Blocked and caught.

In this procedure then, out of summer into fall, you are on the very opposite to spring. You are going out of predominant light, but you are still in predominant light. And you are beginning to enter an approach, a warning of darkness. But the happiness, the evolvement, the vital violent hold, is still the predominance of Uriel, of light. A danger. Therefore you must nominate it 'day into night'.

Here you have the first approach into the conversation concerning *inhalation* and *exhalation*. You might very well say, that the spring is an inhalation, for the first time, out of sleep. And the fall is not an inhalation at all, it's an exhalation. You have already perceived that the whole of the plant world lives totally differently, with a totally different aspect, towards total Nature to what we have. We look at everything participle. But you watch and see, and observe at dawn, in the morning, in the evening all the plants, and it is the whole aura, area, of this stellation that is being looked upon. Therefore, you must give up—as we do, forgive my saying so, with the Bible[4]—write it as we feel makes it possible for us. We must give up making plants live the only way which we can conceive that they could or should. They must tell us this astonishing angelic magic by which they do this.

Therefore their whole breathing is a different consummation altogether. And although, in a certain sense, they are, in most cases palpitating faster than we are, they nevertheless do the periods of various inhalations, which we do—when you sleep you know something of what happens—the whole of that inhalation changes tempo. If it didn't, you wouldn't wake up as you do. You would wake up as you went to sleep. And you do not. You are opposite. The whole thing has become opposite. But you didn't do it. You must look at that between spring and fall.

Now that inhalation and exhalation concerns the opposite that ocean and land does. That the soil, and the procedure on the plant below the soil level—the area of discontinuity of the Earth—where the dominance of the angelic stellation takes command over the physical procedure of ahrimanic, is, as it were, a complete opposite. So this truth, that you have an electric current in the atmosphere, and a positive and a negative in the soil.

Therefore you must perceive this procedure that takes place in day and night, as regards growth and breathing. There are the periods at which the foliages, the stalks and the blossoms breathe, and are facing like that, down, into. And the other is resting. It is only by a gradual change that that opposition takes place, of waking up. And then the other does the opposite. They also go in epochs, as we do. You do not sleep the same throughout the night. You would think you do, but that is only because you're not aware.

There is a change all of the time in that, as there is in the *présentement* of the year, and a century—and many centuries are in great groups as the year is a group. And the twelve months are a group. You cannot limit by this construction of the calendar the whole perpetual procedure of Nature, which is perpetual change.

All of this is to get to an understanding of *when* to water. You would not awfully like, were you in the middle of your sleep, for somebody to come and pour a bottle of beer over your head. Or to put it down your throat. Or perhaps you would. Now you will see that there's a huge falsity in the appropriation, that the plant is really for water both ends at the same time, always (root and stem). That is complete nonsense. The procedure through the month is not any quality at all. Nor, through the cycle of the year. Nor, in the upgrade of the inclination cycle. It is a continual change. So if you think you could have a beautifully hammered out system of watering every day, laid out in a book, you will see the ludicrosity of it.

You have noticed by now, and you must proceed to notice much, much more, those flowers which do *that* (turn upward and outward) the moment the Sun comes out and says, "Hello everybody!" And they say, "Hello Sun!" and they all do that, practically all of them. However, there are some, like the *Nicotiana*, it does *this* (turn downward and inward). "Get away, you beast!" So there you have these intrinsic opposites. So you can't water all your plants with one great douche of the hose.

Now you must have noticed clover. Clover is one of the predominants of this matter, as are a whole bunch of them: *Melilotus*. All those do similar tricks. The moment a cloud comes over—*whhaaaaa, must get ready for this*—what? Ah yes, but why? This is not merely an instinct. It's an obedience of an angelic procedure to the domination of the leaders of Archangels. The Archangels have said, "You know your duty, don't you? Do it." And all the angels say, "Yes of course we do." And do it. It is because there is going to be a shower, and shower has to go to the roots, not the foliage—it's daytime.

So these procedures, according to the plant, according to the area, are obedient, and they're totally obedient. I won't say that in some of the pernicious areas of the world—such as those we won't nominate—things aren't a bit deceiving. That's rather unaccountable.

Now, I draw attention to what I said about winter, spring, summer, fall, and that matter of night; night into day; day; day into night. Now you may say if you like, you may take that into a bed, into a box. And of course you could say *fall* is *evening*, and *dawn* is *morning*, which is *spring*. And so now you also go into those opposites that come out of the middle every time. The middle of the 'eye'. You will find this key throughout. That when the foliages and the blooms do *this*, which is saying to those four elements, "You behave yourselves, because we've got the whole thing under control." And then they do *that* and they say, "Well, you can go ahead. We're behaving. It's all under control." The moisture applications are going to where they should go, and the plant is performing its angelic obedience. You may very well say, that

when the plants are open, and the leaves are exposed like this: over—
no; under—yes. And likewise the reverse when they're closed: over—yes;
under—no. You've got your opposites there.

You must have noticed, when you don't quite water the plants
enough, they hold their leaves up above to get every bit of moisture you
can put: "For goodness sake! Can't you see? I'm holding up for you!"
And then the moment they've got enough, or a little too much: "Ok,
don't you see I'm asking you to stop." And it's all right, of course they
do. Normally.

Classically, we mustn't proceed with this beyond a certain point. You
understand, what I'm trying to do, is to lay before you horticultural
truth that concerns Nature. Whereby you must find, on your own—as
with total, proof, truth—what the procedure is.

Classically, the climate of horticulture is: warm, moist summers; cool
to cold, dry winters; and in between. But if you live with that, you
proceed on a classical line, for that is a classical climate. And all classical
moisturing is done in the late afternoon, so that the plants can be able
to breathe via the foliages, and shall have the roots also moistured, as
required. And that it shan't be dis-integrated obliquely, but shall have
it's full scope of period of play.

Now in this you must look at the growth in an orchard, for this gives
it to you very clearly. In an orchard in the spring the rains have fallen
through the winter, and your moistures have made all the growth of
that tree, in the spring and the blossoming, rich with lush moisture, for
a chick coming out of an egg must have the white, and the air, to keep
that moisture. Later, it will be abortive for the chicken to have moisture
all around its feathers when it wanted to go in and lay an egg. It would
be upside down and back to front.

With this orchard that is going to produce fruit and seed, it wants the
moisture in the spring. In the beginning, in the uprise (spring sap rise),
in the inclination. In the period of light, of totality of light, that must
begin to over-balance into the opposite. And the whole attitude of dryth
unto wet-th will produce what is known as exquisite flavor, taste, sugars,
and ripenesses. For if you have those sugars, tastes and ripenesses in the
blossom, you would have a fantastic mess. But the Archangels do happen
to know, and they're terribly obedient to what they are doing.

That same application then concerns night and day, and the plants. Where you have got an un-classic climate, you have got to go into reverse. That's the whole answer to that point.

Presumably for seed beds onwards, dusk to dawn is when the moistures should have been applied into the soils. Warmed by the coming out of the opposite. Therefore the sleep was in a moist warmth. But if, on the contrary, you have an un-classic climate, with nothing but coldth rising, then you have got a malevolence. Then you must have dryth at night, and moist in the day. But that is not going to suit the plants in the long run. Totally. You are living where you shouldn't, and you have got to come to know it. And we shall always be told.

You will notice that seeds germinate principally in two periods: pre-equinox spring, post-equinox fall. There you have two variations of the lifedom of the plant life. You will find that in both of those periods, in what you call all classic climatics, the clouds are totally different to what they are at the rest of the year—they're all in ordinance with the Archangels. They're all behaving in obedience. You can't regulate it. It's never the same. And the whole stellation makes a slight variation all the time. The ordination of what shall be born and what shall not be born is not in anybody's hands, except that divination.

Therefore, you will find that the cloud formations that fly at those two times are totally different. The spring clouds are low, very low, big sky nimbus, that come along, and when the little plant that is just beginning to hatch, suddenly is panting because of the young Sun energy saying, "Come on! How are you?" And the little plant says, "Well, I'm not quite sure. I'm getting a little bit exhausted. I am so tired." And this Mrs. Cloud comes out between them and says, "Hey, pardon me." And the Sun says, "Wait half a minute!" And it says, "Ooooo." And suddenly the little plant is moist. And just as it is beginning to get moist it says, "Oh my God! I'm cold and wet. What the hell is this?" And the Sun hands a towel to him and says, "Here you go. What a fuss. Well, here's some more. Come on Bergie." And the next moment the Sun's a bit strict again.

Those are the procedures that you get with those astonishing performances. Those are what you've got to deal with. The more you can water your seedbeds—the more frequently you can water them—with that kind of water, the more that you see the resultant performance. Therefore, you are again doing the opposites. And as we have found here in the aspect of this culture, you only water to dryth; and you only beg the dryth, that you can water. This can be a complex argument, as you might say, but it's not. It's coming out of the middle of the other, to meet it.

When you do prick-outs and plant-outs, do you realize that you have performed a huge duty that the Archangels perform, that the angels and the elementals perform? You are performing an angelic performance. Divination has created us to pop things in our mouths, and we have energy coming out of the ends of our fingers from that popping. It's all a divination. When you eat you don't destroy anything, you create. It's a very beautiful, wonderful procedure. And if only we get this right, and have the right attitude, what an exquisite thing it is, this energy from the popping. Don't you see this is what plants do when they die. They're full of giving. Absolute succulent-ness of the whole procedure. And so are we. Or can be...*mon dieu*...

Well, this prick-out and plant-out which many people would turn around and say, "What are you doing? Is that natural? I thought you said you followed Nature." Are we really only meant to make alarm clocks? And aeroplanes? Isn't it a perfect ordination, to drive some wonderful great cows out into a field full of herbs, which they wouldn't have the sense to get to, if you didn't do it? And so, it is the natural ordination. But Nature doesn't do it on its own. And that's the whole answer. The angelic quality of man is this obedience. The obedience to natural divination of artistry. An impulse, a come-forward. Therefore, that prick-out is an actual performance, that we perform. And you will see, astonishingly, that the plants actually enjoy it—although they collapse, to a degree, and seem to suffer a shock. The resultant is an improvement, and you see a huge happiness, for they love to be born, as you know, all close together, and breathe together. And then they begin to say, "Well now, this is a bit much. I mean, it was very nice when we were three days old, but it's now a week and you've got to get out. So get down!" And they don't all succeed, in fact almost none of them sometimes succeed; as participles all require something. They absolutely require...they require...they require what? Your reaction. Us. Our obedient duty. And so you must prick it out.

Now when you've done it, you've also got to know what to do having done it. The whole artistry has go to be, proceeding with it. And that artistry is that you must not use the human sympathy that you would use on a motor car, when you press down on the starter, or making the ice cream and putting it in the refrigerator. It's not the same bag at all. You've got to say to the plant, "You and I know all about this rotation. And I'm going to help you. And you will see, because you know. Don't you?"

And so, when you put it in the bed, you will give it enough water for two or three days, to make it start to be at home. Then you will leave it to the stars and the elements to perform their mercy. After that you will enter the scene and say, "Well Gibbs, how are you this morning? Are you ready to get going?" And they say, "Yes! Yes!" "Well so. Here you are. *Squaak!*" And away they go. So you must remember this thing: the moment that you see a plant when you prick it out, this mad sympathetic thing, it is us that's got to be put right.

Now we spoke something about this watering procedure, about the plant growing: during that growth period that comes—and again we must put things now in their proper positions, not the utilities—the growth, the procedure of annual, biannual, perennial, and you know we spoke the other day about buds in trees with doglegs, and that explained a whole lot I'm sure. That out of a child on a tree, of which there are millions, the next year come children out of that child. You see, it's the whole difference of this angelic procedure of plants. It's extraordinary, fascinating. And the same on plants as trees of course.

And so, when they're budding up—and you know now what I mean when I say *budding up*—they want all the fruitious-ness on the irrigations of the spring. If they're of that variety, if not it's the fall which is the opposite. And therefore they must have this performance.

Now I draw to your attention to this matter. We spoke some time ago at one of our studies here about certain flowers such as the *Daphne*, the *Scillas*, and those endless little blooms that come when there is obviously no effect of the Sun bringing it about. It is absent. And you realize that it is more planetary than the Sun. As you get late in the fall, considerably. The Sun is no longer the total master. The other planets are now having a say in the exposition.

157

Now you must perceive a very fascinating matter and it concerns the growing of seed enormously. I'm rather deviating from irrigation here, but it does connect with it. *You must look at the quality and the quantity of light.* Which is forever throughout those four cycles changing perpetually in the same way that I described night; night into day; day; day into night; night. So you have got to look at light, quantity and quality.

Now you see why it is in the summer you have to shade those qualities and quantities, for the angelic bloomings of anything are destructive. If you take anywhere in some of these regions, you will get a disruptive of intensity of quality and quantity, which in the tropic on the equator, you will not have any of at all. You will have a beautiful equilibrium. Those places where the temperature, which has a certain amount of conformity in its nominality over this matter, is always between seventy-five and eight-five, never below and never above. The Seychelles, where the coco de mer, the double coconut, takes *ten years* to form, from its birth to a nut. And three years to germinate. Do you begin to see?

Therefore, your watering procedures must look into this realm too. As your flowering comes into play, according to your horticultural manipulation, so can you formulate the mathematics. Retard, or increase them. You will give your plants, absolutely as much, possibly a little more, of the moistures, of excitement. And they will sense that there's going to be a procedure. They will *know*. And that when the blooming—which is what you're after—in the flower bed—oh, but not in the French bean. No, you'll want to hurry that over; you'll want the bean to come. You want the seed. So you'll apply water when it's in bloom. But in the flower bed where you want the flower to stay, and you don't want Mrs. Simkins to come next week and find the whole flower border over, or she will say, "Well, I'm not putting any money in this." And so, you would hold your water up and the flowers will stay there for week after week after week. And they'll say, "Well my dears, we're in no hurry at all. We're really enjoying it here enormously. It's a nice holiday."

In the bean bed you'll say, "I'm not having any of that holiday business with you, my dears. You're going to get on with this and I want some beans." So you will apply (water), and it will rush over and produce beans. Now if you want those beans for seed, and not to cut up green to eat, you don't want that. They've got to have the oils, the varnishes, and the veneers out of the Archangels' nominations. You must remove your artifice—artistry—and allow them to lead into the orthodoxy. Then your seed is telling you its leadership. Now you see there's a difference in crops, and the production of seed, in that direction. That is appropriation of obedience, of observation.

You will see that just as you go to a hen, and you say, "Dear hen, you laid twelve eggs and hatched them into chicks last year, if I give you some nice food, and some water, and a roof over you, will you lay me twelve more eggs?" And the chicken says, "Well, if the ordinance says yes, of course I will." And you go see (a milking cow), and you say, "Will you give me a gallon of milk extra if I pumped you?" And it says, "Yes, of course I will." And so you get all these things. So it is an ordination of obedience.

Now you see when you come to your herbs, you see which way you've got to turn. You've got to tell yourself to keep your artifice and your artistry within bounds. Put your hands behind you and give it up. And then you must fulfill it. For the herbs, like the seeds, have got to be absolutely obedient to the four Archangels. If you place a great deal of your desire—and will—in place of your destiny, they aren't going to have the same instruction to it. They're going to re-reflect your instruction that you give to them. If the plant is entirely in its own domain it will reflect the Archangelic content of procedure to us.

Whenever you plant new trees, they should be watered on planting, regardless of the soil. Let us begin to, as with strikes, extract air. Keep air under control. Later you want some air to the roots. When you first plant you should give plenty of water in the beginning, and indeed every week, regardless even of rain, very often, unless it is heavy rain. Normally speaking, especially in what you would call dryish summers— I'm not talking about total dry summers, I mean dryish summers— certainly water once a month to any trees planted that year, or the former fall. Now you must see how imperative it is whenever possible to put all trees and plants—and even seeds—in the fall, do you see. Day into night, into night, is so absolutely opposite to night into day, into day, where everything runs away. Do you follow? You have got a root, an ahrimanic hold over the luciferic. In other words it is far better to have a good pair of legs, than a very wise head.

As regards watering, there are two scorches that are prevalent—
we've just mentioned one, which is the Sun scorch—which is quality
and quantity of what we call heat. It's the Sun energy and the Earth
energy, that if you're in certain areas like this, which is a frost pocket
and a Sun pocket, in opposites, you are going to get what is called Sun
scorch. The quality of the Sun is too much for the angelic quality of
bloom. Of any bloom. Likewise the element of wind does likewise,
and you will get scorch. At both of those times, and within the areas
of those periods, watering is malicious. For the plant will breathe
more and more, will be more what you call open to recipiency, and
will suffer infinitely more.

If you study the fact that if you remove a tree during its growing
period and plant it, you will inadvertently, however much water you
give it, observe that within a few days, the leaves will wither, perish,
and shortly fall off. And as you know, every idiot laments, goes on their
knees and begs for forgiveness for having done an idiotic thing. The
latter is excusable, but the former is ludicrous. The answer is that if the
leaves did not wither and fall off, the shrub would. And the leaves, being
beneficent, and fulfilling the obedience of their angelic procedure,
whither *happily*, and fall off. In order that origin respect, more origin all
the time, goes back through seed into the invisibles.

The temperature of waters. When one spoke of the ocean and the
land, one has put the key on the table. If you go from there, as you will
go from your classic sonnet, you will see that everything else follows out
of it. Origin position that contains utmost energy. In the *divertissement*
out of that first position, is a division of that energy. Until it becomes
so diverse, as with hybridization, you will have nothing, almost. Almost.
I suppose it's impossible but sometimes it appears to be true.

Oh yes, temperatures of waters. So you realize that whenever you have
formations of intensities in the glass house, your water content must be
within there (that temperature range). Thereby it is held. Not that you
wouldn't do it someway else, and bring it in, but then it wouldn't be
suitable. Not convenient, not economical. But when you have frames
that are not an outdoor procedure, where you have any covering over
anything—and the whole of the procedure of horticulture is a covering
over something, as an intensive bed is!

Now you begin to see that this temperature of water is utterly, and vitally important. The ocean, to the land, is absolutely important. And you see what one was referring to about rivers, about lakes, about water with horticulture. It's always been said in classic horticulture, you can make as many artificial fountains, as many artificial waterfalls as you like, but somewhere something in the sylvan doesn't ring. The bells don't chime, and the flutes of Pan are not sounding. You look and you say, "Yes. Yes, it's very pretty. Hmm. But there's something not there." It is obviously an *in* to *out*, otherwise, this is *out* to *in*.

The whole procedure of water connected with horticulture is an indescribable magic. It pervades the *environnement*. The very insects, the dragonflies, the plants, all become enriched, and part of *environnement* and atmosphere. Therefore it is very important that it is this that brings about temperament, maritime, temperate performance. If you had a lake just here, right now, you know as well as I do, how warm, how wickedly hot the Sun is at noon—it is as hot as you would ever want in the summer. And you would say, "Please don't get any more. It's a bit outrageous even now." And the whole of that water would warm up, and if you sprayed it all over your beds they would all go, "MMMMMMM," like that and the scent would come out, and the manure would start to steam. And so would we. On the contrary, what do we do? This ice water comes up from this ahrimanic devilment, and you spray it on as they've been doing this morning, and all the seeds which were about to germinate go, "O my god!" And they all jump up, and you got them acting the opposite of what you want. So this temperature of water is absolutely vital, absolutely vital. There's no pretending with this. It's really far better to put only one-twentieth of the seed in, and go out with a warm water can. Because you will get a result. The other way you won't get a result. Until the intermediary of the absolute minimal of an area's capacity says to you, "Well, you can go now boys. But you've only got ten days, so hurry!"

Well now, I mustn't keep you any more. Have you got any questions?

Q: If you collect rain water in barrels or cisterns or something, how long could it maintain the quality of rain water, I mean rain water works much better than...

How like you to ask such a question. Ever since my own personal upbringing, wherever we were, whatever the roofs were, we always did this. And believe it or not, we even drank the water off the roof, regardless of birds and other things, people weren't quite so pedantic then as they are now. As far as I know, it remains permanently. You know we've often said here, *what is fresh air? What is fresh water?* Do you see? Do you not realize that the very stars, the whole changes that are going on with the Archangels all the time are manipulating water? They manipulate the air; they manipulate the water. Do you see? Of course there's no question if you keep water for six months in a tank, you would say it would go stagnant. But I would tell you we have someone from New Zealand where they must do it I'm sure, but in Australia you probably know, where they have no water for such a terrible long time, they will drain all water off the roof when it pours as it does here as you know for a hundred inches in three days. They have nothing but enormous concrete tanks under the houses. I mean it goes right down to Beelzebub. These things fill up, and all the frogs are in there, and the newts, and you can hear them at night, croaking like mad. And for some months they use that supply, and drink it without any purification at all. I must say I was very bewildered with that and rather questioned it.

Q: Was that ever done horticulturally, for frames or glass houses to collect the roof water?

Always! Never not, in the days of sense. But they have gone. Every glass house every tool shed, had a roof with a gutter, with a barrel. Rain water is...it is again angelic, do you see? And again this monstrosity today, you see, money rules everything. If you can have a pipe and a pump that you don't know where it comes from, that's the whole answer to go upon. Do you follow? As long as you can pay for it, that's the importance. And the whole country pays for it, it's so clever.

---

1 American marine biologist; founder of modern environmentalism (1907-1964). Taken from the CBS program C.B.S. Reports, entitled "The Silent Spring of Rachel Carson", originally broadcast 3 April 1963.

2 Swiss novelist, poet and dramatist; became president of the Anthroposophical Society after the death of Rudolf Steiner in 1925 (1884-1963).
3 L. H. Bailey, American Horticulturalist (1858-1954).
4 Safe to say that Alan has an issue over how Genesis 1:26, "Let them have dominion...over all the earth", has played out for us.

Raised Beds

Covelo Village Garden
1975

May I pick up from last week? I tried to bring home an enormous focus which has got to play through not only all our work, but all of these talks that we're going to add. We want to apply it. It's this astonishing friendship marriage. So I spoke of the Sun from that point of view. Of the miracle of dawn, of what happens, and out of absurdity and verbosity and talking about light and heat—which is so false a word-ism that we just accept it and don't perceive that the miracle is a marriage of the leader over one of the family, the Earth. Marrying each day the ego and demanding that the ego of the Earth come out and meet it and expose itself in all its good and bad, that its functions may formulate and live.

It's important to bear that in mind with the whole *présentement* of the French intensive bed. You understand that that word 'French intensive bed' is a coined phrase, just like 'biodynamics' is, and you must start to entertain it as a performance. It is the great performance of introduction to *revolutionibus*. But you must also perceive now that it is not from soil that the plants grow as a food issue. It's more out of atmosphere. It's *revolutionibus*. Therefore, the soil must come into the entity that it is. Changes take place in that soil every day, every week; and they're opposites at different times of the year. It's difficult to place that in our mind today because we are so mechanical.

I want to refer, before I go into the French intensive bed and its formation, which is going to be highly practical: we have to comprehend the *totem*-ism of Nature. That when you burn something, or when you compost something, the gases out of that compost heap, the gases out of that fire, disseminate into totality.

As an introduction to that, we think we make electricity. We make a dynamo, we make a turbine, a dynamo, and we say that we create and make electricity. It's complete rubbish. It is nothing other than the performance of the energy, God flowing. You could not make any electricity at all if this energy did not flow out of space. And therefore, do you perceive the calumny of making all electricity in one place, and sending it out everywhere? You have got a thing like a vortex going on! The energy of God is flowing in like mad into that machinery, and coming out as energy, just as food goes into us and comes out as energy. You see the idiocy of thinking that the president of the government could eat our food for us, and send us the energy. It's the same thinking.

Therefore, I want you to look at this thing called lightning. Now do you see, there's a word, you've immediately thought of it. You're quite wrong. You've stopped yourselves from knowing anything about it. Because you immediately said, "I know. Yes, lightning. Yes, I know." Rubbish! Lightning is the same matter. It is *totem*-ism reversed to *conservatoire*.

Now the performance of all the plants, the performance of the dog, the performance of the tree, is an issue of ego, *conservatoire*. That ego is like the Earth according to the Sun. It has its periods of when it must restore itself to make conservation around itself. And that all the time the great leaders are trying to open out and share everything equally. All life is a *conservatoire*. It's a performance. It's a destiny.

Therefore, referring to lightning, you would say, "Oh, we haven't had a storm for a long time. I haven't seen lightning." Rubbish. Absolute rubbish. The only reason that you see lightning is that it has come to the excruciating point in the area where there are actual pockets of not-total-ism. That either in the soils or in the rocks, deep down or shallow, or in the atmospheres, there are actually pockets which are not total-ism. And that what you see is a *pfsst*. "Oh! It's the electricity. There's lightning. Goodness!" Well of course it's going on all the time. It's going on *all* the time. It's merely that that is an excruciating, eccentric period because of sudden changes in climatics of temperature, and such like.

Therefore, do you see, when lightning is forked it means that there are cavities in the deep rocks in the soil that are not *totem*. And when you see it as sheet lightning, it means that there are pockets in the airs above the ground. They are immediately thinning out and you see a flash; which means that it's immediately *totem*-ized.

I want you also to look at this matter which is not often easy today: the Moon is silver and the Sun is gold. The Sun pushes and the Moon pulls. Here you've got these opposing forces. Now you must realize that the Moon operates and magnetizes nine-tenths of the moisture. Now you begin to see what the Sun does. It's nine-tenths of the opposite to moisture. Therefore, you will find that all the springs rise in the very tops of the mountains; right up at the very top. And there it lets loose the little, tiny veins which run into the arteries, which run into the streams, that run into the rills, that run into the rivers, into the deltas! That's exactly the same as we've got in us, in our veins.

Therefore, this matter of—it's in a sense a part of the word 'capillary'—is always being drawn up, and if there weren't mountains, it wouldn't. So you begin to see that you can forget the word 'mountain', and you see a whole divine principle of performance of the flow of the four elements. And you must not think of fire, which Prometheus brought to us in the stick of fennel. This word 'fire' that we use, which is electricity in the kitchen, or lighting a fire; that is fire. But you must think in the elemental form of firmament. That is the alchemistic term for it, which is entirely different. You must think of your moistures, in contrast to that. Because to understand the French intensive bed, that is necessary.

Once more I refer to—and this is all an interplay in the beds—these are the keys. You will not need statistics if you consummate the inner understanding of the performance.

Life gives life. Death gives death. And life into death, into life. You understand in the whole homeopathic principle—and they're beginning to discover it again in veterinary work, that you give the most intense poison when the disease is intensely poisonous at its worst moment. You give an intense poison like hellebore (*Helleborus*). And instantly, you'll get a flashback into a positive; and then you must apply a positive. Therefore, I repeat the word: life gives life.

I take you back to the carnation bed. That when you have a carnation plant in bloom, the first one in a whole bed of carnations, if you pick it, the rest of the carnations will not come into bloom as quickly as they would if you had left it. In other words, if you pick that carnation, you will have to wait, shall we say, five days for any more to come into blooms. If you had not picked that carnation, there would have been more carnations in two days. Likewise, if you go to that carnation bed when it's in full bloom, and there are dead blossoms in it that have not been removed, you will find this matter: a dead carnation to age.

167

It's surrounded by beautiful, full-blown blossoms dying because of the vicinity of death. *Totem*-ism.

Everybody rides a skateboard today; all the kids, every one of them has got a skateboard, *totem*-ism. They don't think. They don't know whether they want it. They just do it, thank goodness. Likewise, you will perceive in that carnation bed, not only are the beautiful full-blown blossoms around that dead blossom dying, but you will even find buds not open at all. Now do you see the idiocy of verbosity? We're only thinking of words in our minds—buds, flowers—we cannot see the cycle.

Now you must live in this. You must give up thinking in words. Your mind must become a corridor. And from it must flow eternity through this corridor into fulfillment through *techne* through the visible. So that carnation procedure is very important in this view of the French intensive bed.

The real gardener is a reflection; not made. You see the importance of this. How delightfully that rings in the ear like a bell; instead of another instrument. Are you aware that the growth at night is the very opposite to the growth of day? The growth of night is lengthening, latitudinal, longitudinal. The growth of day is totally different. It's just like the magnetism of water, or the Sun doing that. You see all through the day it's—*woof, woof, woof, sniff, sniff*—open, blossom, fruit.

They're too difficult to put in words, they're too secret. But you must survey into this, and you must sense it and feel it. This is where you must empty your mind of this word-ism and come to be what you might call pictorial visionary. That performance in the day is totally different to night, there's a key for you, and a vitally important key. So don't put it down because the world is not looking at it. The world of agriculture today has not seen what this is.

The growth at night, which is the very opposite to the day, is an elongation, and that the growth on the dark side, the shade side, during the day, is more than twice the amount of the other side, light.

Now you must go into this because you can't think it in words. These are visionary matters. That immediately must explain to you that if you can see you've got two different growths going on a stalk, you will see what happens. It must turn over. And then during the day it says, "Oh, crumbs", and does that. You see, you can't go into a laboratory and discover that because they can't tell it to you. They will tell you the mechanical is different that side to that side. How very clever. You understand that, I'm sure. Well, I don't.

Now you must look at something. These growths, day and night, are most exquisite during the two equinox-ial periods. Do you understand that there are the winter flowers, the summer flowers, the spring flowers and the fall flowers. Some of them do it in both. Some of them entirely, are credited with one. Some plants are social and some love to live singly, refuse to have anything to do with anything else at all. And the others simply can't live without an *ambuscado* of everything. Some live only by three or four variations. "Oh, do come in today, will you? And yes, you. No, no, not you. You. Come in, yes. That works." These are all because of the planetary procedure, the government. You must discover those. They're very secret. They're not written today. Nobody understands them anymore. We're too busy. You can't do it if you get in and out of a motorcar all day long.

Those behaviors must be looked at in your French intensive bed because they must work your interplays. And those interplays vary in areas. You can't write it for the world. All the soil in the world is never going to be six, six, six[1].

Now, I'm going to say this to you which is a key also. You only water your garden, that it shall dry. And you adore it to become dry so that you can water it. Now you must look at that, because that's the whole key of your performance. And here is a balance which eliminates the absurdity of good and bad.

The two equinoxes are the two beautifully balanced periods, when there is neither excessive light or excessive dark—they are equal, light and dark become equal. In the spring equinox, that equality is an opening out, all the time, and is the voluption of falling in love. The fall one is equal light and equal dark, but is a closing down, slowly, of adoration of sleep and rest, and death—the very opposite. Therefore, if you will look at that, you will begin to perceive that those are the two periods of what you would call lush performance. The elements are not vindictive. Here is the whole reason of the arithmetic of the French intensive bed. Do you perceive that when one talks about this growth of one side in shadow, coming out of dark, being different to the light side, it is too singular-ized. The more singular-ized you make a plant, the more you're going to get that extraordinary, almost, you might say, mis-performance.

When they're all close together, and have an atmosphere, you get very little of that. In other words, this beautiful thing of equality in the garden is a *conservatoire*. And this *conservatoire* is part of the whole embellishment of the garden itself, of our approach to it.

So, now, you must not imagine that the performance of Nature is out of accord. The exquisiteness of the human being is a *directoire* on this Earth, of the whole angelic performance of the plant. Without the angelic performance of man in the garden, the plant is wild and has not true destiny *directoire*. And that when man has lost his own sense of *directoire, idée*, he can regain it through the manipulation of this and the discovery through it.

The French intensive bed, then. The proposition is to take soil, to produce the requirements, and to have that soil in more perfect operation, and condition, and nutriment than when you began. When you take the crop out of a French intensive bed, if you have worked technically correctly, that bed is vastly superior in every manner to what it was before you sowed the seed or the plant. You must look at that because it's very important. It's very opposite to today's procedure, which is piracy. "I don't care what I do to the land as long as I get the money out of my pocket out of selling the beans."

Well, I'm not being vulgar. I don't want to be negative. But today there is no performance of the positive, so you can only look at the positive because you are aware of the negative. This is very disastrous because that's the whole reason of most people's organic focuses today, and therefore, they're falsely placed. It's the beatific joy that is the matter.

I will give you the technical performance of this bed in a few minutes. I want to talk about its actual performance. It can be constituted in several ways. Primarily you must think of these different beds in the areas relating to each other at large, and relating to the area. You must think of interplay of deep-rooted beds running between the shallow rooteds, and even deep-rooted growings in shallow-rooted growings; but very largely, the beds alternating. In that way you get your worms operating throughout the area, even in beds that are entirely shallow. Also, it brings

170

about a constitution of the performance of insects and worms that no other system can possibly come anywhere near its achievement.

Since you get an enormous multiplication of insects out of this method, you will realize it is very essential to run some form of livestock in the dormancy periods to keep the balance. Something like geese or guinea hens, or a few fowls now and again, at the right time running through the area, and cleaning it all up. If you look then at the fertility of this bed that you are going to produce, you are going to increase fertility. And fertility is the marriage of cultivation, fertilization and propagation. When those are balanced and interwoven, you have the word fertility.

Now please understand, and I explain something of the ancient Greek here, that when you plant a grove of trees there comes into that grove of trees the invisible bodies: nymphs, dryads. You could all laugh if you want to, but most of you here already have a sense of that; you're aware of it. You've only to stand within the perimeter of an evergreen oak, and you realize that it governs the smell and the atmospheres, and that there are things performing at times when you're there and when you're not there, which we've got no intimate control, other than, within its area. We are inclined only to be able to look at enormities. If you will see then, the plants do exactly the same thing, but much more finite.

Therefore, when you have a group of plants that are performing like a grove of trees, you have a birth performance going on within it. You must know how delightful it is in a huge water meadow on a hot summer's day, that extraordinary sense of vibratory, odor, moisture and everything going on that's living madly with delight; and of bodies that are not visible. This is a performance of Nature which it adores. And man is the great ordinator of it, the great *directoire*.

Therefore, as you have here, in groups, in pools, you will sense this matter. You put your hand inside a bed of potato plants, as you've got up there, or a closely grown row of peas, you will feel an elemental atmosphere inside when everything else is either scorching, or wind blowing, or freezing, and it's totally different. In other words, the plants are performing their duties to the utmost of their angelic procedure because man has played his angelic procedure into it. And therefore, the foliages and the roots have the performance either in the negative or in the positive of dealing with the elements. But the internal structure, which is the high sense of the nervous system, is two inches under the soil and two inches above; an area of discontinuity, the very skin of the Earth, the delicacy.

Now you understand that when you appropriate yourself and you damage the top—and when you water it, it becomes congealed in no time—there's something wrong. Your technique isn't working. You understand that when the Sun shines heavily in the noon, it is making this huge marriage and it can't stand this enormous amount of love. It isn't meant to, because the angelic performance of the plants is meant to make the most exquisite mantle over it. "Oh, do get me a Sun shade, please." But in the evening it wants it.

Now you must look at this whole matter then. You've got to produce in the soil, and you've got to produce in the plants, thermal control, induction of capillary, and that the very foliages of the plants themselves will ordinate this control of the violence of the elements. Now, so that you can understand that more, you might understand this is very technical, and it's very difficult to follow it in words. If you're having difficulty, make murmurs and noises and I'll try and go in a different direction. Are we alright so far? Are you sure?

Then let us look for a moment, since health is so enormous, let us look at the word 'disease'. This will give you a whole answer to the French intensive bed. What is disease? You see, you can't cure a disease. A person is ill: you can't cure the disease. We've all got it. We've all got every disease there is. You cure the person. They're out of balance.

Now you have this matter that is within the plant. The plant comes out of a seed, and seed comes out of darkness. Therefore, in seed is the utmost *idée*, and the least metamorphosis. As the plant grows, you increase the metamorphosis around the same amount of *idée*. Therefore, think you of the word *idée* as the very central juice that was in the seed, the embryo. If you can think of that, and having to extend into roots, and extend into branches, the protein of that *idée* is traveling out into metamorphosis. And all of the elements are in agreement; they are beatific. But the moment that those juices that we are calling protein is not supplied from the atmospheres, from the gentility of the atmospheres, and the control of the thermal controls, the moment that those juices, one particle of it, gets separated from the totality of the body of *idée*, it is disease. You have immediate disease. And it is the duty of the four elements to become malefic, and destroy. That is death. And what a beautiful thing it is. It puts right a mistake. If you could comprehend that, you will see the balance of health, and the interplay of man in this performance in the garden for the plants.

You will produce in the performance of the soil, of the bed, capillary and control, so that the contents of the soil and the atmosphere and the plants themselves will interplay and preserve an equinoctial amenity. It isn't a word, but you understand it. Inability. That the moment that the plants begin to grow, they should be sown or planted in such a manner that they will keep within the bed the warm, moist gases. It is both the roots and the hairs and the leaves that live upon warm, moist gases (inhales, exhales as an example). They're feeding all the time in this. This is their life force. The more there is of that (inhales, exhales) throughout the night and the day, the happier they are. The more luscious is the growth. This is what you must look to. This is what you must be highly sensitive to.

Therefore, the construction of those beds leads to the preemption that you are going to produce all the time warm, moist gases that those roots will be excited in, and travel, during the periods of reception, for there is the inclination and the declination. There is the period when the plants put out into the air, and there is the period when the plants take out of the air and put into the soil. And the plants vary in this performance. Some do it much more than others. There are the givers and the takers. But do they all give something, and something that you cannot discriminate between. So you can't throw out a plant because it isn't a giver. We have to learn from it. Part of the further discovery.

Therefore, when you have made those warm, moist gases perform in that bed, the control of the foliages of those plants must now enact as the protections. They must cover the whole of that area as quickly as absolutely possible. You must do this with your weeds. Your weeds will give much more vital breathings than your plants. They have more strength, more resuscitation to *totem*-ism. The plant is somewhat addicted to the egotism of the mind. It's been cultured by us, and is meant to. Here enters *conservatoire*; a beautiful thing, really.

Therefore, you will see that the foliages of these plants then, will perform a suffering. They will perform an action that is sacrificial. When the wind blows in burning darts, or when the wind blows over-cold or over-wet, it is the foliages duty to say, "Ta da, you keep off there. Keep up. Keep up. Throw it up." And when the Sun shines too hot, it is their duty to be fed by this breathing and held up. And likewise, according to frost, according to too much sunshine, according to water. Do you see how dangerous it is, to water splashing on the bed? You know that you must always water, even the roses of a canvas do that, and not *that*. For the moment you start that, you get seizure. And seizure on the skin of the Earth, it's like having plaster all over your arm! You skin is going to suffer in no time and will break out in diseases. And just the same with the soil. It is the very neck of plants, the neck of plants which is the crown *présentement*, which is just coming out of the soil that is the whole danger area of throttle-ization, which plants can't tolerate. They can't bear seizure on their necks. It's like us, here, with the diaphragm.

Therefore, that area is most particular. It's the most dangerous area in everybody's garden because of cultivation. That must tell you that you may only cultivate at certain times of the year. However, with these beds you can cultivate it almost any time for the simple reason that that cultivation is done in a few hours, and then performed and planted. You are over-riding the exactitude of the ordinary performance of the cycles and introducing man's great art of his vision of Nature and bringing into a beatific management. A multiplication of marriage which is the word 'fertility'.

The construction of these beds then. Here you have got the utmost performance of those plants breathing the warm, moist gases down in the soil, into the area of thermal control amongst the foliages, and held by the deep roots and the surface area. Therefore, your sowing and your planting of those beds must bring about immediate coverage. And you must, indeed, sow weed seeds with those crops when you sow carrot. However much you may dislike that business of getting on your hands and knees and weeding for two days, it's imperative. For the performance of those weeds will occupy a performance in that bed that nothing else will.

Certain plants are as hedges to produce shade, that you can have spinach and things growing underneath right into July before you go on to your north slopes. And your snow pea will grow excellently on a north slope or a west slope, and shade your salads and your spinaches in those beds. And that that pea can climb up a wire in the middle of a French intensive bed, let in, in a slight trough with your bed.

Understand that so many plants are really semi-alpine. They all love hillocks, they all love raised positions. Now one of the huge importances of this French intensive bed is not only now that you've got perfect drainage, and also drainage up, the interplay of capillary, but far more than that, is it will play in winter as well as summer. That wherever you have got a variation in height, you have got movement. You will notice that as you go up a hill, you run into drafts and little breezes which you never get in stagnation of a hollow. In a flat you get a stagnation. So that you not only get what is known as a frost pocket, but you get a scorch pocket because both the freezing and the heat sits and does *that*. But you see, the moment that you have an escalation, you've got flowing air going on, you've got change, you've got the interplay of the *revolutionibus*.

Now the more you use escalation with these beds, perceive that you have an area of the bed which is exposed to the utmost *revolutionibus*, if you have all your beds with walls either side.

And so now we're back at the Hanging Gardens of Babylon, which is exactly what they were, though on the sides of the Euphrates, where every year they had the most calumnious storms that brought down vast sluices of mud and water and wiped out everything. So what did they do? They built exactly these French beds on top of esplanades on pillars. They used reeds underneath, they used a bitumen-astic on the reed, a natural bitumen-astic, and on that they placed the French bed. But the whole of that was the very first semblance of this matter.

Do you realize how beautifully begonias grow in baskets, hanging? To all sense it doesn't add up at all. You know, a boiling hot day, and there's a basket hanging up. And do you realize how very little water they use? You know, you water them more than the other, but you water very little. And the whole of this is *revolutionibus*.

So you must get out of your head that either deep soil, or flat soil is the answer to growing. The most beautiful way that you will ever grow superb wheat is in these raised beds. And they're so easy to handle.

You can make them oval or round or elongated; anything to suit your purposes. But let them be manipulate-able.

May I talk with you about the potato for a minute? Nobody knows today how to grow potatoes anymore. You should be able to get between ten and twenty pounds of potatoes from a tuber, if you grow it properly. And you should be able to get a potato that has a superb flavor, and it has a beautiful texture, and it has health. The only fertilization required for a potato—and you can apply to Doubleday research who've been a hundred years on this—is the composted *Symphytum* (comfrey). *Symphytum* will compost when cut, within six weeks, summer or winter. There's no difficulty in making it.

Now, the moment you give manure to *Solanum* (nightshades), you're into the realms of disease. There is no point in doing it. The plant that is *Chenopodium* completely makes such a matter unnecessary, and *Sonchus* (sow thistle), and fenugreek. Those plants, in particular. The only fertilization that you really require for a good potato is good turf loam, good compost, and sharp (sand). However it is the method of growing that is the importance.

Now this belongs to the world of the Andes; for that ought to answer it immediately. Also, you must realize that the tubers come from the roots. And the roots are made by the plant, and the plant is made by a parent.

So here's your first notation. Whether you want early, middle, or late potatoes—and you can have potatoes all through the year here—you can grow them in frames perfectly, but you must get the right potatoes. You can't get really good potatoes in America any more, the varieties have gone, the beautiful varieties. I can't talk on that right now. I will tell you anything you want about that; I will try to tell you what I know.

The method of growing, then, is to take your potato and chich it. Chich it for at least a month, or even six weeks. Full light, no exact sun scalds, in trains, with the navel of the thing down and the eyes up. Facing, facing, facing in seed boxes, and place in full light in warmth. That will produce the eye, and the eye will not run. The potato will go violently green, as it should, and become highly poisonous.

When you are ready to plant, prepare your soil deeply and allow ample room, for you have got to increase these intensive beds by hoeing; got to. You've got to produce *this* structure as big as that for your potatoes. Without it you will never get good potatoes. Therefore, you plant your first potato almost at ground level. Your beds are already slightly thrown up into mounds, that high above ground level, shall we say, with ample of the other soil mounded between. So that you've actually got a hollow in which you're planting. You are that much (indicates depth) below ground level when you begin to plant. You take each potato—here you have a bucket with lime, half live-lime, and soot if you can get it. Not oil soot, of course. If you can't, wood ash. You take a very sharp pruning knife, and you take a little chink about the size of my index finger nail out of the potato at the base, near the navel, not removing an eye. Take it right out, like that and nick it. And you dip the potato in that mixture, and with your trowel— you have, of course, put your fertilization into these beds before and worked it into the soil at the sides.

And you place that potato in, and you allow ample room, more room than you ever dream of, the more room the better. You cover, and if this is the very early, and you're liable to frost, cover that area with *Pteris*, bracken. Bracken will refute all injury of frost. Bracken will refute all injury of scorch. It's an incredible disinfectant. It is the only thing to mulch a strawberry bed with, if you must mulch. Never mulch a strawberry bed. Allow the weeds to grow; they're essential to the strawberry.

That potato will come through, and the moment it is through, say a couple of inches, you go down the sides with your trowel on either side, and you bring the soil, mounding over, entirely bury the growth; but just, not upper, just. Cover the growth the whole way along so you've started to get a pyramidal form. That you must go on with ad-infinitum the moment they are through.

Now let us just look at what we've done. Why bother with the chich out and the dip in that mixture? The parent potato, when it's planted, is an egotist, like we all are. And so when it makes the plant, which it does first, the roots come off the plant, not off the potato, remember. The potato does not make roots. It comes off the plant. And all of the babies are going to come off the roots, not off the parent. You have to look at that, it's very important. It's totally different to other plants, like dahlias, totally different.

Now, if the potato were put in whole, it would be quite happy and make the plant and start to make roots, and the more it made the plant and the root, the happier it would be. It would sit down in the arm chair, smoke the pipe, get out the caviar and say, "Isn't life wonderful?" And would go on like that ad-infinitum.

However, it's had an operation. And what's more it's had some lime, and some soot in the operation. Now that wound, if it didn't have the lime and the soot, would rot very quickly. The potato is inclined to rot in the soil, with a wound, very quickly. But the lime is a disinfectant. But during the period that the disinfectant of say, six weeks, it is also an eater. And so it is eating into the area which would otherwise be bacterial disintegration. Therefore, after six weeks it's become venomous to the parent. And it attacks the parent, and destroys it, and it rots. The moment the potato is rotting, the plant and all the roots say, "Hans! Father's dead!" And the plant says, "Don't worry, children! Jeeves, children!" And it immediately starts to think of blossoming and producing all of the children on the roots, which come in this way, at least six weeks, or even in many cases two months before they would.

Now this earthing up is that the children adore to be right next to the sides. You must know how potatoes love to get out of the soil and sit in the Sun and become un-edible with *Solanum* poison. And they are very poisonous. Just like the rhubarb leaf. Even a green tomato can be quite poisonous. That's why they should never be picked unripe; it is monstrous to behavior. That unripened poison does not depart. Oh boy, I do go off the track. Therefore, this earthing-up must go on until the potato is in bloom.

Now the stages of collection are—that's for the early potatoes—the moment it has bloomed you may use the potatoes. They'll only be that size if it's the little kidney potatoes, or the little, tiny French one. You don't want size. Plenty of mint, and cook with the utmost care, a few minutes only, and the skin just falls off.

The next one is the middle area. These must bloom and begin to turn yellow. When a yellowness has invaded the plant, you may lift. With the late potato, all of the lates—which includes your 'Russets' and such, and the old 'Edward'. With those potatoes, you must allow them to bloom, to go yellow, and to die right down. The whole of it must go absolutely brown. You then may lift.

In all cases of lifting potatoes it is dangerous in California because of scorch. But they are very well ripened for a little while on the ground. So if you can choose a dullish day—you see you couldn't do that in scorch with your earlies and middles. But it adds an enormous flavor, that ripening of the potato is very important. Do you understand, for instance, with all your apricots, peaches and nectarines, and figs, do you understand that there is a moment, only, there's only one moment, usually on a certain morning, when all of the acids turn to sugars. And that only with the supply of juices and the performance of the planets with the flow of the juices does that sugar-ization happen. It very much also concurs with strawberries and berries. But particularly in the stone fruits.

If you ever pick any of those fruits before the acids have turned to sugar, they never work. You cannot ripen any of those stone fruits once they're off the tree. The acids do not turn to sugars. Therefore, the whole calumny of today there is nothing that is sold, literally, today, that is reasonable to eat, at all.

The principle plants for the composting, and to create the compost and the stratification for these beds: when I spoke about those stratifications, some people would say, "Oh, my gosh. As if I have every day of every week to put into the garden." You may use, naturally, that basis of the stalks, an excellent drainage; and your hot bed or your coolth bed for summer or winter. And on to that you may place an entire constitution of a third, a third, a third[2] on your bed. You don't have to worry about the other starts if you don't want to. They're a little bit persnickety. They're artistic. Every little touch that you give in the garden makes an enormous difference. And you want to lead into more and more of that.

Therefore, these are the particulars and some of them are vastly particular. You will see that you must have a ley area. Everybody who has a garden must think of a third of that area for ley to produce composts. Even though you grow an enormous amount of weeds where you shouldn't. In my language, where you should.

Urtica dioica (stinging nettle), one of the most important of all: the most invaluable compost maker, the most beautiful texturizer. And you must look at this matter concerning the word humus and textures that produce capillary. It is the texture of compost. All the different composts made of different herbs have totally different textures. What is the miracle of clover, grass, turf loam? It's not comparable to any other soil in the world. This turf loam is a magic. There's no other soil that comes anywhere near turf loam. And you have to look at it. We're just inclined to say, "Well no, my soil's not very good. How is yours?" That is incredibly stupid.

So, *Urtica dioica*, or *Urtica pilulifera* (Roman nettle), either of them, excellent, easy to grow. Grow under a hedge, anywhere; in the shade, in a ditch.

Pteris, bracken. *Alfalfa, Lucerne*, twenty percent protein; two percent more than any beef and seventeen percent more in protein than milk. Sainfoin (Holy hay, *Onobrychis*), the most important ley plant in the world. Nobody knows it. You can grow it in the most desolate, dislocated, adjunct, idiotic area imaginable. Like this. Anyway, if you came here before there was anything, and you had seen this derelict soil, exposed, and you said, "Nope. What shall I do?" I would have said, "Sainfoin." Plant it with sainfoin and within five years you would have the most articulate soil that you can get in the world. It's a perennial. It will grow for forty years. You can crop it five and eight times a year. The compost is incredible. It creates bacteria.

I forgot a most impeccable matter, that in the formation of those beds, and in the soil you must never leave out the composite of bacteria. The bacteria of those five principles being: the clovers, the *Vicias*, the *Vicia sativa*, the perennial *Vicia*, three *sativas* in particular. Most of all the fava bean (*Vicia faba*). The fava you can cut off, compost all the top, and this is a complete negative to all *botrytis*, and has more of the bacteria on the root than any other.

Lupinus, the little annual *Lupinus* (lupines) creates quite a lot; and of course, the pea family. In other words, the pea family, the bean family, the principle and utmost are fava bean. You can never grow enough fava bean.

Whenever you have the two dangerous illnesses of the tomato, *fusarium* and *verticillium*—I had it in Santa Cruz terribly—I grew fava bean in the same area in the winter. I cut it all off and composted it. I dug all the bacteria into the trenches. I work all of the compost of the bean back into the beds, and I never had any *botrytis*, *verticillium* or *fusarium* again, ever.

So, all the clovers, certain of the *Menthas,* which are very disinfectant, particularly *Mentha acquatica* (water mint). You must realize that some of these in the soil have a huge matter in the gas as insect dis-relation, and in the growth of the plant as insect dis-relation.

The bark and twigs of *Quercus* (oak), and certainly the flush of all of the *Fagus* (beech), including the little beechnut. Not much to be had beside, but you can grow a *Fagus* here.

Symphytum, the *Sorrels, Nasturtium, Equisetum* (horsetail), principally burned, it produces potassium. Many of the ferns—particularly the *Osmunda—Fenugreek, Senecio* (groundsel) and *Sonchus. Stellaria media* (chickweed), one of the utter importants; it contains all of the chemicals you can ever create, or think, or have known names of.

Melilotus (clover), *lotus,* sometimes known as Lady's Slipper, there's the one that creeps along. *Medicago denticulata* (M. *polymorpha*), very important one. *Chenopodium auridum,* and many of the *Chenopodiums.* The *Amaranthus hypochondriacus* (Prince-of-Wales feather), and others of the *Amaranthus. Armeria,* in particular. *Armeria* grown by the sea (sea pink) produces intense iodine, and *Armeria* grown inland produces intense potassium.

Forgive my using vulgar, stupid, idiotic names that don't imply anything.

Plant *Borago* (borage), and above all, in all of those beds, no matter what else you plant, for our own beneficence, and for the whole beneficence of the garden, *and* the good behavior of dogs and cats, plant vervain (*Verbena*).

Q: Inaudible question.

And this is exactly why the whole of the herbs have gone into disrepute. For this very reason: that the plants are not known any more. Everybody invents some stupid name and they pick up a totally different plant and say, "Chenopodium." And I say, "But that's not *Chenopodium*". And they say, "Well, that's what I call *Chenopodium*". And you give it to somebody to cure something, and it does the opposite. They have to go to the toilet all day.

So, botanically, in books, do you understand there are what are called common names? It's a family of goosefoot? But, you see, you will have in America, all sorts of plants called 'goosefoot'. Do you see what I mean here? So I only research one name. You can look that up in any true, classic book and you'll find you're right.

The herb garden of the world, where every herb is grown *en suite*. And that for all of the library of the ancient books, and all the names, you realize, most of the names of the Celtic and the facts, we don't know what they are. You see, Broadway—if you say Broadway to anybody, they say, "What, New York?" But this, of course, is major, minor and middle *Plantago* (plantain).

Do you see also, you must look that this changing of periods, for instance when the French, the Norman Invasion of England took place, say, like Hitler would have done, they were so angered with the enormity of the past, do you realize that at that period of the Saxon movement, they had a hundred times more plants than the whole of Europe had in culture. Most people don't realize this. It's a very astonishing fact. And then, Europe simply waltzed away with it. And England went out of fashion altogether. Until I came into view. (laughter)

Anyway, *Chenopodium*, which is one of the goosefoots, and you can't call it lamb's quarters, because that's another plant altogether.

Now, do you see, in this herb garden that I'm relating to, you must have a card from the library. You must all work at this. You must get your Indian pens and your ink, you must get your paint brushes and your colors, and you must make your colors from the herbs and from the soil. And you must have *illustrae*, endless, endless *illustrae*. All the little roots, the stalks, the hairs, the anthers, the pistils, and the notification of if it is medicinal or culinary, and its relationship. Do you follow? What a joy this is! And here you escape from entirely those notions, and at last you're able to say, "I don't care how much you talk. That's *it*!" And it can be in dormancy in the garden, and you will still find it. Alright?

Q: Is there a specific for the culture of cucumbers in the stratification?

Yes, distinctly. Cucumber, governed by the Moon, therefore, you understand that it is virulent to the performance of water. It should never be planted in the soil. The raised bed should be above ground level and should definitely be even set on...it's superb, on stone, or little wooden rafters. Do you follow? The bed? And it should be well composted, rich manure; preferably pig. Next to that: sheep or cow, and then rabbit or goat; not horse, ever. And that should be thoroughly mixed as a lower stratification with a small amount of turf loam and a great deal of sharp (sand). The cucumber should be placed in a little dell in the mound. That is the perfect way to grow the cucumber. Again, you can certainly use in your compost in that soil, with the turf loam, *Chenopodium auridum,* for they love extravagant feeding. Is that what you wanted to know? Water frequently and evenly.

Q: In what plants should I use horse manure?

Horse manure should always be used only below the soil, never near the surface. It's too much of a burner. And I think that I can answer you perfectly simply by referring to Pliny. Pliny says every domesticated animal's manure is almost useless. You see, it's incredible. What a wonderful thinker; and all of a sudden you've got everything, you know, the whole key fits the doors. Therefore, it depends where the horse lives. So if you go to the prairie and collect the original horse manure, you'll find that it's, you know, it's just like using goat. And in some cases where you want what you call a very hot burning, therefore, I use it myself, very much, to feed the hot-beds, on the frames, and in the trenches. For the early pea, nothing like it. It will produce a vehement amount of peas.

---

1 Refers to the chemical additives of equal amounts of N-P-K, nitrogen, phosphorous and potassium.
2 One third turf loam, one third leaf mold, one third sharp sand.

Fertility/The Merchant and the Seer

Covelo Garden Project
11 September 1975

In the area of discontinuity between the salt water and sweet land is the shore. In that area grows sedge. Sedge produces an herbage of no value to any insect, or bird, or animal: nor a blossom that will produce a nectar, nor a seed of any apparent values. It's just sedge. It just grows in the area of discontinuity between the two, just as iodine cannot be found in the ocean, because it exists only in the factor in-between sea turbulence and air, known as spew. That is where iodine is made. And only the oysters and the seaweed know how to get it.

This sedge grows. It does have a kind of blossom and a seed, but is barren otherwise. But, it does produce a decadence: it perishes and proceeds and is born, and it perishes and proceeds and is born—life into death into life. And it does produce a de-compost. After it has grown for a number of cycles in the area of discontinuity, it has produced a soil. And having produced a soil, it can no longer grow; it must perish. Having produced a giving, a seed from the sweet land blows with the winds, falls upon this, germinates, grows into plants, produces foliage, produces blossoms that the bees come to, seed that the birds eat, and foliage that the animals chew, and they all likewise produce their giving into the area. And so you enter the first scene of fertility. But note, and remember, that the whole of that procedure could go in the opposite direction, just as easily as that can happen—so the sedge can disappear, and the salt sea take over.

The subjects that we have been over this week—cultivation, fertilizations, and propagation—intermarried with man the horticulturist, with the four elements in control, produce, as with sedge, in the area of discontinuity, the beginning of fertility. Fertility is this total marriage. It has no end. It is ever. All the color, the forms, the textures, the lights, the shadows, the edges—the beneath these, the above of these—are all matters conjunct in the word *fertility*.

When you place those fertilizations that we spoke of into a bed, into the soil, the average householder and the average gardener are inclined to say, "That will feed the plants," thinking that they've had porridge for breakfast, followed with an apple. You already perceive that this is macabre. It isn't real. You know now about the *revolutionibus*. You know about the intervals between the planets and the stars. You know about the cycles, and you know about pulsation. Therefore, you see, when you place manure in a bed, you are really placing atmosphere. There are quite a lot of plants that actually don't get the manure, and there are quite a lot of plants that often don't quite get the moisture. Some get more and some get less. But if the atmosphere is created, they enjoy it and they get it. And that's exactly the whole procedure of fertility in a bed. It is a marriage of moisture, of air, of earth, of fire, in their controls, and controlled by the approach of the word *fertility*. Therefore, it is equally important to look at these quantitives. You will see that this word fertility is delicate. It requires the most careful assumption and manipulation.

The whole of the culture that we have been focusing on this week and the basis of it of the week before, brings to your vision that the higher the note, the more carefully must you play it. For if there is any error in the production of it, it will be hideously obvious. Whereas, if you make a great quantity of grotesque noises, it doesn't matter what mistakes you make, because nobody would notice anything. Therefore, in the whole approach of this, in this very acute fertility, is the utmost necessity of the perfection of technique. Oh dear, what have we said? What is the perfection of technique? This is utterly important.

It is this matter. It's one of the reasons that all art is essential to us as a steppingstone into horticulture. Technique is the fulfillment of the method of playing and using the instrument, having been brought to such a perfection and fruition that it is invisible. The world of visibility and the world of invisibility. And here, all visible technique altogether becomes finally invisible, and a magic. Therefore the technique of the high art of horticulture is invisible, and you won't see it. You will look at the horticulture in the garden and you will be eclipsed, you will be delighted by a magic. And the whole joy of it is that you can't understand it.

Therefore, the application of technique in the whole adaptation of this marriage of moisture, fertilization, cultivation, must be absolutely succinct and obedient. Obedient to the law of Nature, and obedient to the system, whereby the technique is appropriated. If there are any mistakes, they are going to be horribly obvious, and the plants are going to scream. And that's where Nature and the whole of horticulture are different to the whole art and craft. In horticulture with Nature, it is inner to outer; and in the whole of art, it is outer to inner. Go which way you will, it is so. It is in a sense a mechanical, so that the whole of the horticulture must be obedient to the law, which responds in its exemplification and tells you *how*, *which way*, *yes* and *no*.

Therefore it is essential to be on the tips of our toes. And you understand perhaps a little more clearly now what was said, and what was meant when one said that you could damage soil more easily than a plant. Now you have a breathing matter that is full of life, which doesn't appear to be full of life, because the technique in it is so perfect, that you can't perceive it. It's the perfection of the technique of life into death into life. Therefore, at all times, the approach must be perfect and utterly considerate. The outcome of color, the outcome of texture, the outcome of nutrition, are all an ever-building resultive of the never-ending flow of the word *fertility*.

You can't ever think that you will attain fertility. It is a commencement that goes on. It builds on its own laws with the mastery of the horticulturist constructing with it.

Therefore, this essentiality of approach of technique—you understand that if you build a certain size bed for a certain size crop, shall we say lettuce, you would apply this amount of wood ash, that amount of stratification beneath, that amount of fresh manure upon that stratification to set up a decomposition of heat, a certain amount of top soil upon that, and stratifications upon that and upon that, and they will all contain fairly well-measured quantitives. If you applied less, you might as well apply none. And if you applied more, you had better apply none.

Indeed this is what the French did, actually, out of the French intensive system. And even Lorette, with whom I studied, did so in the world of pruning. He went into defoliation, against the law of

Nature. He overstepped the mark by saying, as Plato would not, "I know what I am doing." And that is impossible. The French in their procedure brought about the whole of this culture of these applications of excellent cultivation—this deep cultivation—this bringing about of breathing, of pulsation, the adding of excellent organic manures, of the use of wood ash, and such matters, all applied in the right areas at the right times, and the use of coverings such as glass in the winter to maintain the perfection of the growth. They achieved what they were after, and they were not satisfied. They wanted more, because, unfortunately, having achieved that out of the mastery of the adoration of creation, of plants, money entered the scene. They found that the world wanted what they produced, and needed it and wanted it very badly, and that they could demand much more money than was adequate as a balance in the matter.

Therefore the whole entry of the word *fertility* flew out the window, like Tinker Bell. And in through the door came the bank, the adolescence and adoration of money. And out went *idée*, and in came intelligence and reason. So they added more and more quantities of manures, of fertilizers, and more manures and more fertilizers. Finally they found that if they had a whole bed of manure they could get more money out of it still. And what happened? Very much what you've got today. Nothing whatever in something that looks like a vegetable. The lettuce and the young beans and the little spring turnips and the baby Chantenay carrots hadn't got any nutriment in them at all. They were bogus, and empty. But they still got their money. But at that time people still had palate, and the palate told them they were eating mush, and so they turned around and made a noise about it. In swept the chemical world, and out went the whole issue. But that is what happened over un-balance. Therefore you see that in the construction must be a taking into account of the requirement of the balance of Nature.

It is exactly the same with the use of the watering. Now the old system of what you'd call hack gardening was not to have more work than necessary, therefore you put the hose on the darn thing, and you kind of did what they do at the Gezira Club in Cairo. They simply turn a huge cock there, and the Nile comes up, and the whole of the tennis courts and the rose gardens and the polo ground is under water to that extent. The Nile just comes up and does that, and then they turn it off and it goes down. Well that's all right in Cairo, and it works. But the point is that when you come to a garden and you water once a week, and you water extremely heavily so that the water goes down three or four feet, you of course leech out everything that you've put in. In other words, you drown the word fertility. The whole *présentement* is to keep all of these and you in balance. Therefore the less water you have to use, the better, is the approach of your fertility. And a small amount of water very continually is in most cases the obvious answer.

However, you also understand that the application here includes the planting of the plants and the observation of the utilization of the interpolation of weeds, whereby the whole thing is brought to the finest picture of manipulation, so that at all times you have conservation. Equinox and maritime.

In this area of thought must also enter any attitude we have to livestock. You see, exactly what has happened if you read Page's[1] book that he has granted to us, on the chicken. You would see exactly what has happened. It has happened exactly the same as we spoke about the French intensive system. The chicken agreed to lay an egg, a clutch, and when we said to the chicken, "If I bring you some cereal, would you manage to lay another clutch of eggs this year?" And the chicken said, "Well, if that's the law, yes, of course I must obey. I will." And so she lays another clutch, and we have them and get them. And then we said, "Well, that's wonderful you can manage another clutch. What about another one?" And so the hen said, "Yes, certainly, if that is the law, so I will." And of course all the duns would have done the same, the elephants would have done the same with milk as cows do. So it goes on, so long as you don't disobey the *idée* within you, which is your link with the conscience of the law of Nature. The moment you do that, the Father has stopped and turned round. Because that is the end if you do.

I'll talk about this with an instant story. Just afterwards, if I may.

All livestock must come into this view of fertility. You will then find that there is no end ever to what you will receive; to what will take place; to what will be given. And you do realize you must be seeing that you could never enter the whole of this with a commercial attitude. Out of it can come profit. Out of it can come gain. Most decidedly. But with commercialism, you would lose everything immediately. And this is a very succinct point, because most people will come to the gate of the garden and say, "How do I grow a crop that will make profit here?" The answer is plain. And nobody likes it.

Now perceive that when you have built these beds, when you have composed your garden as an intermarriage of plants: the inter-relators, the dis-relators; the deep-rooteds, the shallow-rooteds; the correct moistures, the correct drynesses. Why do you water the seed pan? Oh, I will tell you. So that it will dry. But why do you let it dry? Oh, so that you could water it. You see you have an *idée fixe*. You think that you're really there just to water it all the time. But this is all change. This is the whole matter. It's the whole inference of using these things, together in marriage. It's perpetual change. And these changes are all interpolating. We can never totally understand them—they're too vast. But they're operating. And the more that you operate with them, the more they will operate and lead you to operate with them, the more into the invisibilities.

Therefore, when you have interpolated your orchard, your soft fruits, your butterflies, your insects, your lizards, your tortoise, your seaweeds, your soils, your airs and your waters—when you have interpolated them, and behind it there is a technique, and the technique has become invisible—by then, an astonishing thing begins to happen. In the cycle that takes place, the birth of fertility has happened. There is a cornucopia that connects with eternity. And it is no longer in your hands, and certainly not within your intelligence and reason.

You are going to find—for find you will—in each cycle, a change that comes, new things you never suspected, you never planned for. Perceive that if you take ten acres and plan the whole thing, what do you get? Exactly what you planned. Or less. But not more. When you leave the planning and the administration of the leadership of Nature, you cannot calculate that planning, of the resultant. It is in eternity. And you will even get crops that you didn't plant. You will even get results within you that you never thought you would get out of a crop. They are things that are related to the necessity and the desire of the sowing. So in this marriage in the garden of the word fertility, the very birds in their song will speak of this fertility. And it will be heard. The very insects will convey it; and the bees, and the breeze, and the wind—a long, long journey away. And the moistures will be aware, and the clouds, and the stars. And with the cycles of change you will be induced to find and to observe and to receive new cycles of insects, new butterflies, new birds, new plants, new weeds, out of the magnification of this fertility.

In the compost heap of this year, of this cycle, will be certain resultants which you know, many resultants which you will guess, and many resultants which you will have no knowledge of at all. In the outcome of that composting to the soil of next year, with fertilities—with fertilizations and with fertility—will grow certain weeds and certain plants that you had no suspicion of, had not even heard of, and knew not of the values of. And they alone will, in their own fertility, speak of insects, and butterflies, and life, and moistures. For there are the coolth givers and the warmth givers; the sugar givers and the oil givers; and the potassium makers and the magnesium makers. They all have their duties and they all have their techniques. So that under all these comes this effect into the gardener of the garden, and it goes to the area of *image*. And here the individual is lifted, so that the *image* is in a new strata. It perceives what it has not perceived, and is lifted. And out of this lift a further perception invokes that into the re-creation of the fertility of the horticulture. And again into the art and the craft. Here enters the eternal, everlasting magic of fertility.

It can go in the opposite direction. How careful, how careful we must be in our approach, that it be reverent and obedient and full of sensitivity and full of observation. For we shall get what we bring about. And inconceivably more.

So this fertility then, is a cycle, as you see. It has not an end. We, because of our perception say we have found the world—there is nothing more to know, there is no more land to discover, and we have sailed every ocean. Well, what about inside the Earth? And so you see there can be no question, we must never pretend, and we must never delude ourselves that we can foresee this. This whole attitude of the *clairvoyer*, which is the essence of the herbaceous border, will lead you into this vision. And that is what you might call the architectural formation of the vision of fertility.

The enormity of this matter is that there is nothing artificial, there is nothing built up or false in the whole of this system and study of it.

It is unutterably true. It does not take any individual to tell another individual about it in words. It is all there. It is all discoverable, and it is all self-relative, by the very growth of the plants, the manipulation of the soil, and the deep study of human nature within it, as a marriage matter in fertility.

And here you have one of the huge answers of the great sorrows of today. Whenever mankind—almost whatever nation, not quite with some of the native tribes, but with the majority, certainly, of civilization— whenever mankind begins to live either in a village, or a farm, or a hamlet, what happens? All the rare plants, birds, and the animals are gone. It's ludicrous. When you go into the jungle, when you go to an island where nobody goes to, when you go to the Arctic or the Antarctic—*Oh hello. Hmm, very interesting. All gather round. It is perfectly natural.*

But we have to face the fact that wherever we go, even the plants all go. And this is utterly, utterly, utterly, hopelessly erroneous. It's got to be put right. And it's got to be put right in the exquisite matter of children. Why should the magic of children be destroyed, and they be turned into machinated machines, and lose all of their contact with that with which they were born, and have it driven out, that they shall not see, and not know, and be hidden by the travesty of this matter. The whole of this attitude, the whole of this approach brings in, because of fertility, the whole of life. It belongs. It is science. It is the vision of the understanding of the law of Nature: of relationship and dis-relationship. And invites it more and more to come and explain itself, if such explanatory is necessary. It should be found and perceived, and given life and shared. And man, in his great majesty, as he is in the world, shall be a great leader of it, and a great ordinator of this manipulation of fertility.

Well that's a bit of a lecture I'm afraid. Do you want to talk about it?

Q: In the plannings I wasn't quite clear on the point you were trying to come about as far as I understand what you think you don't see that you get out, but like there's an example over here and an example over here it seems like we're...

Yes. The intermingling of everything in the garden? I will give an example that should explain this quickly, in toto, but I'll take a single example to do it, if I may. Let us take fruit trees. Let us take apples or pears, or all fruit, it does not matter what. You are going to find here a system and a technique. You will not meet it, unfortunately, in America at all. In this system you will find that every tree is trained, exactly. That all its buds will have an exactitude that is equal. You will find that all of the *revolutionibus*, that is light and air, will interplay equally around every bough. Every fruit will have the same perfection of totality. You will find that the tree, placed within the garden, will have cultivation and fertilization every year as a growing fertility extending with it. Each year the fruit trees are manipulated a little further, and a little further, and intermarried with the garden; all the relators are interrelated. Did I bring to you the matter about friendly pollinations in the orchard? Well, I must bring it in here then.

In the culture of fruit today, we have brought about fruit such as apples and pears that are so far removed from their origins that they cannot intermarry themselves. You may have an entire orchard of Cox's Orange Pippin, or an entire orchard of the Comice Doyenné pear, and they will be absolutely full bloom, the whole orchard packed with blossom, and not one fruit will ever set. Not one. Because, being all of that variety, and coming out of man's *image*, have too far-fetched a self from origin. Such as dogs do when they become highly bred. Do you understand? They can't breed anymore. Fantail pigeons can't breed. They've gotten too much tail. Parisian women have got them in their hats.

Now, it is simply got over. In an orchard of Cox's Orange Pippin, you bring a Worchester pear main, or a James Grieve, to the tune of one tree in ten, and you have got what is called inter-pollination. And with the Doyenné du Comice pear, if you bring a Conference and a William Bon Cretian—either of those two, or both, one in ten—you will have every fruit literally set, or every fruit that should set. In all cases, all blossom and fruit is not intended in Nature to set, and does not and was never intended to do so. It wouldn't and couldn't. That is an error in the first place.

Now, the average agriculturist would say, "They're up. Isn't that wonderful? Do you see how clever we are today? We know it all." I'm sorry, but you've missed the bus completely. And it's this: that when you have an apple orchard of all apples, if you have a few pear trees in the vicinity, and a few other fruits such as stone fruits and so on, there will be an inter-pollination that must be termed friendly inter-pollination. The whole crop of fruit will be superior. Not only will the whole crop of fruit be superior, but also the whole growing of the trees and the district will be different. Does that confer something to you?

Now I go much further. In the training of these trees, we have talked about this equality: the equality of the boughs all having the same amount of juice, all of the fruit the same amount of light and air; none of them in the shade, and some in the sun. Do you follow?

Observe this matter. When you just plant the tree and you know little about culture and fertilities, what have you got? A great mass in the middle. Huge great mass. And on one side is the south, and on one side is the north. I ask you, when a jay eats apples, what does he do? Pecks a few of the red cheeks of some of the apples, and goes from one to the other, eating the red cheeks. And everybody says, "What a beast! Shoot it." And of course it knows exactly what it's doing, and is telling us, and we don't hear. The point is that those fruits are ripe in that area, and not in any other area. No other fruit on the tree is ever going to be ripe. All fruit ripens from acid to sugar—this thing we are talking about all the time, this change—at a certain time when the light—which after all is all sunlight, literally—it is a certain degree, and gives it. Therefore, for correct ripening, fruit must be in the full light and Sun. And these are beautifully sweet and sugared. All the fruit on the north is worm-eaten. Just go and take an apple on the south side of the tree, and go and take an apple on the north side of the tree; go and take a peach, a plum, a prune, a fig, and what do you find? This very matter. Therefore perceive that in this aspect of observing Nature, you grow the tree in a most articulate shape, so that this equality can take place.

Now perceive the extra lunacy of the commercial idiot. He not only grows a tree with the whole center bunged up, but he grows a whole orchard with the whole orchard bunged up. For what else is the whole plantation? And it is nothing but the south row, and the southeast corner and the southwest corner that can ever have a ripe fruit on a tree. The rest may as well be thrown to the pigs, and they wouldn't eat them very much. Do you perceive what I am getting at? Now you begin to see about this interpolation. Do you see that because of that pollination procedure, we say, "Oh, it only takes an apple to pollinate an apple. And there's the answer. We only have put it out and read it." Oh, what about these most delicate flavors? What about the little wild strawberry and the cultivated strawberry being married? Do you follow?

Back to origin every time and intermarry it with your culture, yes. But go on with your cultures and your cultures and I'm sorry, you're quickly over the horizon and gone. The interpolation of weeds in the garden are the sustenance and holding of the most articulate anchorage you could ever pray for. They are the breathing into the atmosphere of the very word fertility. Your cultured plants are never going to produce the cultured atmosphere of fertility on their own.

The interplay of all the plants is a love and a hate. And you can't live without it. The interplay of the tortoise, of the slug, of the caterpillar— you can't live without it. What is soil but total life into death into life? Soil is dragonfly's wings, bird's beaks—students in the compost—heat, skin, everything, the droppings of wind, the droppings of birds, and the manuring of the earwigs. And all of these are articulate with a traveling of this fertility. Earwigs do belong at this time; they may not belong very soon, where you have developed a fertility that is above the necessity of the earwig, that is above the necessity of the slug in the lettuce. At present I defy you to grow a lettuce without a slug. And if you do I'm not going to eat it. Because it wouldn't be safe. Do you begin to see? Do you see that grass grows better when there is clover there? Do you see that grass grows worse when there are buttercups there? We are going to talk about this all throughout the year. We are going to take every herb that we can, we're going to look at it; we're going to see what its inferences are, how it is governed by this changing *revolutionibus* that says to it, "Reflect you, what I am saying." And there it is. So you don't need to be an astronomer, but you must be either a horticulturist or an astronomer, or both. Does that answer your question?

Q: In speaking of conservation, you said equinox and maritime? I didn't understand.

You see, we mustn't jump our hedges. I've got to keep a few little secrets up my sleeve for you. *Conservatoire.* You will seek what an incredible magic this is, fertility. You see, I spoke of sedge, on purpose to open this. We went from sedge, which you could begin to call nothing, of no use to anything, into a compost; into a desirability; into the commencement of fertility. Do you see? *Conservatoire* enters there. The sedge, in its growth, made a *conservatoire*, and deposited, and held, and said, "I will give more than I've taken in this world. There you are. Now I must go and leave you." And the other came in and made more of that, again.

We as horticulturists must perceive the whole of this law. And this is what we do not do today. We make inarticulate bags and boxes and stuff it with rubbish, and eat the bags and throw away the contents, as we should. And we don't know what to do with all this drivel. It's drivel. You can't do anything with it, you can't even destroy it. But everything in Nature *is something*, and you can't destroy anything in Nature. Every stick, every leaf, every little capsule of a seed is essentially important. And the totality of Nature says, "*I did it all! Grow up! Bang!*"

Where are the leaves that fall off in the fall, within a month after when they fell. You go to collect them and get: "But there is such a laugh here! I've come to get them. Where are they?" Everywhere. They've all gone. *Konplunny! Conservatoire.* This is us. This is our intermarriage with it. "C'mon please, collect the money. Into a big, big, thing. Put them there. To hell with God!" Think of all those little bits of weed you take out. You could leave it. Good gracious, if you leave the weed in the Sun today, what on Earth is it going to look like tonight. What's happened? All the gasses, what's up? "Oh, they're up there. They've gone over your neighbors, they've got them all." I'm awful sorry, we want them in here. You take the eggs, you bring the shells back. *Conservatoire:* connect everything.

When I was at the university, and began that garden, everybody looked at it and said, "Poor muddle. Come from England, he's obviously mental." This was a bank of poison oak. Nothing but sog-hopping students jumped over it. And they all got poison oak as a result. And, within no time, we grew the most un-propitious little plants. But those un-propitious little plants made a compost heap. And that started it. They started making leaves, they started making seeds, they started making pests. And they all built life-into-death-into-life, and we collected them assiduously. We even collected the most pernicious garbage from the kitchens, and brought it in to get it going. Later on we threw it back at them. But we brought it in, and started this *conservatoire*. Everything is *conservatoire*. The whole French intensive system is the most intensive *conservatoire* of technique imaginable, only the technique is perfect so you can't see it. You understand now a little?

Except the words equinox and maritime...

I see. Now, in maritime, let us take an example of the Aegean, the whole Mediterranean coast. It is backed by the great Alps—the Dolomites of the alps—and there is the ocean. And here is a great south slope towards the Sun, the government of all of the planets. And that government orders that all the beautiful effusive collaboration of Nature—fertility, which is let lose ad lib—shall be *conservatoires* here. Into this bed. And it should become a fertility, and is. The most beautiful fruit grows there, the flowers. Everybody travels from blooming England in November when they don't want to be frozen anymore, and they want violets, and they want mimosa, and anemones, and beautiful peaches. They all go to the south of France. This goes on ad lib. This is what a conservatory is. It is a *conservatoire*.

Perceive the inter-relators are the four elements: earth, fire, air and water. They are forever obeying the gods. We call it destruction: creation and destruction, and creation and destruction, but the whole area of maritime means coastal belt, means a controlled *conservatoire*. Cancer and Capricorn is a *conservatoire* of the poles and the equator. Indeed the equinox is a *conservatoire* of the dormancy of summer, of mad proliferation, of burning heat, and the obtuseness of the burning of winter, and the dormancy of winter. The two equinoxes are these wonderful areas, *ahhh*, where you just float. Equal day and equal night. You see that everything in this horticulture, in this system, is an observation of Nature. It is not a manipulation of the intelligence and the reason. It is *idée*. Does that answer you a little? Good.

The days are early. We've got all this terrible talking to do. But a lot of discovery, to make it real. You see, the reason only that we do this talking is that our periods here are what they are. And we have lost vision. We've lost inner vision. Not because it's not with us; it is because that as children it was driven out. They pulled the blinds down and said, "Hey, c'mon my boy; c'mon now my girl. What are you going to do? How are you going to earn a living? Now you stop that playing about. Now you stop playing the piano, stop drawing those silly pictures; now you stop running out looking at those damn birds. You c'mon now, you've got to make something, You've got to sell...what about petrol? What about a motor car?" It's not funny. It's terribly sad. The vision is gone. The enchantment of childhood is driven out. This is the reason that people do not have vision and are not able to look anymore.

You must be aware that even in 1500 some of the botanists said, "Do you know, people no longer have the capacity of seeing the seed of peony?" You just don't quite understand that, but you will when you study the peony. Its seed, and the blossom is governed by the moon, and it shines at night. It is quite different to what it is by day. It throws light off it at night, and you can see it. Indeed the shepherds of the Aegean only collect the seeds of the peony—which grows most proliferously there—only collect them at night. Because, they shine when it is dark, and they can pick them up galore. They wouldn't see them at daytime at all.

Oh dear, what are we talking about now? There is this thing we speak of. The reason why we do this talking is that we can throw stars in the air, and you could look up and see them. And once you've seen them, you can go and find them in the garden. But we don't go and hunt for them in the garden anymore, because we don't want to. We are satiated with mechanical blowing-up boxes, and all the rest of the rubbish. And of course this intense verbosity which never stops. You've realized already, that you really can't enjoy gardening or be a good gardener if you are thinking in words. You've go to stop it, to have a touch. You can't look at one of those flowers and smell it at the same time. You can't eat an apple and look at it at the same time. Does that explain a little?

Q: Did you have a tale of the East?

Oh, yes. Do you want it? Can you manage it?

Oh dear, I haven't prepared this and I should. I always have to. However I will try and do justice to this tale.

It is an ancient story from the East. It is called the *Merchant and the Seer*. On one occasion a merchant had lived for some time; and he was a young man. He had been very unfortunate in his business, and had not improved his situation, and had very little in the way of possessions left. Indeed it had come to one camel, and a small quantity of goods that could be contained upon this camel. And he set off by himself, to travel the desert, to try and find a town to do business in. After he had traveled for a few days, he saw in the distance, on the horizon, dust and a caravanserai.

He bethought himself he would as well make force, and catch it up, so as to travel more safely. So he spurred his camel up and by evening he caught up with a caravanserai of twenty camels, and a very old man, with them. He hailed the old man, and the old man did obeisance, and said, "Welcome." And the young man said that he would travel if he might with the caravanserai, as he was not safe on his own. And the old man agreed. As they sat at their evening meal, whilst the camels had been tethered, the merchant explained the position of his misfortune.

And the seer watched him and observed. The merchant said, after some time, after leading into the matter with a considerable purpose, and a careful gaze, he questioned whether the old man knew of any town or area where he could do good business for a change, and make some profit? And the seer said, "Oh yes. Of course I do." "Oh!" said the merchant, "You do?" "Oh yes," said the seer, "I do." "Oh," said the merchant, "In that case, I wonder if I might either come to terms, that is a sharing of any profit that I might make, or, on the contrary, any terms that you might suggest, but if you could possibly lead me to this, do you think that this could be considered?" So the seer said, "If you wish this, of course."

So the merchant was a little nonplussed at the easiness of this. Didn't seem to him quite the usual way that business proceeded. And he began to have his misgivings about the whole thing, as he observed. He thought that this was a very old man indeed, but he looked intolerably well-to-do, and yet too utterly simple to be acceptable. And surveying all this, he said, on thinking it over, before they retired, "Now you...you said just now that there was a place that you knew of, a town. Is it far?" "Oh no." said the seer, "No, it is not far." "Well, you say in this town, that *even I* can do good business—whilst I have done no business for ages and have made no profits at all. But you say that even I could do business, do you mean that I could do *much* business? I could make a really big profit, do you mean?"

So the seer said, "If you wish it, yes, that is so." So again the merchant felt more nonplussed than ever. And he said, "Well, since you seem so free about this, to what extent could I make a total profit? To what degree are you talking?" The seer said, "I can show you all the business of the world, if you wish." The merchant really thought now he's got a looney. So he thought anyway, quite obviously this man could do business, and had done very good business, so he thought he would hang on to it anyway. So he said to the seer, "Then since you tell me that you can lead me to all the business of the world, you will do so? And tomorrow?" And the seer said, "If you wish it, I will."

The merchant said, "Well, I've lived in these areas. I've never heard of this town. I've never heard of such a city. And we can be there tomorrow?" "Tomorrow." "How do I know," said the merchant, "How do I know that what you are suggesting is true. That there won't be a murder tonight? Or a robbery?" And the seer said, "I have here a phial. In this phial is an ointment. If you place one finger of your left hand in the ointment, and apply it to your left eye, you will perceive all of the business of the world."

The merchant roared with laughter. And he said, "You're telling me that if I put my finger in that ointment and I apply it to my left eye, that I can see all the business of the world? And that we could be there tomorrow?" And the seer said "If you wish it, that is so." The merchant said, "Give me the ointment! I'll do it. And then I will know."

And the seer said, "I will give you the ointment, and you may do it if you wish. But beware. *Beware.* And again, beware. Apply the ointment only with your left hand to your left eye. For if you go any further, you will be destroyed." The merchant said, "Well, this is no matter! Give it to me and let me see!" And he took the ointment roughly and grabbed it from the seer's hand. He undid the little cap, and he placed his finger of the left hand in the ointment, and applied it to the left eye, and looked.

He saw a city dazzling with all its possessions; and he realized that on seeing it, it was within his total grasp to have everything that he ever wanted.

And the seer said, "It is time to rest." And the merchant went to his rest, but could not sleep, thinking of this that he'd seen, of how he would get there, but he did not know the way. He must wait for the seer. He wanted every minute to get up and get his camel and go galloping over the desert to the city. But he did not know the way. So he had to rest, the whole night sitting and aching and worrying, and thinking and wondering, "What was this all about?"

And the seer slept soundly, and eventually awoke. They greeted. And they prepared their camels and they set off at an easy pace, and galloped over the horizon, and arrived at the city. And the merchant said, "I can't thank you...I don't know how to thank you. We will meet." And so the Merchant went and did his business, and in a few moments he was covered in riches—of every kind imaginable, so that the camel could hardly move, he was so laden. And by the next evening he met the seer, with twenty camels loaded with riches. The seer said, "Since we travel part of the way in the same direction, let us travel." And the Merchant said, "Willingly." For he knew now, that he was so laden with the utmost riches, that on his own he would indeed be likely to be attacked and robbed. And so they traveled.

On the second day of their traveling, they came to a point in the desert, when the seer halted, and turned to the merchant and said, "Fare thee well. That is your direction, and this is mine." And again the merchant endeavored, in his grotesque way, to say his thanks. He turned his camel and galloped as fast as he could towards the north, and the seer, gently to the south.

As the merchant galloped, he began to survey what had taken place, and he was again full of the misgivings of the extraordinariness of the whole procedure. But none of it seemed to hold water. It all seemed so utterly false, so hideously unreal: it wasn't a dream even. He then began to suddenly think. He began to realize what an utter fool he was. What an idiot he'd been made! Here was a virile young man with endless capacity with one camel with riches, and there was an old decrepit idiot with twenty camels loaded—*loaded*—with fabulous wealth. And although he had enough to last a long time, there was enough for a lifetime traveling in the opposite direction. He stopped his camel like that, and about-turned, and galloped to the south.

And as he eventually came up and saw the seer in the distance, he shouted and said, "Heeeeeey!" And the seer pulled up and waited, and the merchant came galloping up, somewhat threateningly, and said, "Listen, I have something I want to talk about to you. You told me all about these riches, you took me to this place, and indeed you've been kind. But I perceive how clever you are underneath. I perceive how you've made a fool of me; that you've got all these camels—there's twenty camels loaded—look at it! And look at me, I've one poor camel with the riches. How could you do it! How could you do it!" And this the seer said, "What will you?"

And the merchant said, "Well, it is obvious. If you were really generous, you would give me ten of them, and let me take them. That is half of what there is." The seer said, "If you wish it. Do." The merchant said, "Well, you mean to say you will give me ten of these camels with the riches? You will just give them to me with...oh then indeed, I must thank you indeed, for this is most generous. I...in fact I of course don't know how to thank you now. I do apologize of course." And without more ado, he turned the ten camels and his one, and galloped to the north, knowing now that he had enough riches for the whole of life. And away he went.

He galloped until he was back again, where he was before. And on the way he was again bethinking, and was overcome with all these extraordinary fortunes, of how unreal this was—when suddenly the whole thing was clear. He saw the whole thing now. He saw the trick. It was such a clever trick it wasn't true. Here was this seer, traveling to the south, with a guard of ten camels of riches. It was nothing else. It was a cover, a hide, for in his girdle he held the whole secret. He had the ointment whereby he could see everything that there was in the whole world. And these riches are nothing. Nothing! The seer's got the mountain and he's getting away. He's an old decrepit fool and he can do nothing about it. I'll shall kill him on the spot!

He galloped to the south as fast as he could, and within two days he caught up with the seer and he hollered to stop. And the seer pulled up and said, "What is it now?" And the merchant said, "I see it all. You're as clever as a fox. You think you are going to get away with that ointment." The seer said, "Beware! I warned you." And the merchant said, "You have no capacity against me. I can kill you in an instant. Nobody will ever know. You'd rather had give it to me." The seer said, "I have warned you. Beware." And the merchant said, "You can't deceive me any more!"

And he grabbed the girdle and he snatched the phial, and he tore the cap off. He put his left finger in the ointment, and he applied it to the left eye, and he applied it to the right eye, and he fell down blind, and could never see again, and was a beggar in the desert for the rest of his life.

There is the story, I believe from Persia, of the Merchant and the Seer.

---

1 Page Smith, *The Chicken Book: Being an Inquiry into the Rise and Fall, Use and Abuse, Triumph and Tragedy of Gallus Domesticus;* taught history at UC Santa Cruz when Alan Chadwick was there; (1917-1995).

Art

Covelo Village Garden
25 May 1977

The subject this morning is so vast that there is no preface. Also I have no means in this subject of referring to anyone else, the one and only area where that takes place. The subject is art. Art and craft are always put together. We will talk a little bit about craft, as craft is a separate entity as well.

We have considered the seasons. We have now perceived what is behind the tangible, separated, *touchingnesses* of time and place, and we have discovered the mystery: the four Archangels. If you will hold that in your attitude, the *avenue* will lead to the distance of the *avenue* of art.

Art is classic, beyond all accessible limits, forever. Art can never be amateur. It is not created in the mind. It is not reason, nor is it intellect. It is visual. Craft is in technique, reason, and intellect. Art is *idée*. The marriage of the leadership of art, demanding the ego—separated magnetic force, within craft, technique—to come out and use it: is creation. The craft and the art married are horticulture: the visible hand of God. Art is seed, is *idée*. Craft is plant, metamorphosis. Art is the utmost *idée* with no metamorphosis. Everything that we have in life is that, except growth. The art of color, the art of sound, the art of form, the arts of the senses, can all be in ratio, divorced, separated. The art of horticulture cannot be separated. Lives within itself.

Art in the human aspect—which as I have already mentioned in the first statement is beyond all accessible, forever—therefore in the human element is the attempt to touch *idée*, the invisible, into birth, unseparated. There is no reason in it. Oscar Wilde[1] made the astonishing statement that bewildered everybody for a long time. They scattered on their heels when he said, publicly, "All art is useless!" When we look deeply into this, we discover further methods in reflection.

Art is without question joy, and joy is without question mystery. Therefore, technique is craft and is the procedure to physically, in separation, fulfill the art in a tangible form. Art is invisible. Art is then, within the kingdom of the stars, and is within the essence of seed. And seed contains the essence of mystery.

Look then at what we call art. You have a participle of separations: that the more classic that your focus becomes in art, the more classic does the art, of course, become. And the more that you create separations, the more that you have to cross the bridge—which your very voice has to cross when you speak on your level—you have to cross the bridge that links the visible to the invisible.

Today, we are so utterly tied up with ahrimanic, that luciferic, although it is playing the utmost, is completely bewildering to us. The whole laboratory, the whole mis-art of agriculture, is this ahrimanic action: only that which is touchable by the physical, that there is only physical, that there is only death, not birth. It is this that has become stagnant for us. It is this whole mystery that art leads us out of. The whole of the arts that concern separatenesses are color, sound, and form, with the senses; they are the whole permanent and perpetual leaderships that are the radii of mystery that never leave us alone. *Never* leave us alone. They are our entire *environnement*. They confuse us, they worry us, they trick us, and all our senses inwardly are reactive.

And the great envision-ments of classic art always strike to the very center of each individual, whether they accept it or not, whether they can perceive it or not. Just as the trees and the grass and the plants are the resuscitators and the forgivers: thus is art. The whole connection with what we must assess as religion, which takes the pomegranate as its fruit: being all seed and no fruit, therefore being all mystery, therefore being all essence of *idée*, and no metamorphosis. With the whole astonishment of humanity perceiving this, ad infinitum.

In the B.C., the whole attitude to gods and goddesses under God and Olympus, the whole essence of forms of Olympus, came about after the A.D. to become the cathedral, the monastery. Within the very essence of the focus of that is almost the center point of the approach to art. Was not the whole form formed by the tree, of the building? Was it not a majesty of this separation of *idée*? Was not the color, the light, was not the sound of the instrumentation, all *separatenesses* of *idée*? The art in ascension, wholly, in essence within a seed of the belief in mystery beyond all accessible limits. The whole beauty of that matter was that the cathedral, true mystery to total birth, creation of God, should be the greatest achievement of the art constructed through craft, that man could reflect. More so the feeling that this held, more so than his self, his family, everything around him, his possessions.

No art can possibly be empty. It is not. It is the reverse, the opposite course to separation. It's a total marriage. The whole concept of every person who is called a 'great artist'—and of course, none of them have the right to be called a great artist—there is no consideration of return of balance in the scale whatever to the ahrimanic, to the luciferic. It is utter *image*, *idée*. When everything is sacrificed to the *idée*, then everything can be sacrificed to the technique, the craft, to bring it about.

The whole astonishment of this therefore, in music: how like a copy of the bee hive is the whole orchestra that we know of today, where every single entity in the hive operates upon her reflection to a leadership. Not one of the female workers require to have the sexuality of life, but they all do, through the queen. How interesting that all the musicians in an orchestra do not wish to compose the piece that they are playing. It has already been composed by art. And they are performing craft. But in performing craft, they have in their very essence, in their heart, the seed of art. Creation is there and they are fulfilling it.

But every one of them is one hundred percent obedient to a conductor. And the conductor did not compose the score. The score was composed and thrown in the air and written on the wall in notation. That notation is craft, technique. And it's the possibility for every technical ability to follow it, compose it into paper. How astonishing that you can take a score of music and everybody can play it. It is only black dots on a piece of white paper, and this is verbosity, and this is wordism. They can play nothing themselves, nothing whatever. But out of rhythm, out of true art, true language, comes creation.

The whole of consideration of the art of medicine: when man lived in balance, his food was his natural balance. The word 'medicine' did not exist. It was compete. It *was* complete. It was art. And as man separated his reason and intellect, his mind from *idée*—art—his internal organs became unbalanced and required more focus from the craft, technique, of the juices of plants, to restore, and the doctor came in. Before the doctors came in, it was the participle of the Druidae, who of course, as you know, were vastly B.C., it was them whose duty it was to be what is called the priest and the doctor, who attended to the spirit of man: the vision, the seed, the art, *and* the craft; the health of the people. It is the duty of the Druidae priest to be the priest and the doctor. And then reason and intellect divorced, till it limits the art. Too hot; too cold. And the medico, as the family doctor, was no longer valued, and became a specialist, and then became a specialist dietician, and then became a mental specialist, and well you have got some idea of where it has got today.

Remember, then, the statement that origin essence contains the utmost energy. The more *divertissement* of that origin contains less and less degree of the energy. Now you understand why herbs are moral forces. They contain the utmost energy. The figure, if you like, of the modern horticulturalist, the self-appropriated, divorcing horticulturalist, who is thinking more of himself and his fellow men than Nature, produces a plant that has less energies. The herb is a moral force. The herb is art, contains art. Plants of the garden, generally, not as energies at the present, contain less art and more craft.

Now enters the word 'arty-crafty', what you approach in that, what it is. And then invariably you say, "Oh that person. Brilliant, absolutely brilliant! Very clever. Terribly crafty!" Hmmm. So much acumen, that looks so wonderful to the physical eye, and contains no essence, so little *idée*. Very crafty: complete bewilderment, do you see? But also perceive that all craft, technique, completed with the marriage of *idée*, is so perfect that craft cannot perceive it. You cannot find the technique of perfect art through the imperfect art. And what is imperfect art? That craft which has not been properly married to *idée*.

It was in this matter that Leonardo[2], as a huge informative within, which he realized that the silhouette of the great Dutch period that followed the van Eyck[3], where van Eyck, the van Eyck family, placed the whole background of Nature to the background of the human being, marrying *idée* with metamorphosis. And that following that, metamorphosis came into the major picture of wanting a subject. *It*, that we can see them, we can touch. And so they painted everybody's face on brown sauce. Nature was gone. Essence, *idée*, was beginning to disappear. You couldn't go 'round the back of the head, it was just brown sauce. And you can't go on swimming in brown sauce.

Leonardo, the enormous observer all the time of the scene, as Plato says, "I do not know, but I do perceive": he looked always at Nature. He realized that the whole attitude of draftsmanship was a basis and that it was deceptive in that it was touchable, like a photograph is, that is so acceptable to the ice cream palette. The children may swallow it, but the aroma of *Angelica* is not. And in his perception he realized the nearest that could be got with color and form was that it must exhibit the vision of *idée*, the almost bringing of invisible birth into the very painting that is completely a constriction of patterns.

For the astonishing thing is, that when you go into a gallery and look at a picture, you never go up and touch it. But everybody does want to. They go right up and try look 'round. And because they can't make it out, they have to look and see what is written underneath to tell them what the painting is about.

This whole matter that he realized, where he perceived Nature always, because he lived in *idée*. He never really lived in metamorphosis, as when he proceeded from the plan he made (of flying machines), flying in the height of the sky, and led his vision right out of himself, and left it there. And so he realized that all of anything he wanted to paint as a subject, must absolutely be lost in totality. In this he discovered that he must use some synergist that would make no silhouette, no edge, no line. For there is no edge in Nature. There is not an edge to the stem of a tree, which only our educated parental mind pretends that is there. It's a pretense.

So he discovered that the juice of the fig was that magic synergist. And so secret was his discovery, that of course, like all great artists, as they must, must hide it in the dark and never reveal this. All great artists are secret. They will not confide. Nobody is ever allowed into the rehearsal of a great player. Nobody is ever allowed into the studio of a great painter whilst the painting is going on. When music is being practiced, it is not open to the public. It couldn't be. That would become amateur. But nobody must perceive the craft, the technique, for that is going to surround and be obliterated by *idée*. This then is art. This is classic art.

You see something of it in Aeschylus[4]. Aeschylus wrote this play *Prométhée* (*Prometheus Bound*), which today, how interesting, nobody can sit it out because they can't follow it. The whole mind of the thinking of metamorphosis cannot permit the reflection of *idée*. For it doesn't add up. "I am sorry but I can't hear. I'm sorry but I can't see. I'm sorry but I can't feel. Because I have no sixth and seventh senses or inner touches. All the movement that is a lizard in me, that is the flight of an aphid, I have drowned. Because I hate, and it is no longer in me to touch it. It is in me, I know, but I can't any longer touch it. Because I am of such vast separation from *idée*, from art. But, I am only craft, and I am utterly crafty." This vision, then, in this *Prométhée*, which is so profound, it probably goes beyond the other great dramatic works that are concerned in the whole mystery of fable, parable, mythology, fairy story—that connect with this whatever, inestimable, un-accessible vision that is art.

Nobody knows where fairy stories come from. And you can't write one. Why? Oh, because it is too full of very obvious metamorphosis. And everybody says, "He just thought it up!" A fairy story, basically, is around *idée*. And as you can't touch *idée*, you can't make it come out and say, "There it is." Oh yes, there's a moral there, but you can't take it out. And when you hear the parable, or a fable, or a fairy story, you find yourself not listening to words at all. You are traveling to unknown, un-envisioned worlds. And they all connect differently with different radii of personality, of individual. Fairy story is not the same to any of us, any more than is color or sunlight. It is not the same to any of us. It's mystery.

In this *Prométhée* then, is the enormous envisionment, such as Puccini[5] brings out in the unfinished opera of *Turnadot*, and as Wagner[6] brings out in *Parcival*, the search for the Holy Grail. Only the Pure Fool can find the Holy Grail. Not anyone with reason. Only that one who can resolve into art, *idée*, can find it. And so in this *Prométhée*, we get this astonishing story, revelation, when you consider when it was written, four hundred and fifty years B.C.; that here is the whole word that we use now, 'love of humanity', stretched on the furthest extents of the unvirtuous world, of cruelty, on the rocks of the highest mountain, for the vulturous bird, the destructive bird, to tear out the liver every day, that it should grow again, into another. And that this agony must be survived, because it reflected art, seed, to the gods, who change, who under God, who are all governed by God. That those gods were unchangeable is nonsense.

And because *Prométhée* represents the utmost vision of art, seed, in his great love of humanity, in which he brought this fire in the (hollow) stalk (giant fennel stalk—*Ferula communis*), the story is that he must be stretched in this way by all the basilisk of the world, the steel bands of hardness, of the furnace that produces the movement of steel, the hardness, the most resilient, of infamy. That he should be bound to the highest mountain, to the wickedness of the utmost bird, to strike at the midwinter of Zeus, to bring his vision to God, to art. What an astonishing thing to be able to put in words. And that all the ancient Greeks went to it and to a degree comprehended it.

And yet today, there is not a performance of it that can either be given or be accepted. Just as in the enormity of that other drama of Aeschylus, the *Oresteia*, the great judgement of Orestes, for killing his mother, for his mother killed his father. And Orestes, being led by Apollo to perform the act, now has to come before the whole jurisdiction of art, to be judged. And that judgment is like the hundred keys, with the last key of the hundredth room. And that key is now the place of the ordinate, the judgment—not the mind, within the reason of Orestes.

And so it is to Pallas Athena, the epitome of female, who when she comes to give her evidence and cast her decision, which is to make the final decision for or against the existence of Orestes, she says to the Furies, who emancipate and stand for all of the basilisk of humanity, all of those things that bound Prometheus for his love and duty, it is that she stands forward and says, "There is only one edge, and that the mother killing the father, and the son killing the mother, are not equal." That she, Pallas Athena, does not represent that mother, for she was created out of the mind of Zeus, and was not a person in herself. Well these enormities are visions, and this is art, classic art.

We are always trying to say today, because we live in this wonderful world that we have these wonderful motorcars and airplanes and everything at our fingertips, we can do just what we like, when we like, in every way. We are so clever...so far. And we really look upon the world as our discovery. In fact, you have just had a centenary I believe, or a bicentenary. But how different is that bicentenary to a birthday? A birthdate was a seed, an art seed. The bicentenary: it's an illusion. It is a craft.

In the matter of what we are inclined to construct as art, we mix in craft. Craft is utterly incomplete, and cannot exist at all without art. But craft can be over-divorced, over-separated and applied to the visible and married. And where people are exemplified by living tangibly and visually only: carnal. Then art, an *idée*, a gift, is of course there. It has never changed its position at all. It is the sedge in everything. But it is not perceived; it is only a mirror. Therefore, you see, a person is not a person at all. A person is a technical achievement around art. And if you can consummate the huge vision of art, you are part of the reflection of the firmament. The other is only a part of a reflection of metamorphosis, which is very perceivable. And, only being seen, is very difficult to be unseen.

How very fascinating that everything that we have in this world, then, is even a slight metamorphosis, partly, of everything that is in horticulture, in the individual. Nature is without a doubt the craft of God, the technique of visibility of the art of God. And that is what that statement is, as you know, in Pliny and Virgil, and certainly out of Ptolemy. And the great mystery of Solomon. Where they all said that the teaching of the plants, of the herbs, was the teaching of God. This, then, is a very astonishing matter, that when you play your piano, when you sit on a carpet, when you put a jacket of green upon you, when you comb your hair, you are fulfilling the reflections of the metamorphoses of art. There is nothing that can be performed in the whole world, by anyone, that is not participle of art.

But, if the balance of craft is not of the reflection of the birth of art, then it is limitation, and can become sick. Is this not the tinned pea? Is this not the frozen pea? Looking at food then, do you perceive that out of the essence of horticulture, the garden, is the whole envisionment of all forms of the senses into the world of art. That is the invisible vision. And that any form of technique, of craft, that is reflecting that vision, will be creative. And it must be that way 'round: within to without, and never without to within.

Referring to these matters of the carpet and its texture: "Oh!" you would say, "I am not thinking about trees or leaves or the hair on the plants." Aren't you? How do you know? For when you see a tree in the middle of a meadow, you would look at the tree and say to everybody, "Do look. It's the most beautiful tree! Isn't it wonderful?" And everyone says, "Yes, isn't *it* wonderful?" But *it* isn't *it* at all. It's the approach to the tree. It is the light. It is what is behind it. It is either the blue sky, or the clouds, or the stars shining that is making the tree what it is. It's totality in it.

For that is what must concern us now so deeply. It's humanity that must concern us, for that is classic art. And then when you come back to us, well, alright. We're in the position of being able to see fully again. If you take it out from one's self, you have got the division of the circle into an angle of separateness. And it is unbalanced, has no proportion to view, to focus. What was Leonardo talking about this edge? It is all part of this vision. You can't find it. It is not like today saying, "I know it." Because that's a wrong way of living. But how interesting that when wordism became so terribly dominant, instead of drawing, or music, which after all is so much more speaking than words, for that is why composers and painters do what they do. They are born with the absurdity of words. And poets are born with the absurdity of words, and they write poetry. They are putting art into craft, not craft into art.

Then a person studies with professors at a university, and they understand the craft. But nobody can understand art, because you can't understand it. So they study craft, because that's something they can do. And it is very important to do. And when they have done it, they do it. That's metamorphosis. It hasn't got any birth. So you get pianists and musicians and composers who write corpses. But even a piano, even a violin string that is catgut, stretched on pieces of wood, tied together and stuck: they're all technique. They're all craft. And inside it the original was *idée* and you can't find it. You can't find it *inside* a violin. I had a Stradivarius: I have often taken all sorts of microscopes and telescopes to look inside and try to find out where this happens. It did nothing.

How interesting then, that beautiful poetry, the beauty of words, was brought through *idée*, into metamorphosis—the gurglings we make in our throat: "Huh, huh, ooo, ooo, ahhh, ahhh, blub, blub." An yet you all understand each other. And even the birds comprehend this, because there is *idée*: that's the connection. How fascinating that at that time, in those idiotic guttural noises, within drawings, and we call them a vocabulary, you can read it with your eyes, and you can hear it with your ear. Do you understand me? I don't. How can you see a sound? This is the metamorphosis, it is a technique and a craft.

You can do it. You can make a propeller go 'round underwater and tear along. But it's all about *idée*, quite literally. Yet if the technique and the craft is placed before *idée*, you can be sure there is something wrong. You have got the idea quickly. Then those guttural verbosities, put then in the formations of drawings, which we call words—they were a little ashamed, and as you know the Druidae wouldn't allow it. They would only have it done through the guttural noise of the possibility. And then as little as possible. For they understood mystery. But when later it was done, and written and drawn in black on white, which is what we call print on paper, ha ha...you understand it clearly, don't you? Yes of course. Do you? It is incredible, isn't it?

None of this is really touchable. How interesting that they may have done that: black on white, print on paper, that they were a little ashamed, like Adam and Eve that had to put a fig on the wrong place. A fig leaf, I mean. (Laughter—someone jokes about the synergist of the fig juice.) So it was necessary, as you know, to draw vine leaves all around the pages, in order to say, "This isn't the drivel that comes out of my spittle, this is Nature." And so the books all had beautiful illustrative figures, and even the letters were violets coming out of the ivy leaves. And the whole of the front, which was made of *Fagus* wood, as you know, was all embellished with carvings that were of tree stems and leaves and the veins of leaves and so on. But all produced one, art, vision, that was to say to you, "Please understand that what is in here is idiot metamorphosis, but that somewhere within it is art!"

Do you want to talk about it? I have always loved art, within everything else in the world.

Q: Alan, you asked a question that you didn't answer. What has become of the individual?

The individual is a mystery.

Q: Alan, you spoke about the 'over-craft'. Where you were going out of the temperature zone. Is that where the craft becomes to the point it is copied?

The ætherial world, *prima mobile*, the *secundus mobile*, the visible, and the invisible. You know what you're trying to do? What I have, in a sense, suggested to you, I have deprecated. You are trying to put a cage to put the bird in. For every one of us we have different Cancers and Capricorns, the areas around the equator, and different poles. You couldn't survive very long as a person at the North Pole or the South Pole. As you come down towards Cancer and Capricorn in either area, you could begin to reflect. Every one of us would have a different area where that could happen. Do you follow? There is not a cage for the person. The planets do concern with arithmetic of the reflection of our lives. We are married with totality. The person is Nature.

I beg you, you must forgive this study. As I say, it does not refer. I did want to get this study in, because I said it does not refer. It should not be reasoned upon our intellects. Best to do it a little bit slowly.

1   Irish dramatist, novelist and poet; Alan performed in his plays; (1854-1900).
2   Leonardo da Vinci; (1452-1519).
3   Jan van Eyck, Flemish painter from Bruges; (1395-1441).
4   Aeschylus, ancient Greek playwright; wrote *Prometheus Bound*, which Alan prefers to pronounce the French title of, and *The Oresteia*, a trilogy devoted to Agamemnon's return from the Trojan War, his death at the hands of his wife Clytemnestra, Orestes' vengeance for his father's murder by killing his mother, and Orestes' trial by the gods for the matricide in the final play, *The Eumenides*; (~525-455 B.C.).
5   Giacomo Puccini, Italian opera composer; *Turnadot* is about a Chinese prince who must win a princess through riddles, but she can destroy him if she learns his real name, *love*; (1858-1924).
6   Wilhelm Richard Wagner, German composer; his opera *Parsifal* is somewhat based upon the epic thirteenth century Grail poem *Parzival*; (1813-1883).

The Garden as the Mirror of Man

Covelo Village Garden
20 August 1976

The subject today is a continuation, and you'll have to bear in mind, if you will, the previous talks that we've had, all of them play into this last one. You may find this loose, but I'm going to try to knit it together.

We're at the last stages of what you might call the extremities of wordism, whereby we can even touch any more, reality with words. Therefore you must understand how I try to treat this. And one expresses one's incomparable ignorance in touching such a subject. I am merely trying to put my finger on things, to try and throw things in the air that you might of yourselves discover it. It is nothing more than this.

So, one begins by saying: we give each other a name. Forgive me, I always contend that the age of twenty-one, what is called 'coming of age', everybody should then have the permission—not necessarily to undo what was given—but to elect a name for themselves. They go right through life and even write it on tombstones, but they are underneath, still that name. You must realize instantly that nobody is the same any day of the year. We are not the same at all, and therefore, that name is so ludicrous. Really, as you know, I never know anybody's name.

You must likewise—and we all have, because one has heard the remark so often—have been mystified by the fact that we have establishments in life. That those establishments are utterly broken—such establishments as a horse race, and a game of chess, and billiards—three balls on a table, with a stick, with some pockets. Now all of those games, as they were, have a ruling, a principle behind them, that you do this and that happens.

An extraordinary thing is that—as with athletics, in a race, as in a game of tennis—it is so astonishing to everybody that at some time, somebody comes along and beats the record. A man runs a race with other people and somebody suddenly says, "Broken record!" If you're running, there must be a limit to running. It's merely the movement of two feet. How is it that you can always go on beating a record? You must be aware of this, you know, how much one says, "Well, you know, they can't go any further and that's that." The next day you see in the paper somebody's beaten the record. High jump: there must be a limit to what a person can jump over a pole and come down again. They must go on up! And how incredible that people at billiards can go on hitting three balls around the table for three days and not finish the stroke, you know it goes on, and then suddenly somebody makes fifteen more. And everybody had then said previously, "It was impossible." What is this delirium?

Let's look at it. And let us look at the whole of horticulture in the same area. What is this delirium that today we have discovered everything? We've been around the world backwards. We know all the stars in the heavens, and we can calculate the atom inside out. And there's really almost nothing then left to know at all except the very odd way in which certain very unpleasant insects behave in their life. And having no interest in such unpleasantness, we don't bother to solve it; we don't want to. Apart from that, we have discovered it.

But if you realize that nothing is the same any moment to the next, then you must at least have undone the lock of the chest. If you begin to survey what we laid before ourselves then, about the leadership of the Sun under the Sun, and this cosmic radiation of energy—life force— which in its vitality draws out of this Earth a life force, and becomes a marriage, a fertility in atmosphere. And that that fertility taking place out of a marriage must spread itself, as lightning, finally, where there are pockets that won't behave, so to speak, must spread itself in Nature's form of non-*conservatoire*. And so you get life and death out of marriage.

Therefore, try to arrange in your approach to this, that word then, *radiation*. That it is an attraction of a greater power to another power and marrying it in affiliation. That the Sun's Sun has not affiliation with the energies of this Earth, but through the Sun it has. Totally so: through the Sun, via the Sun.

So that when one says that this change is perpetual, you will suddenly see that breathing in as we do, and breathing out is a mystery. It's a complete mystery. We take it absolutely for granted. We take everything in the whole world that is absolute magic, that is complete mystery, we

218

take it completely for granted and put it down the drain and pull the plug. Utter disinterest in the most incredibly magical things that are happening to us every minute of every day. And we pass over it because we are incomparable bores.

Therefore, breathing in and breathing out is coming to life and dying. It's a whole regular procedure, and you do it more or less, according to your breathing, all the time. Perhaps you will see, some of you, how very important then, is breathing. How you breathe, how it affects the whole circulation of your approach to living, even to moving. Quite apart from the silliness of speaking.

Survey then in Nature. Look at the trees. How fascinating it is that in the whole family of the ash and the willow you see this change going on so enormously. One thinks, "A tree: Oh well, it was once a seedling. It was a little sapling, and now look, it's a huge tree." And you think of it there from the day it is born. Oh, you are very mistaken. There's none of the day it was born there, literally. There's none of the twenty-year-old tree in the two hundred-year-old tree. It's practically gone. The whole thing practically has disintegrated. In the ash and the willow the whole middle always disintegrates. It's the outside goes on outside and sends up new branches. All the old branches that were there originally have gone. And so you get these different ages. Oaks: one thousand five hundred years growth; the metasequoia, known so well over here, at two thousand being nothing, and it grows as you know, it can grow to four and five thousand. But it is not the same!

You see, the whole production of that tree in those eras that go with the age of the tree—and now you've got to survey that—the eras that make that great age, or the little age, throw it into an encompassment of enclosures of what we call years. There's a characterization there. And those characterizations have their complete changes. The whole shapes of that tree change: the degree of foliage, the degree of wood, and the circumnavigation of those barks.

The astonishing matter that is a tree, that this sawdust that appears each year in some miraculous way that does that with the tree, and the whole thing is compressed and is timber. And they can actually build a table and you can't bend it, and it doesn't fall to bits even when it's dead. It stays together. What a mystery!

Now there is a matter—we have talked here a great deal about hedges, how we've said we're going to study again lawns, and how to look after them. You clip and prune hedges. You must. Why must you? Why must you look after and dress the lawn? Well, because in Nature, this change, this non-static, depends upon everything. When animals eat a meadow, that meadow goes through a change and begins to grow different plants. Generally speaking, those plants are taller. And if the animal were to go on, and man were not there, they would become shrubs, and then would become trees, and the meadow would go. And that's what happens very largely in Nature. There is a horticultural procedure going on, and it is this that the horticulturalist is based upon.

When you cut and prune a hedge, you are doing several things. You are doing many things to an advantage, and certain things to a disadvantage. The pruning of that shrub means that you are going to make it grow in certain ways more vociferously than it would if you allowed it to run. And if you only prune it or clip it in the dormancy period, you are doing maledictions because it can't respond. It has to respond in a season, making that response a violence, not a gentle re-interplay.

For instance, as if an animal chewed the shoots, it would immediately start to re-enact. But if you chop half a hedge off in the winter, it is only in the spring when the sap rises that it is going to say, "Oh my God! My head's gone!" and start to put out some new heads. But the whole thing is out of a timed balance with what was happening. Therefore, that change that you bring about either way, and you see that one is good and the other is bad, is also affecting the roots and the root procedures in the soils. That those root procedures are perfectly happily going on, saying, "Munch munch," to the gases and blowing them up the stem. And all of a sudden the bush says, "Don't be silly. That business of two courses for dinner—I've got twice the size up here. I'm playing twice the game of tennis and I need much more energy." And the root says, "Well, I'm very sorry but somebody's been mucking about with you. They haven't mucked about with me."

That, of course, is largely the approach today of the huge error of watering systems. They're trying to affect the roots to affect the growth so as not to prune. You can see what happens. You've got a restriction on the life altogether.

What I'm pointing out to you is that if you cut a hedge, you've got to do something to make up the root procedures. So it needs dressing. It needs cultivating, and dressing. And this is exactly what goes on with a lawn. It's the faithful thing and well-known in classical horticulture that you never cut a lawn below two inches of length. Why? Oh, because you're cutting the grass too low, for numerous reasons, for the life of the plant to be able to comply. There is a certain classical area at which an animal and life is *destined* to behave, and the horticulturalist has to apply himself to such a destination. Therefore, when you go on cutting the lawn and removing the grass—as you should—if not you merely mat the whole area surface with dead stuff which would seize it up anyway, with being unable to breathe. And no, almost no, plants like their own death around them, which you are already aware of. Therefore after you've cut a lawn a certain number of times, you've darn well got to put something back in order to supply the plant with its satisfaction. And so you have to dress a lawn.

And that is why I've explained to you about the toothed row. You insert that into the soil right through the whole lawn. In other words, it's like putting a prong all over the lawn, and thereby it lets the *revolutionibus* in, the gasses, and then you can dress it with some new soil, which is a combination of what you have removed—which an animal would do by doing its duty, to a degree. Not always—that depends on how many animals you run on how much area. And here you get the same implication. So you begin to perceive the essentiality of ley, connected with horticulture. Now you must begin to perceive the essentiality of Nature connected with ley, connected with horticulture.

Very interesting that we cut our hair and we cut our nails. One is always surprised when you cut a nail off. You think, "Well, I must die." But you don't. You can even cut your eyelashes. I had all mine burned off in a fire once.

Now let us look at something else. You must manage these jumps, they are not necessarily affiliated. Let's look at this statement about annuals, bi-annuals, tri-annuals and perennials. Oh, you've got it all beautifully categorized, I'm sure. Well, you'd better discard it because this is what happens.

Let us take a mignonette. And you know the family it belongs to and what plant it is. There is much in a certain key here that you must look for. If you will take that mignonette and grow it in the spring from a seed, you realize that it likes warm weather, it will be killed by frost. If when it sends its bloomspire, first of all you remove it and stop it from doing what it wants to do—in other words, pulling its destination, but stop that destination—it will send out what is called branches that will then all attempt to fulfill its destination. And if you remove those, believe it or not, that you can, if you will house it from frost, from inclement weather, you may have a twelve foot shrub which has yet not bloomed. But that's just one small item. This can go on. Geraniums will do the same, and likewise. However, the geranium is not an annual. But the mignonette is said to be an annual. Said to be.

You must look at that. You can do exactly the same with any plant. If you go on clipping the blossoms off, and not allowing seeding, you will get more and more and more plant, and what is more, every annual will turn into a bi-annual, and will turn into a tri-annual, because it insists upon fulfilling a destination. That is one way of putting it. It's not the true answer.

If you take the century plant. You probably know it under that name. It's an agave. You realize that it's called the century plant because somebody, some botanist or naturalist observing it, said it bloomed once every hundred years. When it blooms, it dies. When a female spider beckons to a male spider, which she does very audibly and very ostentatiously, and having got what she wanted, she eats him instantly. That's quite a procedure with all of the spiders, not all of them, the majority. That plant, actually blooming, does die. And it has spent one hundred years coming to the matter, and having got to the matter, immediately perishes. The whole attitude of living is a bringing about death.

The interesting point is that according to how that plant grows—I'm talking about this particular agave—it is a very interesting matter. According to the area in which it grows, according to the soils, according to the lightnings of the area—in other words, the atmospherics, principally—so will it bloom in a totally different cycle of areas of years. It will not very often take a hundred years. That was one naturalist's predicament, in spending a hundred years watching it. Frequently it blooms in fifty; sometimes they will bloom in fifteen. I have watched these on the coast of Africa, on the Cape, and the astonishment of them in their behaviors. Therefore, those things that appear so set, and that we think must be, you know, the ruling principle in them, is not so.

The whole appropriation about fruit trees, you begin to perceive, that if you prune in a particular manner, the life of your tree can be three times the life if you don't prune, and vice versa. And equally so in line, according to the way you prune—well or badly—the life of that tree will be totally changed. Not only the life of the tree, but the giving and taking of.

This matter concerning to flower, and to seed: now it is well known that if you sow certain plants which are known as bi-annuals too early, you will ruin your crop. And this applies very much to the beta, should we say. You sow it too early, by all rights the beta should grow for one year, and having grown for that year, that so-called thing that we idiotically called a root—and become so established in differentiation of the root and the top as two totally different items, because you eat one and don't the other, or some such idiocy—that root, by all rights should go into dormancy and then change completely, which it does. It changes all of its textures—its whole life forces go into another realm altogether and it turns into different materials—and produces a long stalk and a huge radiation of flowers which all develop into seeds. Now if you sow that beta too early in the year, it starts to do that at the end of the year. And so you have ruined your root and you have also ruined it blooming for the next year as a seed, because it's thrown out of ratio. You have begun to turn it back into an annual.

In the whole establishment of the herbaceous border, in our studies you have been carefully led into the correction that none of them are perennial plants. You remember this? Many of them are a type of bi-annual, some are tri-annuals, and all of them, indeed, are not perennials. Not one of them is a perennial. That crown *présentement* will not go on blooming by any means forever. In nearly all cases, a crown *présentement* will bloom for one year and perhaps two, and that actual crown *présentement* perishes. It is a family that proceeds.

Now I go to the matter of the Sun again. I go back to the matter of the Earth and its forces, and the marriage that takes place in the atmosphere. In that marriage and that atmosphere, do you realize, there is the issue that remains over, during night, when we would think that there is no light and nothing prevailing? The resemblance that you sometimes find in very early spring day of last fall, and the discoveries in the middle of summer of the awareness of fall being in there. They are all respectably interwoven. Of course we have four named nominalities (the seasons), which give us a completely false proposition.

Therefore, in this atmosphere—which is a marriage—a birth goes on, and that birth is changeable all the time. Not only every moment, particularly every day and connected with seasons is that changeableness acute, in whole areas bunched together. Do you understand? This is very intangible. In those atmospheres is a word called 'hydrogen'. That hydrogen is, according to science, naught point oh three of the content of the atmosphere. You realize that changes, that naught point oh three changes all the time—a little more, a little less—but it's one of those vital matters which science pretends it can separate, which of course is ludicrous, you understand. It pretends that it can separate it and read it. But it is that matter which is one of the principle excitements, as you might say, is somewhere towards the embryo that is in a seed that you can't find and touch. It is one of those matters that is the embryonic food in the gaseous form, upon which plants get a principle of focus of life, a particular acceleration of focus of life.

There is music that is in the stars. You can't possibly, with words, read the music, but it's all there. It's perfectly clear, and it never goes wrong because it can't. The thing that goes wrong is our acquisition, misapplication.

Therefore you see that the stalks of different plants are a huge key, if you like, of information about the plant. It is a total informing of. Now do you begin to perceive that fish are in water, that birds are in air, and that moles are in the earth, and worms are *in* the earth? And, of course, those are only the categories that we've inspected and deemed worthy of. Do you realize all those that we haven't?

Then to add to that list there are a number of animals, and there is man, who is able to move two parts of himself, that he is not fixed. And that is, just in that atmosphere, a very important position between what we call the air and the earth—where the marriages so much take place.

Therefore perceive, plant life is alive, interrelated with all the other, but it is a life under leadership. And there is bee life which is not really connected with insects. We put them all as insects, but they're not. There are some insects that don't need their legs. There are some that don't need their wings. There are some insects that are really birds and some insects that are really rodents. And we call them all insects. They're given atmospheric attitudes, if you like.

And then there is human life. Now, you must apply this to perceive destiny. You must interrelate all those, whereupon you should perceive revolvement, change, in place of evolution. Now do you see that *idée* is each of us? But that intellect and reason is our name, and all we know about each other, the day that we were born: the fourteenth and a half of February, 1876.

Do you not see, commercial horticulture isn't really the key at all? It's not how to raise plants. The key is the visualization of the mystery of Nature. You see, that even with this thing that we call 'voice'—and voice is not words: in fact, with voice, we can't very well remove our words at all, it's very difficult, almost impossible—the voice is music of intervals, and it can only be brought about, as something, by relaxation and tension. It is the air flow by human power into sound flow. You see, again, we have taken it completely for granted. We don't even look at what noises we make or how we make them.

It's quite un-understandable to us when we listen to a nightingale; we can't believe that it can happen. You cannot in any way conceive how this idiot thing covered with foolish feathers, with a most grotesque beak, and that incongruous neck, when you look into it, it can't possibly make anything so exquisite, of which there is no instrumentation in creation that is equal.

Therefore out of the word radiation: if you can perceive the meaning, then, the radiation that is color, the radiation that is sound, is of course bloom. And you realize the healing qualities contained into the movement of this. When one says 'healing', one speaks principally of what you might call the maintenance of health, if you like. That it can wholly heal them, in a balance.

Do you realize that the attitude of conquest, which is making money, is a game, in reality? It must never be in life, because it can't be in life.

It is not in life. Therefore the destiny is all for all, around a life, Nature, which is the city, which is the garden, which is vision.

Therefore, quickly re-establish the Sun forces, with the interplay of the planetary forces screaming, calling, singing, coloring, requesting with all of the vastness of senses unknown to us and known. Such same senses of similarities that exist in this Earth, come out and meet, and establish fertility, atmosphere. That performance demands the relationship in all living. There is nothing on the Earth that is not interwoven in that radiation and emanation taking place of marriage, of life force creating. And that is the production of light and shade.

Now do you perceive that you can grow a plant in the winter and apply three times the amount of light, and it will be better? Grow that plant in summer in a pace like Covelo, and the light is three times too much. It will grow much better with a third of that light. But how will we remove a third of that light is the indictment, because by removing a third of that light, it can, as it were, eat the hydrogen better. It can eat it properly. With three times the light it can't partake of it. It must close. It coughs and cuts off. It can't bear, as we in the winter, can't bear. It is too much for us. We must go indoors and light the fire. We can't go in the summer, it's too much for us, it's too hot. We must go in and get cool. We go off our feet.

So you get the highest high and the lowest low, and then you get the meridian, the maritime. You take a plant out of the greenhouse at any time and put it straight out of doors, and it will literally perish. You have to harden it off, as it's called, in the maritime. We're doing it all the time with everything. It's even what cultivation is. Therefore, in a certain sense, the equinox, and likewise the position in the world of equinox, with the angles, is the maritime. It is livable. It is the open, of those that close.

Therefore you can surely see the word that we now arrive at: 'fertility'. We must begin to see an enormous marriage of matters, that we began to allude to, very caustically, is now an intimate marriage that produces a major, total life force. And you see now how it applies with what you might call the alchemical statement about 'raising the vibrations'. That's all that it means. The alchemists also were trying to use words, and how frightening these words are.

One refers here to that astonishing story of Balzac's[1], about an orphan, Pierrette, who because of being an orphan was left in the hands of two peasants of utter poverty, in a little country shack, unhealthy, ill-fed, ill-provided, ill-cultured. And the sadness of this enchanting girl, placed in these improbable hands because of orphanage. And Balzac's story unlifts the human focus of civilization and places her in the hands of two 'excellent' people; the one, is inwardly despicable in jealousy of this beautiful creature, and a husband who is blind with the knowledge of citizenship. And both of them are applied to Pierrette, and her life becomes an intolerable sadness instead of a complete happiness. And she dies.

The whole story is very astounding in that it carries you all the time to see and believe that these two citizens are in perfect accord with living, doing the utmost best for this dear little girl, to bring her to the good life as she should; only to die of utter sadness, for it were better that she had been where she was. That, of course, is not said in the story.

One plays that story right here, and realize, every one of us, our fallibility. And the one, true, hand-in-hand hold, that restores one's complete belief, and the comprehension of capacity: the garden, Nature. It is always there.

We must learn of a unity which links the garden of our making with the garden of the world around. The more we prize and comprehend our garden, the more we'll become that of the Nature uncontrollable. Each supplements the other. To understand either, we must contemplate both. The physical senses are implements of comprehension. They must be directed by insight, *in-sense*, the birth of vision.

One refers very briefly at the final point of that, to that matter that concerns the William James Association and what they say. As you realize, they talk so much about this extraordinary thing about armies and corps, and about Alexander the Great. And they uphold, as you know, the 'James thing', it upholds this enormous sense that militarism is part of the soul of man, in a certain sense. That the heroic, the heroicness about the ending upon your life, that it should be insufferably given up for your friends, is undoubtedly heroism; but a pacifist, in the refutal of that, almost under-balances, so to speak. And he says here: *All these beliefs of mine put me squarely into the anti-militarist party. But I do* not believe that peace either ought to be, or will be, permanent on this globe, unless the states specifically organize, preserve some of the old elements of army discipline.

Do you see what they're doing? You see, it's the same old story—it's Alexander again. A divorcement. Isolations.

Man walks in the atmosphere. He has a latitude and there's destiny. And that destiny and that latitude are completely in relationship with grass and with trees. And that destiny-relationship, with those, is of course governed by the leadership of the planetary forces. You cannot bring such things into a verbal discussion. They are governed by the whole law that is Nature, and it cannot be separated. And when so treated, cannot make mistakes and go wrong.

I feel rather as though I'm giving you meanings of expressing this in words, but may we talk about it perhaps?

Q: *I wanted to ask about your expression of, in a situation of the building of fertility, that as the lightning discharges from one point to another, involving, and you said, the non-conservatiore of Nature in this process. I don't understand what is meant by this.*

The very thing I've just spoken of in the last minute—totality. The whole procedure of Goethe and the circle, which is truth. And the moment that you try to talk about mankind, not with words, you have a small handle of that circle. Do you comprehend?

Therefore, the meeting of those two enormous governing forces instantly spread themselves out and vacuate totality, with that emanation of force. Do you understand? Do you?

Can anybody who sees this explain it in any other way? Because we use words and you will have a name, whenever you meet anybody, you are introduced by your name. That might enter into it six months later, but you should obviously meet a person *by meeting him*. That's exactly what I'm talking about, or trying to talk about but can't, of course.

What one hopes, possibly, to have opened up through the whole cycle (of lectures), in some of what we talked about this morning, is this mater concerning plants. Do you see? That this mirrorization of Nature, the reflection that goes on, is so utterly and totally connected with man living in it, belonging in it, with it. That his manipulation, as a participant, is a whole matter of result of which at present is not there, both in the garden, and in ley and in Nature. You do perceive this?

I spoke last time, you remember, of proliferation. You also bear in mind, I'm sure, along with one of those enormous keys which we had, about matter in origin taking the greatest life energy. And the further removed from origin into fractured compound, automatically requiring less and less life energy. You need to look at that because that entertains concern, very greatly, with the ordinary, tangible expression of quality and quantity.

---

1 Honoré de Balzac, French novelist; the story of Pierette is part of his *The Human Comedy*; (1799-1840).

History of Herbs

Covelo Village Garden
28 February 1977

We have merely nominated this thing 'History of Herbs'. Now there are certain documents which I have collected during my life which were here, which are gone, owing to the endless moves, and the dissipation of the library and other things. Therefore you must understand some of this comes out of memory. I am not prepared to endorse certain things, since they go back for a few thousand years. But I just explain that now. It's a surveying of plants and man, and his treatment of the matter from the time that any historical fact is recognized.

History of herbs: let us begin with the Druidae very briefly. We know almost nothing, truthfully, of them, so let us not muddle around, and get on with it. They were undoubtedly priests of a religious order of that period before Christianity who were so predominant in their idealisms. One of their great tenets was: *no writing of words*. They would not permit it. The avoidance of verbosity was part of the whole doctrine. Ritual, *festivalia*, observation, and reflection of the soul, were very certainly the essence of their procedure.

That in saying they were religious priests of those orders—you must understand what that covers—but they were based upon Nature. They entertained magic, but it was all connected with Nature. And enormously placed all reverence into herbs, and plants, and trees, and stones. Principally, as there was a period that followed, all of those priests were most emphatically doctors. It was their duty to keep the people healthy in body, mind, and spirit. That was their participation and that's why their idealism was a classic. Since no writing took place you can understand that we have no writings to refer to, and what a good thing.

We now enter a period known as the Anglo-Saxon[1], Later we will come over to this side. The Anglo-Saxon was a period that you could say of the result and the influence of the Druidae throughout living. And that in every little area a Druidae was in charge—like a chief—and that connected with them were those who were rather more physical, such as were later called 'the pharmacists', the herbalists. An enormous amount of their procedure was in no sense what we look at as medicine today. In fact, almost none of it. In every case of allocation of what we would call medicine was enchantment, chanting, and an observation by the patient, which brought about a reciprocation to what they were receiving. And quite frequently, as you know, they had no knowledge of what they were receiving. Neither did anybody fully understand the leadership which they were obeying. Almost everybody of that period had an enormous comprehension of Nature, the elements, and of all of the herbs.

In many instances, the use of medicines—which of course were all connected with plants, trees, stones—were not actually touched to the patient at all. They were often operated in numerous ways. Well, just to give a brief instance, you must have unfortunately read too many books now, which are very dangerous, and that, if you would like to take it as one very clear example, that when people began to lose clarity, of clear eyesight, they were made to look into clear, ice cold water. It sounds extremely silly. You would find on the whole of this subject we are going to try to look at today, that if you will look deeply into it, you will find the subtlest and deepest meanings. If you take it for verbosity, you will find nothing.

Out that Anglo-Saxon period there are just a few books, and in case you want to know what they are: the *Leechbook* of Bauld[2]; the *Lacnunga*[3]; the herbarium of Apuleius[4]—influence from the continent, which the other two were not—and the one very largely an influence from the continent, from Italy, the *Practica Petrocelli Salernitane*[5], which came from the great school at Salerno, which had existed out of time *ad infinitum*. Salerno was the original university of Europe, and the original university of medicine.

The names of *Widseth* and *Beowulf*[6] all connect with what you would call a people of utter humility. They bowed down in every respect to the law, the eloquence, the admonition, the beating, the terrifying, the joyful of Nature.

Now an interesting matter takes place. I just refer to why I say this, that the oceans principally, and the sense of the oceans, was the dominating factor of all. That is not observed today. It is not known that this was so. One thinks of them on the land as vague farmers with some strange animals wandering about the moors and mountains. One never thinks that they've had this absolute, dominant knowledge that the ocean was between them.

You probably know that in *Tristan and Isolde*[7] Wagner picked up the very ancient mythology of this Irish princess, to marry the Duke of Cornwall. And that the whole of the music of *Tristan*, which is, as you know, rising and falling, are the great rollers of the Atlantic Ocean. That is the whole form of the music throughout the opera. You will find such meter in the poetry. It is oceanic, and not of land.

You must survey at this period, that the whole of life, of human beings, was totally dominated by the unrecognizable in Nature. They were absolutely aware—every single person that lived—was absolutely aware of the invisible. If they went out after dark, they went with both terror and excitement—and probably joy—but undoubtedly it was there.

The whole of Nature had not been chopped up, disseminated, interfered with, interrogated into, by artifice. It was total in its reality, in its dominant effect. Try to absorb that, because it's important to understand these people. Therefore, man's happiness and well-being was instantly gotten by the whole matters of Nature, at all times, whether he was ill or well.

The result was that when Christianity came, none of that administration actually changed, not its basic performance. In other words, Christianity rode right in, like a huge wave of conception, but that the whole of the previous, of what is called the magic of Nature, the mystery of Nature, of how to deal with ill and health, were all predominantly administered in the same way. True, the Christian doctrine now claimed its reflection. But that the same principles of Nature were inadvertably predominant throughout. In this way, as I have mentioned before in this history, that the great belief of Mother-Sun, Father-Earth—which is rather reversed to our modern thinking—and that a huge predominant, to the people, was Ēostre, dawn. That was a festival that happened daily, that happened daily through the Druidae's indoctrination. And that that daily, became through the calendar also, into the solstices.

Therefore, when Christianity came, that remained. The priests of the church of Christianity could not change the structure, nor was there any reason to change it, as we will see at the very end of this. And therefore Ēostre remained, and became Easter: dawn, resurrection.

Therefore the ritual of the herbs, after the Christian era, remained, with a new reflection, but in its same natural ordination. So interesting is this matter, that a very important and total lecture of the Royal College of Physicians in London in 1903 stated this: *The Anglo-Saxon period had a much wider, greater knowledge of the performance and the use of herbs and plants beyond the whole great school of Salerno* (which was the medical college and university of Europe), *and even stated beyond the comprehension of the whole of Europe, both for its plants, themselves, and its knowledges*[8].

Now this is a statement that is right every time and obviously can't be denied, that the whole plant and herb proposition of the Anglo-Saxon era was out of all relationship to the plants of Europe. The fruits, and the knowledges of the trees, of both themselves, and their knowledges. An enormous amount centers around the great period known as alchemy. A most mysterious and mystic period. When the Norman conquest took place, the Anglo-Saxon vernacular literature and medicine was obliterated, as with that monster of Italy, who was considered a great religionist, on his appearance, and who was eventually burned at the stake as a heretic, Savonarola[9]. Well, he was a small Viking in comparison to this.

The Norman conquest then, came carrying the School of Salerno, with its great knowledge. And it came carrying the knowledge of Europe, and its contents of plants and fruit. But it came to wipe out the enormity of the effect of the Druidae and the Anglo-Saxon heritage. So vehement was it in its conquest and its hate—as one might say, "Would not Hitler have done?"—it obliterated, burned, all the manuscripts of the world, which were very few, and obliterated the whole language, and most of its plant and herbal lore, and peoples who held them. It was replaced by a most gigantic war-like violence, an entirely new continental issue on a small island of inhabitants.

Let's go quickly into the Ancient Greek, which came as a support into this matter. You understand that the Roman conquest of Britain had very little effect at all, except to bring a certain civilization of how to make roads, of how to behave occasionally, to wash once a week, and certain other matters, but not great introduction—nor interference—in the Anglo-Saxon vision. It did not interfere with it, especially in the north, where, of course, they couldn't penetrate, because the nettle juice which they put upon them, to keep the cold out, didn't work any more up there. It was too much. However, of course, it was not the climate that it is now; it was a very different climate. Two thousand years ago, it is said that there was no ice in Iceland.

The Ancient Greek, leading up to Christianity was a whole perception, extremely similar to what we've just been talking about. That they believed in the gods, but that they were ruled by God, and that God was yet not known, from Christian attitude, or the likes, shall we say, in whatever religion that you trace that's there. That therefore they held the same sensitive reflection to the whole perceptive laws of Nature, that were both perceptive and invisible.

That these teachings and the world of plants and medicines—which is what we're now going to focus on more and more largely, in fact, totally—were based upon Galen[10], Pliny, Dioscorides. Oh they, of course, took it out of others, which we'll briefly touch on. One huge change was brought about in their, what you might call, classic domination, by Constantine[11]. Now Constantine is actually of Africa, the great creator of Alexandria, and he did a translation of the medicals from the Arabic, from Arabia, introducing Orientals. And those became predominant in the universities. None of these names matter very much, except that they are historical facts and links that you can find out.

Now the teachings of them were of Arabic, what was known then as *Materia Medica*. Europe relied upon the Levant for their spices, their herbs, their drugs—which means herbs—extracts, for four hundred years, from about 900. They didn't produce very much. They used the local, but the actual performances of extracts came from Arabia and the Orient.

During during the fourteenth century, two hundred and eighty herbs and drugs—as we would use the word, but please accept it as we call it, they are, medicinal material—two hundred and eighty came from the Orient to the West during that century.

During the Renaissance, which now follows, there was a revival, a complete revival of the Ancient Greek classical attitude of medicine. In other words, they began to find that this import from the Orient and Arabia was not justified. That import was the first infiltration of an attitude of commercialism: it was a business. That's why it was operating. So that this return to the pure Greek tradition, those were the therapeutics of Hippocrates again, and Galen, and the herbals of Dioscorides. And you could say later, Pliny.

Thus many new forms and translations were made, particular to identification of plants of low power, to correct the many errors which had crept in by the imports, and the relationship of the imports to the local area plants which were not true. And to correct these many errors already entered by the pharmacists. Indeed the confusion of plants had already truly begun by this import. And all of that led up to the huge period, when Monardes[12] later, made a publication at Seville of his very, very famous *Pharmacodilosis*.

The major mistake, however, still now remained, of mistaking the Mediterranean herbs of the Hellenic peninsulas, of Greece, of Asia Minor, and of North Africa, for those, again, similar of Northern Europe's, where infiltrations had taken place by emancipation of war. They were confused between the Mediterranean coast and the Northern Hemisphere. In other words they were likened because they had similar names. The medicinal results did not respond.

At this period, the Renaissance botanists were still physicians, and in this way they were still aware of the mistake, and conscious of it, and attempting to right it. Now during the Arabian herb reign, as we would call it, Venice had grown into the center of salesmanship. Business. They were smart, huge, mercenaries. And they had a stranglehold, a complete hold, on the trade of the whole of Europe for those imports of drugs, until a certain period when the Portuguese discovered a sailing trade route to the East Indies. That interrupted the Venetian stranglehold. Thus it was that the expedition of Columbus across the Atlantic was a formed as a direct attempt to circumvent the Venetian monopoly.

However, we must just look at this Columbus procedure. Who and what were they? Although they were hired by Spain and Portugal to break up a commercial monopoly, they were really of nothing but monstrous adventurers. They were not botanical scientists at all, knew nothing of botanical science. What they collected on this travel was riches, and those riches were principally, as you know, gold, precious stones, etc. That's what they brought back. That's what paid the people who sent them out, and themselves. They made vast fortunes, but that was not out of anything else except loot.

They did, however, on coming back, describe all the trees, the gums—some, not all—trees, gums, plants, roots, oils, which were suspected of vast pharmacological importance. However they could, of course, only refer to any of those in terms of what could be found in Europe, for they had no word-knowledge to talk about them. If you dream of a color that you haven't seen you can't tell anybody about it except gasp. Therefore they could only refer to them under European names, terminologies. So they were immediately begun to be connected, and this was the beginning of vast misleadings.

Later, on journeys when specimens were brought back, references, explanations, were that the Indians employed these for various remedials, for wounds, for diseases and for illnesses. Again, those illnesses and the plants, and what was used for them out of those plants was unrecognizable because they were not growing it. But the relations were made nevertheless with the European likelihood, shall we say, possible looking-like. Then, on later journeys, others brought varieties of different names of similar plants. In other words, when they went to the south of America, to the middle of South America, to the north of South America, to Mexico, to the Panama area, and then eventually up to Virginia, and then eventually right the way up to Newfoundland, they met these tribes of Indians, who all used what the Anglo-Saxons used to do: the plants of the area. They all had languages of their own, and they had names of their own.

So they would collect ten or twenty plants, all with different names, and that even looked slightly different, and indeed were variations. And eventually on bringing them back, they were grown in the gardens that were allocated, and they were classified as belonging to the European reference origins. As a matter of fact, the same occurred in the geography itself, for naturally, these areas had not been charted. And in many cases, just as an inference, one of the cases was that one of the travelers went to a place called...you must forgive my language here, because I don't know how to do it...Chip-wee-ah-go. Well, later they came back and said they had also been to Pueblo Neuvo, and then they came back and said they had been to Narcades. Well these became Spanish terms, do you see, and other terms. They were mixed up with the idiom, but apparently, they were all the same place. And they were dotted on the chart as being totally in different places. And people couldn't figure out what they were doing, running on rocks, and going into different harbors and finding it's something totally different.

Well that's exactly what happened with the plants. Now the confusion set in. For all these different names for different uses that the Indians had, and that were predominant, and had cured them for decades of centuries; they had not been false; they were not false. But they were translated as such plants along with Greek plants of Dioscorides school, calling them the same plant.

At the same time Columbus returned from the West Indies with that terrible disease, syphilis. Now the axiom of the time was, as you know, that wherever in the world that a disease existed, and this is Dioscoridean, there God created a remedy; and so there, seek the cure. And this they did, because they were still following, in Europe, the Greek tradition, but they were now mixed up with a lot of imported things that didn't refer to that tradition. And it was now that they found that the wood of the *Guaiacum* tree. The *Guaiacum* tree was the one that the natives used and cured this disease, which they gave to all of the sailors, and cured them. Now it must also be noticed, an interesting matter, that the result of that disease being prevalent, it had very little effect upon the natives.

I remember when I first went to Alexandria and Cairo, I was invited by one of those enormous potentates to go on the great dhow on the Nile, and I was told—and not permitted to go—I was told that if one drop of the Nile water entered me, I would be in the hospital. Well, on the dhow they drank it, boiled it, made tea, washed in it—it's the only water that they had. It didn't affect them at all. If any European touched it—and when I say European, I mean, you know, 'civilized person'—more or less—they literally perished on the spot.

It is true to say that the natives who had this disease, it was so ordinary, the very like effect of measles. This wood was the one that they used and probably had always used, and it may have been this effect which made it unprevalent, or uncapricious amongst them.

However, on bringing this back, the *Guaiacum*, from the island of Hispaniola, as it was called, was undoubtedly a cure. It cured completely this terrible disease, which had now, from the merchants and the marine people, had now spread violently all over Europe.

Therefore in 1508 the Spaniards were using the *Guaiac* wood, and by 1517 it was a universal remedy for this terrible disease, which as you must probably know, had swept the whole of Europe. And Ulrich von Hütten[13] said, and published in the *Medica*, it was a *certain* remedy, complete remedy.

Now, there was a group of business people, merchants known as the 'Ughers'. They were all connected with economic commerce. Business. Commerce. And they contracted with the King of Spain, where this disease was violently prevalent, a monopoly on that wood, its import. They bought the monopoly of its import by giving a huge loan of money to the court of Spain. The court of Spain was in great difficulties at these times, because of the enormous expenses it had gone to on these journeys. It was granted to them. Therefore, nobody except these people had the handling of that wood.

Immediately they entered into a commercial procedure of importing that wood by sending out voyages to bring it. They made those voyages as inexpensive as possible to get the biggest profits possible. In a short time, because of this monopoly, loads and loads and wagonloads all over Europe were traveling the dusty roads, with this wood on carts, to deliver it to the hospitals, to the villages, to the towns, to the cities, to bring this ineffable cure to the people who were suffering from some terrible disease, which is not understood, and not fully comprehended, but of which this was the one and only total cure.

Well, you've already guessed in your mind now what happened. They brought in all sort of bogus woods, in a great hurry, that looked like it— and indeed they discovered later that there were very many variations of this tree, of which none of them had the virtuosity that the one that the Indians introduced to them. Therefore the whole of Europe was now inundated with stacks of wood, with all sorts of interminable, stupid woods that looked exactly like, but were not in any form whatever, held no virtue whatever. People died left, right and center. Hospitals were absolutely piled over with people who were dying and seriously ill, and no cures taking place, and nobody positive of any of the wood, as to whether it was true or not true.

Paracelsus[14], realizing what was taking place, looked into this wood and found almost all of the import of it was absolutely false. He realized that the epidemic had seized the whole of the western civilization, and he brought about a cure, out of mercury. At first, this looked as though it had saved the situation. But it was not so. The situation was worsened, for this mercury did indeed cure the external effect, and drove the disease inward, to internal structure, where it hid. Therefore the applications of such became destructive. They had broken away from the Greek classical, were no longer observing what was the predominant aspect in Nature, and were using drugs by experiment.

Therefore, because death now was so prevalent, and it was indeed a total epidemic, and brought fever with it, that there was a return to the hope in the *Guaiac* wood. But, although it operated when they got it again, when they found the true one, there was now so much business connected, that no one knew anymore what was genuine. Confusion, disease, was rampant; business was brisk; substitutions and cheating were predominant, and deceit, and death. And it was not until much later when Monardes published his book of medicals upon the new world, that they then planted, grew and observed the tree, and the trees and the plants in their own garden. And it was at this period that cocoa became predominant amongst so many others. And John Frampton[15] then translated that writing for all of Europe. And thus it was that the attitude to new drugs for all incurable diseases, became more and more and more and more predominant and focused. Origin attitude was obliterated.

The physicians, which includes Monardes, still clung however, to the classic school of the four humors. This matter of classicality, still, was like a vein, a strata, becoming dim and distant, but unable to obliterated—like Ēostre.

That school of the four humors, as you know, was connected with hot, dry, cold, and moist, and cured by contrary. This they now still used as the basic treatment behind these drugs, behind these new imports, that were not known, and not understood in their origin at all. Thus, they still used these same basic treatments *with* the Indian medicines, which were not true to name and species at all. Therefore they misapplied the hot, and the cold, and the moist, and the dry, because they even made absolute opposing mistakes in the use of them. So that all now fell between two schools: the classic was muddled up, and nobody fulfilled it; and the new drugs were unrecognized, mixed up by merchants, and commerce, and not identifiable. And disease rode the high wave.

Galen, in the origin, had relied upon the symbol, color, shape, touch, taste, smell—the identifiable of locale. Now at this time, as you know, experiments on patients was not permitted still. Even Leonardo DaVinci, as you know, had to disobey the law in order to dissect horses. Therefore, it was impossible in any of the hospitals to experiment with these importations, to find out if they were correct or incorrect. All they did was to administer them when they came, and wait for death. Or for recovery, which was rare.

1600 to 1700: In London, Salzburg, Rome, Bergano, Naples, Cologne, Amsterdam—*Guaiac* wood, *Sassafras*, *Nicotiana*—were all universally accepted from the New World, coming under the heading of herbal drugs. Frequently, none of these produced any results whatever. They were written as authentic, and guaranteed as medical curative. They were applied privately in homes by pharmacists, by doctors, by hospitals, and there was no authenticity of result, but major failure.

What belief could be left in the construction of herbology?

Again, it has to be looked at that in the conquest of the New World by discovery, the originals—even when sent later by knowledgeable people, scientific botanists, should we say, that they were still not aware of this enormous, catastrophic, climatic difference, which is one of the matters instilled in this period, which became a huge abortion to humanity. That the people traveling, particularly to America in the north, felt that having possibly survived, as a few of them did, the first winter, that they had met the most catastrophic happening of eternity of one winter. And of course such a thing couldn't happen again. And of course they had to be re-informed.

You understand that there are moments, days, hours, seasons, in which these can and cannot be of any use. Therefore they were collected in the wrong seasons, the wrong parts, the wrong names, wrongly dried—and that heat and humidity of areas relieved them of their healing properties on their journeys. Seawater in particular, with mildew on those very long, stormy journeys they had to make back. Thus there was very little of value that arrived back at the ports, and sold—every bit of it—at the most monstrous prices, because of the huge demand by the incomparable death and disease. Every bit of it was saleable by merchants. You wouldn't question whether it was valuable or not valuable. And so it was only when used in the hospitals that it was discovered useless.

Regardless of all such matter—and you see how much we have dwelled upon this till you're absolutely bored with it—think of the centuries that this existed in Europe, of life and death it proceeded upon, that even *then* the merchants continued. They continued to send those vessels, in the same way, under the cheapest conditions that they could manage. The druggists continued to make the profits, and the physicians bore the brunt.

Thus it was that in 1570 Philip the Second sent Francisco Hernández[16] to Mexico, where Hernández spent seven years surveying, and produced a *botanica medica*. And brought back, and described and *illustrated* it. Twelve hundred irrefutable plants.

This was one of the final steps of recoveries. However, printing at that period was almost impossible, it was very limited indeed. It was not till one hundred years later than that, that this publication was brought out.

There were attempts at that period, to persuade every traveler to disconcern themselves with commerce, with merchant-ship, with profit; to attempt to restore a concept of herbal lore and result, and propounded, that all such escapades of travel, for the collection of such, should include physicians, surgeons, botanical herbalists, and scientists. In other words that includes the whole bunch of those who would bring about illustrative result, factual, both to the plant and to the cure.

And it was out of this that Francis Drake[17], in 1571, brought back, with full illustration and reference, the Winteraceae, (*Drimys winteri*, or Winter's bark) a huge, complete cure of scurvy, which was so predominant. And Morgan[18], who went and brought back to Queen Elizabeth—for he was her apothecary—*Sassafras*, and the whole entry of that became true and real. And then there was the introduction of *Nicotiana*, which was said to cure ulcers, which it did; it was said it cured gout, which it did; and it was said it cured asthma, which it did. And they made money instantly, again. They made money, and so much money, that immediately they said, "Well, it's a panacea for *all* disease!" And so cigarette smoking came about.

Most predominant of all, to throw light on this matter, *Cinchona*, the story of it. The Spanish missionaries discovered its febrifuge qualities, as a total cure for the fevers. Fevers of that time were predominant, and killed people, as you know, in great ways. This attitude brought an utter end to the Galenic theory of medicine, and this very *Cinchona* was immediately confused with Peruvian bark, which is of the balsam tree. It was occupied instantly by the cheating of the merchants again. And you see it was added to by the concept of great truisms of people again. Such as Honoré Fabri, who in 1607, who lived until 1688, a Jesuit, stated that thousands of people in Rome alone were immediately cured of fever by this bark. And it was correct that that was true. Therefore the merchants were supported in their monstrosity of behavior by the hugeness of the results of the perfections of Nature, which did work when correct.

The results then were obvious: ignorance, commerce and prejudice played a thousand times more against humanity and truth. But that the Jesuit powder, that it was known as, in 1655, still true, complete truth, but now, the whole medical world refused to accept any truth in it at all.

In Charles II's reign, Robert Talbor published a book *Pyretologia*[19] in 1672. This was so concept of truth, so utterly true and irrefutable, that it was unacceptable. It did not endear him to the medical world—and to such an extent that they tried in every case, legally, to get rid of him, to denounce him. It was only because Charles II actually protected him that his life was even saved. And that, after he had cured Charles II of a tertian fever (an intense form of malaria) by the application of herbal. So he fled from the College of Physicians, to Paris. He went to France, purely to escape. That was a considerable journey then, and a very difficult one, especially when you're running from a country.

On arrival in France, he immediately cured the Dauphin, who was an extremely weak, constipated, suffering creature, as you know, perpetually weak. He cured him of a most serious fever. And he cured thousands of people of the most serious fevers. So much so, that Louis XIV approached him, and induced him—and one can't guess what the reason was—but he sold his treatment to Louis XIV. And Louis XIV gave him two thousand *Louis d'or*. At that time a salary was, a weighted salary, was fifteen *Louis d'or* an annum, for one of the court physicians.

Later, it was Ramazzini[20] who admitted that *Cinchona* had brought as great a revolution in art of medicine as gunpowder had in the art of war. Yet, not one *Cinchona*, but many.

Sessé[21], appointed as botanical explorer-in-chief, proved that all of Hernández' findings were correct, curing dysentery, liver disease, yellow fever, and all. And the corruption of the import made the whole thing not valued.

The result of all of this was the New World, the discovery of the New World, and all its magnificent and beautiful plants and herbs, and the Indian lore of its cures, to the contribution to the *materia medica* and practice of Europe was nil.

Do you perceive that in reading Gerard[22], the cyclical aspect to every plant? That was this period. His knowledge of plants, his love of plants was utter. He would with one word have been chased out of the country, if he had upheld the classic principle.

Parkinson's[23] *Theatrum Botanicum*; John Jocelyn's[24] accounts, discoveries—they were all bypassed, in truth. John Talent, who introduced the Seneca, the snakewood[25], which cured, unquestionably, pleurisy and pneumonia, and brought the writings of the hand of Linnaeus[26]. Thus all in all, the enormous discoveries of the New World, the influence on European medicine, was utterly negligible.

The greatest teacher of the whole of this matter—probably the only one who has ever exemplified by his own living what we've talked about today—was unquestionably St. Francis. It was said that he was indeed denounced by St. Bonaventure, who claimed him to be almost a heretic, when he upheld the total democracy of Nature that he found rather naked. It was said that when he lectured the people, and preached to people, that because they did not attend and follow, he preached to the birds. But this was not so. He preached to the birds because he comprehended the democracy of Nature. He wanted to talk to the birds about what he knew, that he felt that God was in everything and man. And it's astonishing that he just related that they flapped their wings and sang, in the hymn.

And there has been relation that there was this wicked wolf of Gubbio, who was so destructive to the people. And when St. Francis was approached about it, he went and pet the wolf. And he preached to the wolf, and the wolf was overcome. When the wolf died it was buried in consecrated ground.

In the whole aspect, apparently, of St. Francis, was the matter that the Anglo-Saxon had, humility. And so it is recommended, the ancient saint of ecology should be St. Francis.

This being a vast diatribe of historical bilkings, do you want to discuss it?

Q: Is the Guaiac bark still used today?

I can't tell you because I don't understand synthetics anymore. Some time ago I did. I know that it has been used up till recently, but whether it is still used now, I don't. I do know that, of course, in South America it is. In all herbals you will find that they will state that it is. But as to whether it is used in...you see where are you referring to? Are you referring to America? Are you referring to civilized Europe? Or are you referring to uncivilized?

You see, when I lived in Africa I found that they didn't know anything about...in fact they never went to doctors. There weren't any in most of the places where the natives are. And they all still used their origins. And their witch doctors. I imagine the answer to your question is, in some places certainly, and in other places, 'no'.

---

1 The Anglo-Saxon period is generally from the 6th century until the Norman Invasion of 1066.
2 Ninth century Old English medical text; 'Leech' means 'healing'.
3 Early eleventh century medical text and prayer book. 'Lacnunga' means 'remedies'.
4 Written by Pseudo-Apuleius in the fifth century.
5 Ninth century collection of medical texts, translated into Old English from the Latin in the eleventh century.

6 These are of the oldest Old English poems, possibly back to the eighth century.
7 Written by Richard Wagner between 1857 and 1859, and first performed in 1865.
8 Joseph Frank Payne, *English Medicine in the Anglo-Saxon Times; Two Lectures Delivered Before the Royal College of Physicians of London, June 23 and 25, 1903.*
9 Girolamo Savonarola, reformist Benedictine monk, burned 23 May 1498 in Florence.
10 Galen of Pergamon, great medical scientist and anatomist; (129-200 A.D.).
11 Constantine of Africa, medical professor of Salerno of Tunisian origin, translated many medical texts from the Arabic into latin; (1017-1087).
12 Nicholás Bautista Monardes, Spanish Physician and Botanist, published books in Seville touting the medicinal qualities of tobacco and *Sassafras*; (1493-1588).
13 German humanist, scholar, poet and church reformer; (1488-1523).
14 Philippus Aureolus Theophrastus Bombastus von Hohenheim, Swiss-German alchemist, botanist and physician; (1493-1541).
15 Sixteenth Century English merchant from Bristol who settled in Spain; he translated Monardes in 1577, and translated the travels of Marco Polo in 1579.
16 Francisco Hernández de Toledo, wrote *Plants and Animals of New Spain*; (1514-1587).
17 British admiral, privateer, slave trader and explorer; (1540-1596).
18 Sir Henry Morgan, British admiral, privateer and pirate; (1635-1688).
19 *Pyretologia, a Rational Account of the Cause & Cure of Agues, with Their Signes Diagnostick & Prognostick. Also Some Specifick Medicines Prescribed for the Cure of All Sorts of Agues; with an Account of a Successful Method of the Authors for the Cure of the Most Tedious and Dangerous Quartans. Likewise Some Observations of Cures Performed by the Aforesaid Method. Whereunto is Added a Short Account of the Cause and Cure of Feavers, and the Griping in the Guts, Agreeable to Nature's Rules and Method of Healing.*
20 Bernardo Ramazzini, Italian physician; (1633-1714).
21 Martín Sessé y Lacasta, Spanish botanist; (1751-1808).
22 John Gerrard, English writer and botanist; (1545-1611).
23 John Parkinson, considered the first of the great English botanists; (1567-1650).
24 English writer, botanist and nobleman, visited Scarborough, Maine in 1683.
25 Seneca Indians taught American settlers to use it to treat snakebite, hence 'Seneca snakewood'. The Seneca are native to western New York State.
26 Carl Linnaeus, Swedish botanist, zoologist and physician; his work is the foundation for the modern binomial system of plant and animal taxonomic nomenclature.

Energy, Color, Herbs

Green Gulch Farm
19 May 1980

In the garden, in the procedure of the garden generally, do not underestimate the use of chalk turned into live lime, basic slag, and agricultural lime, as it is called. Do not underestimate these. They are prepared in such a way that they are either virulent, semi-virulent, operative, or gentle—as you understand those three procedures. You must always, always keep these limes on hand. They are most important in your shed. And you should keep manipulations like buckets, brushes, adherers and so on, at hand for that purpose only and keep them clean. Thereby they will be operative for you.

Now whenever you've got posts, whenever you've got sheds, potting sheds, and wherever there is growth concerning plants in particular, the use of this lime is a little bit more than one comprehends. It has reflection to the light, just as the plants have. And it throws this off. That is why in a glass house, you use white paint. At one time the use of white lime, adhered, was much more preferable to the actual paint. And therefore, wooden frames, brick frames inside, should be washed with lime regularly. Now that lime is also a very decided disinfectant, and keeps the whole thing clean, and the light reflected and bright, and all the plants refer to it. It also creates atmosphere.

That's why you see, on the stems of fruit trees, that little ring of lime sometimes. That is to prevent the fall insects from climbing back up the stems. They don't appreciate it at all. And so, one cannot sufficiently point to keeping lime on hand and to its usages. Now it is very misappropriated also. People are inclined to accept the ministry's sophisticated tabula, that you spread so many pounds per square foot of lime on the ground to sweeten it. That is not a good policy. You should only use the limes when they have become necessary and where you have calciums in the soils, that is quite rare.

You must also be wary that there is a whole collection of plants that are

247

destroyable by the use of lime—the *Castanea*, the chestnut, does not like any calciums at all. It can stand a certain amount of natural calcium in the soil, but it doesn't take lime. Neither, of course, do any of the broad leaves such as the rhododendron, the azaleas, the magnolias, the camellias, and all that family dislike calciums. So never get lime onto those, nor dress them with lime, of course. But, for instance, in particular, in your spinach beds, your salad beds, lettuce, and peas to some degree, and, of course, clover is a kind of self-creator of lime. Wherever you put lime, clover will come up automatically. Therefore I point towards the usage of this in the garden and it must not be overlooked.

Live lime, as it's called, is obtainable, is very cheap normally, and you may make it in to a creamy paste, or a thick paste, or a considerable liquid. And that that is done by firing in a kiln, and it therefore boils when you put water on it. Now this is also the basis of making first-class plaster.

Likewise, to keep your plants and matters clean, the use of Fels-Naphtha, or any very, very natural soap. Be careful of some of those, because they are difficult to mix and must go through a strainer. But the use of soap on many plants, they appreciate it. And, for instance, if you want nicotine, nicotine sulfate to adhere so as to last for a long period on the plants, mix that with a certain quantity of this soap and you will have a synergist to hold it, which is better than using some of the oil sprays. Therefore, nicotine sulfate or black leaf forty, or make your own nicotine, of course, from the *Nictotiana*, and the soap, and the lime are three matters that I point to, to keep always in your shed.

And keep all your appurtenances separate. Don't get them mumbo jumbo, and keep them clean so they're always ready for use. And your sprayers, when you use your spray with your soap and your nicotine, always wash it out the moment you've finished with it, and hang it up well and carefully to drain and dry. You will find that the plants respond—that roses and other plants actually like the spray of nicotine and a certain amount of soap to keep them clean. Insects dirty them and they can't breathe so well. After the spray, they breathe and they appreciate it. And you will see the difference.

I want to remind you in your thinking, that when you come to realize that all cooking, all forms of heating, what we call 'artificial lighting', are artifice. And that, of course, they come from the energy, the cosmic energy of the Sun and the planets. Likewise, you must think in the area of color. That all paint, dye of fabrics, coloring of buildings, is all an artifice and that it is true color that you will find in plants, flowers and trees, which relates to the origin of heat. Do you follow that? Good.

Now regarding moisture, which is one of your big items here. You must go, in this moisture, to keep what you would call an even balance. Do you realize that when you pick a crop of strawberries, when you pick your raspberries, when you cut your cut flowers, that is the time, if you need to, to apply irrigation, water. Now at all times, try to keep that as even as possible, remembering always that you apply water, that it shall become dry. And you beg for it to become dry, that you can apply water. This is this huge zest for change. Always sweet into acid, into acid, into sweet—life into death into life into death into life. Do you understand? You cannot look deeply enough into the laws behind that.

Now you must also balance that flow of evenness and the amount of moistures, with the period of the cycles. There is the period where you want to run on a dry, even keel and the period of moist, even keels. In other words, your two equinoxes are the moist, even keels and the two dries relate to summer and winter. You see, what is called the perfect climate—is it not?—is the dry, warm winter and the moist, cool summer. They are the perfect climates. And to a certain degree, you are blessed with something of that here (northern California), but a lack of clear sunshine.

Also there is a great matter here to look into, that the whole plant world, that is the four Archangels of the seasons, are the absolute obedience to their performance, of their performance. Do not imagine that you can interfere with that. In this I relate that there are all the plants that must be in the inclination with the periods of shortages of Sun. You understand this opening out of the inclination, that little of it begins until it's halfway through. That amount of energy is what those plants are waiting for, what that obedience is waiting to fulfill. And then you come into the dormancy of summer and they require that full flow, that absolute exhaustion. It's nothing to a sunflower to have the whole twelve hours of energy. They like it. And then, you see, the things like the potato don't begin to respond until the declination is on, and they're aware of this slowing down to produce their tubers, as indeed, the *Helianthus tuberosus* (Jerusalem artichoke) doesn't begin to produce those tubers until after the flower has formed and then they suddenly perform. And that likewise, those plants like the Michaelmas daisy, the chrysanthemum: they all don't begin to turn on the blossoming tap until the light is more than halfway closed down, and is closing down, not opening out. This is why I advised you to hold your chrysanthemums, do you remember? And that is the basis behind that technical procedure.

Therefore you must understand that the plants are in obedience to that, the four cycles, completely, in comparison to local climatic. Local climatic will have all its effects, but whatever effects that has, it will not have an effect upon that period when that plant is in obedience to that cycle. Do you follow? This you must look at carefully, otherwise you will trip yourself up on trying to produce things when you can't.

Q: *Better to let it go by. Better to let it go by than to try to do it out of time.*

Well yes, it is malignant to do so. Not a question of better to let it go by exactly, but to learn to behave, to it. To be a gardener, obeying the garden.

Therefore in this manner you will come to understand color flow—careful color flow, flavor and scent—in this astonishing way in which they come and vanish. Take this *Nicotiana affinis*, the way in which it comes, as this flower does in this vase. At the moment there is no scent from that flower at all. And yet tonight, in this room, without taking it elsewhere, the scent will flow out of that. And before the dawn just comes, it will go with it. Now you see, you can't work this out in the mind in words.

And that you realize that the color in all of this does come and go? Did you not? Yes, it is not a static.

If you look, color is connected entirely with flow of energy. And if you will look at any object, if you will look at a leaf, would you not find the majority of the leaf, until a certain period of the day, is major shadow? You can't see color. It is a tone. There's no color. And that on the opposite side of that, there is what you call highlight, that is not a color, it's a tone. It is a whitish blue. It is not a color. Between that light and that shadow is a small area of color. That area of color is changing its position every moment of the planetary change during the day, which is all the time. Therefore at dawn, you see no color, but there is plenty of tone. At the equinox, color comes to its full. Agreed? And at the zenith of noon, color is overwhelmed. Agreed? Then that comes, the equinox of evening, evening out, where all of that color melts together and becomes tone again. This is what Corot saw so much in painting. Camille Corot. His paintings are beautiful. He was one of the only people who could paint evening light and tonality. But you can't find color. It is a vagary and is the perfect complete evening out of amalgamation of what we are talking about: color suffused.

Q: *Somehow I did not imagine that that subtlety in light came so much from the flower. I had somehow the idea that it had more to do with what the light was, rather than what the flower...*

Well, what I am really getting at is that it is the play between the two. And it is this that causes the herbs that we use to have their various times of day at which they are pertinent to collect, and then, certain times of the year. You see, everything amalgamates. That we talk about the four seasons of the year—spring, summer, autumn and winter—birth, dawn, opening out, dormancy, going eventide to rest—you have it in the year and you have it just the same in the day. The dawn comes and the equinox comes after the dawn of that perfect amalgamation, when birth flows into everything. In other words, love again is born. And then love goes to sleep in the evening. Do you follow? How many people look out of the window and say in the early morning, "Oh, oh, isn't this delicious? How I love the dawn. *Sniff.*" And this freshness, you know. And there are others who are still asleep in bed at that time. And they, later on, in the late afternoon, before it's dark, get up and say, "Oh, the peace of this. How I love the evening time." And you see they are related at that time by their horoscopic, so to speak.

Therefore, you must perceive also, this matter of going away from something and smelling it. Now mignonette, we must make a note of that. Mignonette, I feel, might go down on your list of moneymakers. We're going to talk about this more, and I hope you will bring it up, because that's the way we're going to come to it.

You see, it is very extravagant. Most people think of all herbs as either being culinary, or magic, or strewing herbs. And they can't believe that there are periods of the day when they are impotent, when they literally don't flow. Now if you'll know the plant mignonette, you know its exorbitantly fragile and exquisite scent. And yet you will take somebody to it, nincompoop that you are, and say, "Smell." And they will say, "Well, I can't smell anything." And you will go and smell it and say, "Well, neither can I." Do you follow? And you look an awful mugwump. The point is that this plant is under its governance. You see, we still can't clearly comprehend that the planetary influence is either drawing it or filling it—this thing of, into the plant, into the soil; or out through the ego of the soil into the atmosphere. Do you follow? So I wanted you to begin to focus upon that so as to comprehend when we go more into the herbs, how one must discover the forces that rule them. So in relationship to the color flow, flavor flow, and scent flow, you must think of dawn and sunset, spring and autumn, acid into sugar: and that *revolutionibus* is the guiding hand of that. Do you follow?

And, of course, that leads you to the words 'dark' and 'light'. When you have seedlings in boxes, and you get suddenly a quite serious damping off, or damping off is prevalent in certain seedling boxes, as it often is, here is a method that you can use, which very much governs this. Either leave when you plant or sow, or if not, take away a little area of the such plants, put them elsewhere, and place on the soil—you would probably in an ordinary seed box use two little flowerpots, if you like—a tin with a very small hole in it, with crocks or something in the bottom, and you place that just on, or just within the box, as it were, a part of the plants. Then you can half fill that, or fill it, or a third fill it with water, and that will permeate below and not wet the surface. Thereby you keep the crown *présentements* of the little seedlings dry. One of the great things which the horticulturists talk about is, "Don't let them go to bed with wet feet." You understand? And that method of using the little pots puts the water below, and not on, the surface. Do you follow?

For I am thinking so frequently of your business, you know, and what you are speaking of. And when I say business, I mean giving these beautiful things to the public which they haven't got, and through the means that you can give them. You see if you take those sweet peas and the flower, the annual *Gypsophila* (baby's-breath). Now the *Gypsophila* is quite difficult to grow. In actual fact, it is easy to grow in the bed, but it is rather difficult to handle and is difficult to keep up and takes a considerable amount of artistry.

Now, at Santa Cruz when I grew it, which of course I did from the first year on, not only did the public pour up from Santa Cruz to steal it and collect it from the flower store, but immediately as they did, the florists all complained to the chancellor that their business was going. So I suppose the chancellor did say to them, "Why don't you sell it?" They said, "Well we can't get it. Nobody grows it." And then they said, could they come and buy it from us? And the chancellor said, "Here's your chance Chadwick." And I said, "No, chancellor, we are not selling here, as you know." And so we didn't, although it did cause trouble.

But what I am pointing at is that there are many such beautiful things that are not grown, and not handled because they require delicate technique. It is like the growing and picking of berries today. There just aren't any, for that reason. As we said only the other day, raspberries in the Mill Valley market are three dollars for a quarter of a pound. Well, you're not about to sell your coat and buy betony. I don't know what you would have to sell to buy raspberries. Therefore I recommend that you grow, for instance, particularly *Gypsophila*. Now this plant, you pick it by the spray. It's extremely easy to grow. You can sow it every month. You can have it, actually, from March onwards, right up until Christmas. And then there's the cessation of three months, which is not very much.

Now all of those sweet peas, if they were set off with this *Gypsophila*, are enhanced at least three times. It is astonishing what this flower does. And you can even put it with those clumsy old calendulas, even to the extent of marigolds, and it will make them very fey, very beautiful. Therefore, people will get to know this. I assure you in Santa Cruz, they simply poured up—the residents—and stole it, regardless of what anybody said. They just went and snatched it, and asked for it over and over and over again. And all the students learned to love it and put it with their flowers. In other words, there's very little that you can't use it with. It enhances, it is a synergist to all the others.

And also, likewise, the sweet pea, I don't know wherever you can see to buy sweet peas today. I know down there, one couldn't get them. In fact, I don't think anywhere.

Q: *They're on the tables of the restaurant this week. And I visited on Friday. Coming in the door, I smelled them. The Sun was pouring in the window on the flowers.*

Yes. Good.

Likewise I am recommending you get plenty of seed of the *Iris kaempferi* and the *Iris higo* (Japanese irises). They are terribly easy to grow, will grow superbly here. Within a year, you could have any quantity you want that you could dispose of, any quantity, of exorbitant beauty. You never see them in people's houses. You never see them for sale, and are, also, one of those flowers which are exceptional, in the fact that you can have five and six foot stems—four, five, six foot stems—very tall flowers. And you can imagine those, for instance, enhanced with large sprays of *Gypsophila*, and of course, probably with delphiniums. Also, as just occurred to me, and I had thought of it previously and put it on the list, mignonette. You see, for scent, little bouquets of mignonette. People would get so used to giving them as little, tiny gifts. And perhaps it's the small moneymakers that make the big money—little tiny bouquets of mignonette that cost next to nothing. And there you would probably sell plenty.

I want you to think, from a point of view of compost, of this very extraordinary matter concerning seed. Seed, because of it containing the utmost energy, the utmost *idée* and the least metamorphosis, is, of course, what you might call the very essence of life force. And that you will find that if you make compost heaps of seed, for instance of grape pips, of cereal, that is of any seed, you will find a huge growth outcome that you can't understand, and it is no good trying to. The point is that here you've got almost what, but in a natural way, what they are trying to do in making pills out of all the vitamins. And therefore, apply your visionary thinking to what goes on in Nature.

How many poppies can one poppy make? There is a statistic on it which I gave; you don't happen to remember it, I suppose? No. It's not a simple one. It's something like half a million. It's quite incredible. Now, do you ever see those plants the next year? That quantity? What would happen? What does happen is this: that of course, they vary under their dominance as to their capacity of germination; a huge quantity of the life force of the seeds that do germinate. So you see again this application of relationship. Now many of them are too deep, many of them are too shallow. And it is only that little area in the skin of the Earth that is just the germination quantity, which is probably one-and-one-half percent of the total. The others are liable to sit there for a hundred years in some cases. Clover does that, poppy does it. I believe poppy does, but clover certainly does. Some of them can re-germinate after a hundred years. In other words, you dig them up, and they come up near the surface and they will germinate. Therefore, I want you to think in your ley growing of when you want intense performance of soil, use seed humus. Do you follow? Even the shells of the seeds contain more than the average compost humus. Do you follow? That requires quite a considerable amount of consideration thinking about.

So, I want to go on to your herbs. Can I? In the mints, the mints are all coolers, you understand, moisture lovers. Now, where do you buy, little bundle for the soup, a bouquet garni? Where can you buy a bouquet of mint? With potatoes, with peas, with broad beans, with many dishes, mint is incredible. Here is the ideal place for growing mint. This is the very sort of valley and land that it loves, and will grow voluminously. Here is a market produce again. And again I recommend it heartily to your kitchen. The mints, the principle mints for the culinary, are *Mentha viridis* (spearmint), *rotundifolia* (false apple-mint), and *pulegium* (pennyroyal). Those three are the culinary mints. Then there are the other mints for the other purposes. And, of course, there are certain mints that are huge controllers. They will control mice. With *pulegium*, no mice will go. And I have an idea that this must have an effect on, of course, voles, on gophers even, and you know how they travel by root, so it might be an excellent thing to get underway. Terribly easy to grow. But, you want to look up your right varieties and what they look like. So I've got several pages here with reference to what they look like: what the leaves are, what the blossomings are, the color, when the blossoms come, and how they form, so you can't mistake them. Keep them in their different patches for that reason, for they inter-spread.

I don't know how much I dealt with you before about one of the most valuable of kitchen herbs: saffron. The best saffron in Europe was at one time actually grown in England, around London. And that is why you get the numerous places called Saffron Walden and such places, because of the huge business that occurred in growing the crocus, which produces the saffron. You see the Spanish saffron is not saffron at all. It's not a crocus. It is one of the *Helios*. The other saffron comes from Tibet and such places and, as you know, requires hundreds of thousands of blossoms to produce one little iota of dried saffron. The *Colchicum* is not the creator of saffron and many people will imagine that it is and, of course, it is not. Because it's also known as meadow saffron, the *Colchicum*, and it is not. That blooms in September and in October, and it is medicinal, highly medicinal.

The saffron comes from the *Crocus sativus* and only from the *Crocus sativus*. This can always be told, discriminated, by the tongue of the crocus, it comes up through the blossom and turns over and hangs down the side, like a tongue out of a goblet. No other crocus does this and they call that word polyploidy. It comes in the Song of Solomon. It's most enormously aromatic, carminative, and is a herb of the Sun, under Leo. It's therefore a huge strengthener of the heart. Do not ever think of more than ten grains. Don't be tied to that, but it is a statement. *For the Sun, which is the fountain of light, may dazzle the eyes and make them blind*[1]. It can bring on headache, debility and the numerous dangers of aroma—blindness and delirium. Can do, when overused. In other words, the tiniest quantity is the ideal and anything above that becomes very destructive. It is used for coloring. It has intense color. It is used for perfume. And it is used with syrup of rose, with saffron and apple, to produce gentle and wonderful sleep, an excellent producer of wonderful sleep.

A cordial, being taken in any inordinate quantity, hurts the heart instead of healing it. Then to remember that it has narcotic properties and it will blister the skin. It can bring headache, delirium and blindness. And to remain in a room where it is drying for dyeing, it can bring on debility and even apoplexy, because of the vapor. In Asia it is known as *za'faran* and it will be in the Song of Solomon, because it was always considered a valuable product. Apicius'[2] Juscellum (*Latin*), Juselle (*Saxon*) was eggs, bread, saffron and sage.

There is a period, of course, at which that tongue falls and it is that perianth that gives the area that is used for saffron, it is that little tongue. And is collected at that time, when it is ripe, has to be very carefully dried and then stored dry. As you know, its price is inimitable. Well, if you didn't think of a trade procedure, you probably can't afford to use it in your cooking because of the cost. But why not grow it? It will grow here if it grows outside London, as it did so volubly. I would recommend it from both points of view, and certainly, perhaps among the Christmas sale gifts. It could go in a very attractive little container, couldn't it?

Now the next one, which is a very fascinating herb, the *Ocimum basilicum*, sweet basil, belongs to the mint family and must be looked upon as an annual. It comes from India. Highly aromatic. Behind its whole growing—and this plant is an argument—the intense argument of poison and medicine. And for that reason it was frequently looked upon as not for internal use at all. Let's look at it and see why. It's been used in cooking throughout. It's been used in perfumery throughout. It's excellent for wasp stings, by the way. And yet, it is said, by even smelling it you can create a scorpion in the brain. Alright? It is an enemy of rue and they will not grow together. *Ruta* (rue) is as great an enemy to poison as any that grows. Now you must put these two by two, do you see? You have got to do an addition here between medicine and poison. The seed, ground to powder, is the most aromatic for cosmetics. For medicinal use: dry or fresh. For dry, gather in July, preferably, the government of it. An infusion of the green herb in boiling water is good for all obstructions of the internal organs, and to arrest vomiting and nausea, and the seed an excellent cure for warts. Now this argument about its use and values; if you read Pliny, Dioscorides, this one will say this and that one will say that. And now they have all reverted to the same answer on the matter. It's duplication.

The *basilica* was a building, an architectural building, which was manifold. In other words, it was for religious and spiritual approach, and likewise it was for human justice, law and those other things of human kind, which are, as it were, the very opposite to spiritual vision; and that if you go back you will find the translation of the word 'basilica' means exactly royal or splendid; and that the word *basilicum* meant robe, and the basilicum was a royal robe. And yet, in the whole of mythology, that word becomes *bashilik*, which is the Russian, and that means a serpent, and even is a translation of the Medusa.

Now, that serpent, basilisk, is beyond all other snakes, all other kings of serpents, and does not go by the wreathing of the coils, but travels upright. And nothing can face it. To look upon it is death. And here enters the one attacker, the most extraordinary of all, as it would be, the weasel. The weasel attacks basilisk on sight and cannot gain or win in that form at all. And after having made battle, must go and to eat that one herb we spoke of that is the opposer of all poison, *Ruta*. So the weasel eats rue and goes to attack, and has the power, the only one to have the power to overcome basilisk. In other words, the weasel is ermine, the same sort of animal. And therefore it was that the robe of *basilicum*, was always edged with ermine. Do you see? All these things put together begin to bring us out of 'wordism', into what these formations are.

Now the story of basilisk, as you probably know, is part of a very well-known mythology. That the usual thing takes place—the son of a king, the prince, sets out to travel the world and to find a princess and eventually he comes to this court where the king is, and the ideal princess, for him, is. And he asks for her hand. After the conclave of the matter, the princess is given to the prince, and they marry. And everything is perfect and happy. After a short while, the princess' father, the king, comes to the prince and says, "We have to go away to one of our country homes to attend to matters and we will leave you here in the palace and there are the keys of the hundred rooms. We will return in so many days." And then he says, quite nonchalantly, in handing the keys, that there is one quite different key to all the others. And he says, "Use them all, enjoy them, the whole ninety-nine, but that one, the hundredth one, you can't mistake it, never open. Don't open, you understand? Absolutely don't."

So the prince says, "Of course." Away they go and the prince remains. Every day he opens door after door, all the delights of the world, endlessly.

The day before the return of the king and the princess, he has opened ninety-nine doors and there is the hundredth. And then it strikes him: after all, there is such a thing as nobility and glamour. Was the king testing him for his nervous ability? Was he testing him for fear? And then he builds this as an excuse and, as in all such cases, or so many cases, makes up his mind. He puts the key in the door, unlocks it, and throws it open.

And then if you will go back to what I said, that basilisk is the whole Medusa of the world, that you can't look upon it, you are dead. The prince has no power. He is sterilized, whatever you like to call it. And here is this thing chained by every metal in the world to the floor in the middle. It has no hair. Its eyes are fire. The whole thing is descriptive of a furnace: molten and seething. And he says to the prince, "Goblet of water from the fountain." And the prince hasn't any power. He goes to the fountain and brings the goblet of water. And he says, "Another." And then he says, "A third." And the moment he drinks the third, there is this noise of the most colossal thunderstorm, the bursting of chains, spreads his wings, and basilisk flies through the door and at that time picks up the princess who is returning and carries her away into the sky. And there they are left.

The king returns and the irate scene follows. And what can the prince do? Well, like the whole story of Psyche now, there is only one *Saturea* for him, one savior for him, and that is all of the Nature of which he has brought about in his youth, with the world, with all the animals and birds. And so, the bird that he saved gives him a feather. And the fish that he helped gives him a scale. And as each occasion when he comes up and meets basilisk, which is in everything, the moment he meets basilisk, he uses one of these to assist him. And basilisk has to change continually from one form to all the others, one after the other.

And so he is chased over the mountains, over the oceans, into the oceans, into the sky, and eventually comes down to the last little thing left in the world, when he is assisted. And suddenly the egg in the duck, so to speak, is stabbed and there is the princess returned. That is the only way in which she can come back. Did you follow? That is something of the story of basilisk. And therefore, this then is the background of this herb, which obviously, as you must notice, is very potent. It's, in its *double entendre*, duplicate in everything. You probably are aware of it, that you sense in its very smell this danger. So I relate to you that story because it has a huge inference on so many of the herbs. Would you like to talk about it?

Q: *There is a fever associated with this herb. People must have it; they crave it. And we are always constantly being asked to provide it, and the tomato both. That combination has a power that can't be denied. People are always wanting it.*

Yes, culinarily it has more effect with the tomato dish than anything. Again it should be used with great discretion. If used up to that discretion, is exquisite. But beyond it, of course, like the saffron, does the opposite.

Q: *Alan, could you explain to me why, at Santa Cruz, you didn't sell things?*

Yes. The whole approach of the university: you understand that I was taken away from ordinary education at an early age and went under tutors. That had a huge effect upon my view of life and what I followed. And that, until I came to Santa Cruz through Freya (Countess Freya von Moltke) and met Paul Lee, Page (Smith), and then introduced to the chancellor, I was not in any way of fey with university life. I had always looked upon it as being the pillars that held up the temple of education, and truly believed that there was fact in that. But I came to discover that certainly the majority were there for a living and that they were all hunting for salaries. In fact there was nothing but a huge argument for salaries, and that the corruption of the whole university as regards money was absolutely deplorable.

Anything that I wanted for the garden had to go through the management, and they took about one hundred percent into their pockets out of everything. For instance, the chancellor gave us money, a thousand dollars, for a glass house. And it had to go through the management of the university and they just took half of it straight away. And then he appropriated to us one of the chalets, which had been in the fields, which the students used to live in, in the early stage. And they charged more than the value of the chalet, to put into their pocket, just to bring it to the garden. Those things all put together, I came to realize that education in itself was, of course, a religious matter and it could not be paid for, on the basis of a salary, or fought for on a salary basis. Likewise, the whole object of my work in the garden and the bringing about of a garden is the opposite to commercialism.

It cannot survive upon commercialism being its flow. It can be the other way about, of course, but it cannot be commercialism behind its performance.

And therefore, since the students needed this reformation and since they were pouring into the garden to the tune of over one thousand working, on and off, little tiny spells, it was very adamant that at no time should there be any mis-education: only education which concerned truth. That's a huge statement, of course. And for that reason, any basis of money concerned with the selling of the produce, undid the purpose of what their garden was about.

And so the chancellor said, "Well you shall have a box in which people can put the money, where they collect the flowers and vegetables." But no, we did not find that that filled the picture. We were also, as all the students and their president, were very considerably discriminative about where the money came from to support the garden. Now I ran that garden all the time I was there, the actual garden, on two thousand a year. And I gave back out of that always a small sum, up to the tune of two hundred, left over from the year. And, of course, the management pounced on that and stole it every time. But the purpose of this was to bring about the attitude of propagative profit and not selling the Archangel's gifts and turning it into self-possession. That is the key to my answer to your question. Is that clear enough?

You see, in the long run, what can we do, or do we do, other than share? For if you pay for it, you are not altering the sharing. Where does it come from? This is why I wanted to tell you the tale of the gazelle, a gazelle. Where does it all come from? Can you possibly put any sort of valuation, any relative valuation on it at all? You can't. Whatever you do, you share it. So it's only a falsity. And when you look at the calumny that has come out of that selling, do you see the whole of the agricultural attitude has destroyed the continent of America. And if you are going to solve that, it's got to be a miracle. And that miracle, as far as I can see, can only take place by coming to be aware of where it all comes from: the essence of creation.

As the sutra we said over and over this morning, "Don't try to figure it out, trust the immeasurable."

Yes, absolutely. What a huge statement. Enough there to chew on for a hundred years, isn't there? Well, other than the herb connection, which is the idea to set in motion of our thinking, to approach the different herbs more clearly, we need to go very carefully and gently and to come to the comprehensions of how, before we take a schoolroom statistic attitude, that this herb does this and that herb does that, we must comprehend the laws behind it. Agreed? Now we can begin to take herbs more and view them.

Q: *We made a trip to Santa Cruz to see your gardens, at Santa Cruz, at the university, and it's clear that the gardens were on quite steep hillsides, both of them. And there was a great deal of stonework with them, and pathways that worked beautifully with them. I was interested in seeing the beds at the Santa Cruz garden, placed so steeply running uphill and the little raised stonewalls at the foot of them. I didn't exactly understand why they were laid out that way, or what kept them from running down the hill in a big rain. That was one question I had. I noticed that at the foot of our own valley, there's a huge heather-growing operation and the plants run in rows—I guess they're in rows—up and down the hill. They don't run sideways across the hill. And one answer to that I heard was to run machines up and down the hill. Well I know that's certainly not why the Santa Cruz are placed at that angle. That's one question I had; and the question again about elevation.*

It is rather funny that when you mention that slope at Santa Cruz, that when the chancellor, who didn't realize what was going to happen at all, but when, after I had begun, when all the university had packed and gone; they hadn't been gone long, of course, but they were gone, and there I was left with a poison oak hill. Not a weed on it. And I started digging, you see, with a pickaxe and spade. It bounced off and hit me on the head, at four o'clock in the morning even with an overcoat on in July. The chancellor happened to come along and we got talking and he said, "Well I am definitely going to solve this immediately. I can't have this going on, and so, we've got the very thing down on the campus. It is there right now, it is just here for a job." And this was a—it might have been six hundred ton for all I know—tractor. It had a tooth as big as this room. So he said, "I am sending it up and in three runs the whole thing will be plowed." I said, "Heaven help!" I said, "Please don't do that." "Well," he said, "That is what I see and I assure you it will do the trick." He was being very kind, you know, really wanting to help. And he sent this thing up. It did half a run and fell over on its side. And then they couldn't do anything with it and they had an awful job to get it up, like Humpty Dumpty. The man was so irate, he took it away again, of course, at once. And there we were back in the same position, an amusing little story about that.

Of course, you do realize that I went there without any position at all. The chancellor said, "We have all agreed, for some curious reason that we can't put our finger on, that we want this garden." I said, "Good, that is fine." He said, "The point is that this is not a horticultural school, there are no diplomas and there is no allocation of money, nor any kind of source from which we could make a branch to bring it." In the meantime, the work was going on. I had little possessions. I'd left quite a few things in my visit to New Zealand and Australia and I sold those up and got money from that point of view. Then I had to go and see the vice-president, who was the receptionist at the university. And he said, "Well we have been talking with the chancellor about this." And this is entirely secret. Can you switch off? (Tape recorder switched off here.)

(Recorder turned back on for new topic.) I suppose one of the answers to that is: of course, why not? It sounds ideal, could work perfectly. Obviously, buildings would be far better on elevations than in the valley and the growing proposition also excellent. It's a question of your focus and your labor. It would appear to me to be one or the other. That is something which you and the management of your place here must know well what you've got to do, as regards family buildings, if those are required. And that's where they can go. Surely that must be the emphasis of the decision. But if you want to make supply from your garden, and supply your restaurant, supply your entire family here, the clientele, and also to do business, well you must have a force in the garden. Is that not so? So those are decisions which can only come out of the planning of your management.

I mentioned to you, did I not, about the thinking of the *Arctium lappa* (burdock). You probably know it. It is the great burr. All one thinks of here, when there is any trouble, is you either get a trap, a poison bait, or whatever the shop sells. Here you have gone into this thing of commerce. The only thing the mind can do is, "What do I buy?" Not, "What do I invent?" Not, "What do I study in Nature to give me the answer?" but, "What do I go to a shop and buy?" Do you follow? Now I have found, and it is one of the things that the garden at Santa Cruz and other places brought into play, dusting, dusting with ash of numerous plants, particularly lavender. And the flow of seed from *Sonchus* (sow thistle). It is so voluminous throughout the summer that it will flummox insects, grasshoppers and things. It will smother them, in other words. Now there are obviously areas of land in which things grow which the gopher doesn't enjoy at all. And it travels in a tunnel. It lives underground in that tunnel and it fits the tunnel very tight.

Arctium lappa is the great burr. It grows about six feet high, has a huge, tough leaf, looking a little bit like rhubarb, and it looks like a thistle. And it then blossoms and produces huge bundles and bunches of seed in cones. Now any cow, and human being, anything, that walks amongst this is absolutely smothered in it forever. You will never get it out of a cloth, never. It gets woven in and stays there and clings. Do you follow? You know it? Now if you put *Arctium lappa* then, in bundles of those heads, you can grow it, can't you? Any amount of it. Put that in those tunnels and gradually, at least make areas of safety. Drive the gopher out. And then build your roadways, put down all that stuff and keep them out. Do you follow? Let us look to the performances that are in Nature, at hand, rather than going and buying things to cure everything. Agreed?

Have we got other things to discuss? Is there time?

---

1   Nicholas Culpepper, *Culpepper's Complete Herbal*, (1816) p. 161.
2   Marcus Gavius Apicius, 1st century Roman gourmand.

Annotated Bibliography

Adams, George, and Whicher, Olive. *The Plant Between Sun and Earth and the Science of Physical and Ethereal Spaces.* Shambala, 1982. Goethean science, projective geometry and the link between the invisible and plant worlds.

Bailey, L.H. *The Standard Cyclopedia of Horticulture, Vol I-III.* Macmillan Company, 1939. Invaluable extensive resource.

Bamford, Christopher, ed., *Green Hermeticism: Alchemy and Ecology,* Lindesfarne Books, 2007. Essays by Chris Bamford, Peter Lanborm Wilson and Kevin Townley on the history of the Hermetic tradition as it pertains to a true green future.

Bird, Christopher, and Tompkins, Peter. *Secrets of the Soil: New Solutions for Restoring our Planet.* Earthpulse Press, 1998. Compendium of alternative organic growing methods.

Blackhirst, Rodney. *Primordial Alchemy and Modern Religion: Essays on Traditional Cosmology.* Sophia Perennis, 2008. This is a wide-ranging, insightful book, but germane to Alan's thought are a number of sections, especially "The Man-Plant: Central Themes in the Alchemy of Farming", which go to the heart of why he thought mythology is essential to horticulture.

Buhner, Stephen Harrod, *The Secret Teachings of Plants: The Intelligence of the Heart in the Direct Perception of Nature.* Bear & Company, 2004. A beautifully-written book drawing on Goethe and Thoreau showing how we are structurally and emotionally heart-designed to communicate directly with Nature.

Chadwick, Alan. *Performance in the Garden: A Collection of Talks on Biodynamic French Intensive Horticulture.* Logosophia, 2008. Companion to this book.

Coates, Callum. *Living Energies: An Exposition of Concepts Related to the Theories of Viktor Schauberger.* Gateway, 1996. Understanding the deep work of Schauberger on living water and water systems.

Critchlow, Keith. *The Hidden Geometry of Flowers: Living Rhythms, Form and Number.* Floris Books, 2011. A beautiful book revealing the hidden structure of the floral kingdom, by one of the premier sacred geometers alive.

Cuthbertson, Tom. *Alan Chadwick's Enchanted Garden.* E. P. Dutton, 1978. Overview of Alan's horticultural techniques.

Darrow, George M. *The Strawberry: History, Breeding and Physiology*. Holt, Rinehart and Winston, 1966. Comprehensive resource.

Davies, Jennifer and Dodson, Harry. *Harry Dodson's Practical Kitchen Garden*. BBC Books, 1992. Discusses method of clamping used by Alan.

Evans-Wentz, W. Y.,*The Fairy Faith in Celtic Countries*. Citadel Press, 1994. One of the best sources for lore on the faeries and elves that Alan speaks of encountering.

Fuluoka, Masanobu. *One Straw Revolution: An Introduction to Natural Farming*. Rodale Press, 1978. A different approach than Alan's, but equally involving a commitment to, and connection with, Nature.

Goethe, Johann Wolfgang von. *The Metamorphoses of Plants*. Biodynamic Gardening and Farming Association, 1993. Classic work. Huge influence on Alan.

Grieve, Mrs. M. *A Modern Herbal: The Medicinal, Culinary, Cosmetic and Economic Properties, Cultivation and Folk-Lore of Herbs, Grasses, Fungi, Shrubs and Trees with All Their Modern Scientific Uses, Vol. I & II*. Dover, 1971. A resource for Alan.

Howard, Robert, with Skjei, Eric. *What Makes the Crops Rejoice*. Little, Brown and Co., 1986. Contains a chapter dedicated to Alan, including the most extensive biography available.

Jeavons, John. *How to Grow More Vegetables (Than You Ever Thought Possible on Less Land than You can Imagine)*. Ten Speed Press, 1974. Student of Alan's who demonstrates how biointensive methods can be applied to any scale garden.

Johnson, Wendy. *Gardening at the Dragon's Gate: At Work in the Wild and Cultivated World*. Bantam, 2008. Reflections on meditation and hands-on gardening from thirty years at the Green Gulch Zen Canter garden, where Wendy Johnson was with Alan at the end of his life.

Keyserlingk, Adalbert Count, ed. *The Birth of a New Argiculture: Koberwitz 1924*. Temple Lodge, 1999. Firsthand accounts of Steiner's 1924 lectures on agriculture.
– *Developing Biodynamic Agriculture: Reflections on Early Research*. Temple Lodge 1999. Insights from a long life involved with Biodynamics.

Kingsley, Peter. *Reality*. The Golden Sufi Center, 2004. The essential book for understanding the origin and reality of western civilization as brought into being by shamanic philosophers we now call 'pre-Socratics'. The end section of the book discusses this tradition as inner agricultural work. If you read one book from this list, this is it.

Langham, Derald G. *Circle Gardening: Producing Food by Genesa Principles*. The Devin Adair Company, 1978. An amazing esoteric approach to gardening by the mystic who developed the Genesa crystal.

Lee, Paul A. *There is a Garden In the Mind: A Memoir of Alan Chadwick and the Organic Movement in California*. North Atlantic Books, 2013. A lively personal account of Alan's starting the garden at Santa Cruz in terms of the Goethean vitalist tradition in conflict with physicalism. Paul Lee was a great friend of Alan's and was vital in bringing him to UC Santa Cruz to begin the garden there in 1967.

Lorette, Louis. *The Lorette System of Pruning*. Rodale Press, 1946. Alan studied the French Intensive System under M. Lorette in France.

Lovel, Hugh. *A Biodynamic Farm for Growing Wholesome Food*. A practical guide; includes a useful Biodynamics glossary.

Maeterlinck, Maurice. *The Life of the Bee*. Dodd, Mead and Co. 1929. Source for bee lecture. His play *The Bluebird* transformed Alan at a young age and its magic eventually led him into the theatre.

Meyer, Joseph. *The Herbalist*. Clarence and Meyer, 1918; rev. Joseph Meyer 1960. One of Alan's sources for herblore. Paracelsus. *Paracelsus*. Princeton University Press, 1995. Introduction to his writings.

Pfeiffer, Ehrenfried, M.D. *Soil Fertility: Renewal and Preservation*. One of the pioneers and greatest practitioners of Biodynamics.

Poppin, Jeff. *The Barefoot Farmer: The Best of the Barefoot Farmer*. Jeff Poppin, 2001. A terrific book of advice from one of greatest biodynamic farmers in the US.

Pratt, Anne. *The Flowering Plants, Grasses, Sedges and Ferns of Great Britain, Vol. I-IV.*

Prechtel, Martin. *The Unlikely Peace at Cuchumaquic: The Parallel Lives of People as Plants: Keeping the Seeds Alive*. North Atlantic Books 2011. This is a deep look into the indigenous relationship between corn and humans as co-entwined living being. An astonishing book worth many readings.

Frederick Warne & Co. 1891. A source for Alan's lectures.

Schilthuis, Willy. *Biodynamic Agriculture*. SteinerBooks, 1994. Concise overview of history, philosophy and practice of Biodynamics.

Schumacher, E. M. *Small is Beautiful: Economics as if People Mattered*. Harper & Row,

1973. He stated in an address at UC Davis in 1977: "Alan Chadwick is the greatest horticulturalist that the western world possesses today."

Scott, Barbara. *The Joy of Biodynamic Agriculture: Living with the Unseen Forces Behind Nature.* This book is a call to encounter, bless, and be blessed by the spirits of Nature.

Simon, Ted. *The River Stops Here: How One Man's Battle to Save His Valley Changed the Fate of California.* Story of Covelo garden patron Richard Wilson; includes some pages on Alan and his work there.

Smith, Richard Thornton. *Cosmos, Earth and Nutrition: The Biodynamic Approach to Horticulture.* Sophia Books, 2009. An introduction and cosmic overview of biodynamics in terms of food quality and the future of biodynamics.

Steiner, Rudolf. *Agriculture: Spiritual Foundations for the Renewal of Agriculture.* Biodynamic Gardening and Farming Association, 1993. These 1924 lectures are the seminal text for the Biodynamic movement: deep insights into the cosmos, plants and chemistry; not light reading.
—*Bees.* SteinerBooks, 1999. Source for Alan's Bee lecture.
—*The Four Seasons and the Archangels.* Rudolf Steiner Press, 1947. Comprehensive look at the relationship of the Archangels to the seasons.
—*What is Biodynamics? A Way to Heal and Revitalize the Earth. Seven Lectures.* Introduction by Hugh J. Courtney. SteinerBooks 2006.

Storl, Wolf D. *Culture and Horticulture: A Philosophy of Gardening.* Biodynamic Literature, 1979. Possibly the best introductory text on Biodynamics.

Thomas, Graham Stuart. *The Graham Stuart Thomas Rose Book.* Sagepress/Timbar Press Inc., 1994. Rose sourcebook.

Thun, Maria. *Gardening for Life: The Biodynamic Way.* Hawthorn Press, 1999. If you want to turn someone on to biodynamics, this is the book. Beautiful and clear graphics, simple and profound.
—*The Biodynamic Year: Increasing Yield, Quality and Flavour: 100 Helpful Tips for the Gardener or Smallholder.* Temple Lodge Publishing, 2010. Picks up where *Gardening for Life* leaves off.

Vilmorin-Andrieux, MM. *The Vegetable Garden.* London, 1885. One of Alan's sources for vegetable varieties.

Virgil. *The Georgics: Vol. 2, Book III-IV.* Cambridge University Press, 1988. Roman poetic treatise on farming, plants, livestock and bees.

Wilkes, John. *Flowforms: The Rhythmic Power of Water.* Floris Books, 2003. Explanation of these amazing rhythmic water channels, very tied in to biodynamics.

Woodraska, Woody. *Deep Gardening: Soul Lessons from 17 Gardens, Biodynamic Memories.* Aurora Farm Press, 2010. This is a book of deep gardening, fertile from decades of dogged experience, sprouting a wisdom only found through a profound conversation with the soil of life.

Xenophon. *Oeconomicus VIII-XIII, Bristol Greek Texts Series.* Duckworth Publishers, 1995. Source for some of Alan's thinking about the human in relation to the garden.

Acknowledgements

The Alan Chadwick Archive, by providing the ability for Logosophia to make Alan's vision available to the reading world, would certainly not be possible without the dogged dedication of Craig Siska. His dedicated efforts over the course of many years for finding, collecting, and sometimes prying loose tapes and materials gathering dust in scattered closets and attics bears its fruits in this book. In all but one anonymous case, the transcriptions were done by Krys Crimi, Tracey Schmidt and Steve Crimi, with some invaluable editing and uncovering of the inaudible by Craig Siska and Krys Crimi.

Special thanks go to our designer and cover artist, Susan Yost, always there for us to midwife a book into this physical realm with attention, precision and beauty. And we are especially pleased to have the presence of William Price's inimitable artwork gracing the cover.

Thanks to the wonderful writers Martin Prechtel, Stephen Buhner, Deborah Madison and Barbara Scott for endorsements, and to Malcolm Holcombe and Peter Lamborn Wilson for the epigraphs.

There have been a number of Alan's friends and former students who have been supportive with photos, tapes, encouragement or advice. Special thanks go to Betty Peck, Dan McGuire, Nancy Lingemann, Stephanie Tebbutt, Chris Tebbutt, Beth Benjamin, Jim Nelson, Greg Novotny, Fred Marshall, Gregory Hudson, Dennis Tamura, Margot Bergman, Virginia Baker, Bernard Taper, Mark Taper, Richard Wilson, Michael Stusser, Hilmar Moore, Linda Maslow, John Jeavons, Jauquin Hershman, Stephen Decater, Gloria Decater, Raymond Chavez, Dot Brovarney, Emily Mattison, David Worden, David Field, Kathleen Downs, Agaja Enajaro, Robert Howard, Matt Drewno, Paul Jackson, Stephen Kaffka, Paul Lee, Richard Baker-Roshi, Steve Stombler, Janet Britt, William Cambier, Bill Bruneau, Herb Schmidt, Alice Warrick, Dan Crebbin, Mark Feedman, Isel Lise Lamoureux, John de Graaf, Jim Mulligan, Avis Licht, Richard Senior, Nada Miljkovic, William Davis, Jodi Frediani, Maria von Brincken, David Valbrecht, Katrina Frey, Jonathan Frey, Bart Johnson, Richard Joos, Jack Tomlinson, Jean Carol Moore Schwartzkopf, Tom Lawrence, Tom Palley, Al Wilkins and anyone else supportive I may have missed.

CPSIA information can be obtained
at www.ICGtesting.com
Printed in the USA
FSOW01n0839300115
4870FS